Windows Server 2012 Hyper-V Cookbook

Over 50 simple but incredibly effective recipes for
mastering the administration of Windows Server Hyper-V

Leandro Carvalho

PACKT enterprise
PUBLISHING   professional expertise distilled

BIRMINGHAM - MUMBAI

Windows Server 2012 Hyper-V Cookbook

First published: November 2012

Production Reference: 1151112

Published by Packt Publishing Ltd.
Livery Place
35 Livery Street
Birmingham B3 2PB, UK.

ISBN 978-1-84968-442-2

www.packtpub.com

Cover Image by Artie Ng (artherng@yahoo.com.au)

Credits

Author

Leandro Carvalho

Reviewers

Vinicius R. Apolinario

Edvaldo Alessandro Cardoso

Kristian Nese

Carsten Rachfahl

Acquisition Editors

Stephanie Moss

Robin de Jongh

Lead Technical Editor

Azharuddin Sheikh

Technical Editors

Brandt D'Mello

Pooja Pande

Project Coordinator

Joel Goveya

Proofreaders

Maria Gould

Dan McMahon

Indexers

Monica Ajmera Mehta

Tejal Soni

Graphics

Valentina D'silva

Sheetal Aute

Production Coordinator

Melwyn D'sa

Cover Work

Melwyn D'sa

About the Author

Leandro Carvalho is a well-known virtualization specialist who writes and presents sessions about virtualization and the private cloud. He works with Microsoft solutions such as Windows Server, Hyper-V, App-V, VDI, security, System Center, Exchange, Lync Server, Sharepoint, Project Server, and client systems, in addition to helping the community constantly with articles, forums, videos, and lectures about his passion—Microsoft Virtualization. He has the certifications Certified Ethical Hacker/MCP/MCSA+M+S/MCSE+S/MCTS/MCITP/MCT, and MVP. In 2009, he won the MCT Awards Latin America Trainer of the Year, and he has been awarded Microsoft MVP as Virtualization Specialist every year since 2010.

Leandro can be reached at `http://leandroesc.wordpress.com` and `http://msmvps.com/blogs/msvirtualization` and his Twitter handle is `@LeandroEduardo`.

Acknowledgement

I still remember when my cousin Marcelo used to force me to read books when I was young. I wasn't very fond of reading in those days, and now here I am, releasing my own book. It's hard to believe that I could have achieved something that was such a distant dream for me before. So, I start by thanking you, Marcelo, for pointing me in the right direction and helping me to become who I am today.

I thought it would have been easy to write a technical book and that I wouldn't need any help. Well, I've proven again that we can't conquer anything alone. I've had the pleasure of having four friends help me by reviewing this book. I can say now that I could not have finished it as I did, without their help. So, thank you Alessandro, Carsten, Kristian, and Vinícius, for all the time spent reviewing, with such perfection, the chapters in what I call "our" book.

I would also like to thank all of those on the Packt team involved in this project, who helped me right through; first, Stephanie, who was my first contact, and then later, Azhar, Brandt, Joel, and Pooja. Thank you, guys.

And last but not least, my wife, Juliana, and my son, Eduardo. I am very proud to have had your support right since the beginning; you even gave up the time I could've been spending with you so I could write this book. I dedicate it to you with all my heart.

About the Reviewers

Vinicius R. Apolinario has worked with IT for more than 10 years, always working with Microsoft products, managing servers and environments for small, medium, and large companies. He has a strong background in managing Microsoft Servers such as Active Directory, Exchange, and other Windows Server components. Today he works for Microsoft Brazil as a Technical Evangelist, focusing on Infrastructure. As a part of his job, he does presentations for partners and customers about products such as Windows Server, Hyper-V, System Center, and Windows Azure. Before this role, he worked with Microsoft Brazil on the Windows Server and Private Cloud Product Team, as a technical specialist. Vinicius is also a Microsoft Certified Professional on several Microsoft products. He has been a Microsoft Certified Trainer since 2009 and maintains a blog—ADM de Redes (www.admderedes.com. br), in Brazilian Portuguese—through which he shares his knowledge with other professionals.

> Working on this project was truly a challenge but was also really fun for me. The time it consumed was actually taken from the time I spend with my wife. Her support in everything I do is the most important thing I have and I must not forget to thank her for being by my side all the time. I also want to thank Leandro, whom I really admire as a professional, for letting me jump in on this project and making me believe in my skills.

Edvaldo Alessandro Cardoso is a team leader, with expertise on the cloud and a vast knowledge of a variety of Microsoft Infrastructure technologies in areas such as Virtualization and management. His product skill sets include Hyper-V, System Center, Windows Server, SQL Server, Active Directory, Exchange, SharePoint, IIS, and Forefront, and he also has knowledge of Quest Migration Manager, Linux Infrastructure, networking, security solutions (such as VPN and Firewall), and VMware in complex and large scenarios. He has a strong grasp of industry-related datacenter processes, strategies, industry regulations, and requirements.

He has over 23 years of experience in IT, in roles from in application development to a role in the field of network security. He has worked as a system engineer, as a senior consultant, and as an IT manager and has a history of successful enterprise projects in the IT, health, education, and government sectors.

He has been Microsoft Most Valuable Professional in Virtualization since 2009 and is a well-known speaker at IT-related events such as TechEd, CNASI, and User Groups. He has consistently been a presenter for more than 10 years.

An active member of Microsoft System Center 2012 TAP, Australia Computer Society Certified Professional, MCSE, and MCT, since 2003, he was selected as Microsoft TechNet Brazil IT Hero in 2007. He was also awarded the Microsoft IT Heroes Happen award in Los Angeles in 2008. Furthermore, his virtualization project for a government institution in Brazil, while working as IT Manager, was selected as a business case by Microsoft.

He works for Dell Australia as a Senior Technical Consultant. Currently, he is associated with reviewing *System Center Virtual Machine 2012 Cookbook*.

He blogs at:

- ▶ http://virtualizationandmanagement.wordpress.com/
- ▶ http://virtualizacaoegerenciamento.wordpress.com/

I would like to thank my wife, Daniele, and my kids, Matheus, Lucas, and Nicole, for their kind and full support and for understanding my long nights at the computer. I'd also like to thank the Microsoft Virtualization team in Redmond for their help and support, and Leandro Carvalho, for the invitation to participate in such a challenging project.

Kristian Nese started his career in 2005 with no formal training. After some years of heavy training and private study, he has reached a high level of understanding regarding technology, business requirements, and opportunities. He now has 6 years of experience in networking, servers, databases, virtualization, management, automation, architecture, and optimization. Kristian is a Subject Matter Expert in Cloud Computing.

He is an experienced speaker, delivering keynotes and highly technical sessions (level 400), which are often used by Microsoft nationally and globally both as a speaker and writer, on subjects such as Windows Azure, System Center, Windows Server, and Hyper-V.

To stay sharp, he spends a lot of time in the TechNet forums as well, trying to help the community so that they can get the most out of the technology. He also delivers training to local user groups in Norway.

Kristian is also the author of *Cloud Computing - Med Virtual Machine Manager 2012*, published by *IDG/BookWorld*. He has been a part of several other books related to cloud computing, virtualization, and technology in general.

He has also been associated with books such as *Microsoft Private Cloud Computing, Aidan Finn, Hans Vredevoort, Patrick Lownds, and Damian Flynn, John Wiley and Sons, Inc.*, and wrote a review of the latest release of VMM in a famous blog post, *Cloud Computing with System Center 2012 - Virtual Machine Manager*. The *Review*, on his blog, Virtualization And Some Coffee (http://www.wservernews.com/go/1350553154779)

I would like to thank my lovely son, Lukas, for letting me spend my time working on this project. You are the source of my inspiration and happiness.

Carsten Rachfahl started his IT career in 1988, working as a developer on porting X-Windows to an operating system called OS/9. In 1991, he founded his own company in Germany and is self-employed these days. Since 2001, along with Citrix/Terminalserver, his focus is on the virtualization space nowadays. When Microsoft finally created a "real" Hypervisor and brought it to the market, he was all in. His blog http://www.hyper-v-server.de is highly recognized and appreciated within the virtualization community. The blog features tutorials, articles, screencasts, video interviews, and podcasts that focus on Microsoft Private Cloud. Being an MCT, he teaches various Microsoft virtualization courses and his own "Hyper-V Powerkurs" course. As a co-founder of the German Hyper-V community, he regularly organizes events. His efforts were rewarded with the Microsoft MVP Award for Virtual Machine in 2011 and 2012.

I want to thank my wife, Kerstin, and my kids, Ian and Ina, for their ongoing support, their understanding, and encouragement. Without you guys I could not have followed my passion.

www.PacktPub.com

Support files, eBooks, discount offers and more

You might want to visit www.PacktPub.com for support files and downloads related to your book.

Did you know that Packt offers eBook versions of every book published, with PDF and ePub files available? You can upgrade to the eBook version at www.PacktPub.com and as a print book customer, you are entitled to a discount on the eBook copy. Get in touch with us at service@packtpub.com for more details.

At www.PacktPub.com, you can also read a collection of free technical articles, sign up for a range of free newsletters and receive exclusive discounts and offers on Packt books and eBooks.

 PACKTLiB®

http://PacktLib.PacktPub.com

Do you need instant solutions to your IT questions? PacktLib is Packt's online digital book library. Here, you can access, read and search across Packt's entire library of books.

Why Subscribe?

- ▶ Fully searchable across every book published by Packt
- ▶ Copy and paste, print and bookmark content
- ▶ On demand and accessible via web browser

Free Access for Packt account holders

If you have an account with Packt at www.PacktPub.com, you can use this to access PacktLib today and view nine entirely free books. Simply use your login credentials for immediate access.

Instant Updates on New Packt Books

Get notified! Find out when new books are published by following @PacktEnterprise on Twitter, or the *Packt Enterprise* Facebook page.

Table of Contents

Preface

Virtualization has proved that it can help organizations to reduce costs, and the Private Cloud has created a revolution in the way we manage and control our servers with centralization and elasticity. The new Windows Server 2012 Hyper-V release from Microsoft comes with a myriad of improvements in areas such as mobility, high availability, and elasticity, bringing everything you need to create, manage, and build the core components of a Microsoft Private Cloud for virtualized workloads.

Windows Server 2012 Hyper-V Cookbook is the perfect accompaniment for Hyper-V administrators looking to take advantage of all the exciting new features the release has to offer. Through practical recipes, you'll master Hyper-V deployment, migration, and management.

Windows Server 2012 Hyper-V Cookbook is an essential resource for any Hyper-V administrator looking to migrate, install, or manage their virtual machine efficiently.

With all the features of Windows Server 2012 Hyper-V covered, you will learn everything from installation to disaster recovery, security, high availability, configuration, automation, architecture, and monitoring, all in a practical recipe format. The book also includes new features such as Storage and Shared Nothing Live Migration, Hyper-V Replica and Network Virtualization, and much more.

With *Windows Server 2012 Hyper-V Cookbook* in hand, you'll be equipped to manage your private cloud with ease.

What this book covers

Chapter 1, Installing and Managing Hyper-V in Full or Server Core Mode, provides all the necessary information that you need to know before, during, and after the Hyper-V installation, to make sure that you can save time and solve any problems that you may face.

Chapter 2, Migrating and Upgrading Physical and Virtual Servers, covers tasks that will help you to have an easy and a successful upgrade to the new Windows and Hyper-V versions. You will see how to export and import virtual machines, convert VHD files to VHDX files, migrate virtual machine storage using Storage Migration, and so on.

Chapter 3, Managing Disk and Network Settings, covers recipes that will help you to manage disk and network settings efficiently.

Chapter 4, Saving Time and Cost with Hyper-V Automation, highlights the importance of PowerShell. This chapter will help you to learn and utilize basic commands in PowerShell and also to use them for daily tasks.

Chapter 5, Hyper-V Best Practices, Tips, and Tricks, will show you some best practices for Hyper-V and how they can easily be identified and implemented. By using best practices, you can enhance performance, increase security, and improve Hyper-V administration.

Chapter 6, Security and Delegation of Control, shows how to use configuration options such as access control using Authorization Manager and Simple Authorization, network protection with Port ACLs, and Hyper-V auditing, to enforce a safer environment for virtual and host computers.

Chapter 7, Configuring High Availability in Hyper-V, will show you how to create an iSCSI Target server for low-cost storage, how to prepare and configure a failover cluster for Hyper-V, **Cluster Shared Volumes** (**CSV**), and other interesting things, to provide a high availability Hyper-V environment.

Chapter 8, Disaster Recovery for Hyper-V, will walk you through the most important process for setting up disaster recovery for your virtual machines running on Hyper-V.

Chapter 9, Monitoring, Tuning, and Troubleshooting Hyper-V, shows how to use the default tools in Windows Server 2012 to monitor physical and virtual servers, how to troubleshoot, and how to tune Hyper-V servers.

Appendix, Hyper-V Architecture and Components, includes well-explained topics with the most important Hyper-V architecture components compared with other versions.

What you need for this book

You should be comfortable with virtualization concepts and practices, and knowledge of previous versions of Windows Server would be an advantage.

Who this book is for

If you are an administrator who wants to master Microsoft Server Virtualization with Windows Server 2012 Hyper-V, this book is for you.

Conventions

In this book, you will find a number of styles of text that distinguish between different kinds of information. Here are some examples of these styles, and an explanation of their meaning.

Code words in text are shown as follows: "After its download, copy it to the chosen directory, then access it through the command prompt and run the command `coreinfo -v`."

Any command-line input or output is written as follows:

```
netsh interface ip set address "Local Area Connection" static
192.168.0.10 255.255.255.0 192.168.0.1 1
```

New terms and **important words** are shown in bold. Words that you see on the screen, in menus or dialog boxes for example, appear in the text like this: " To change the maximum number of simultaneous storage migrations, click on **Storage Migrations**".

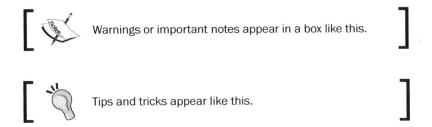

Warnings or important notes appear in a box like this.

Tips and tricks appear like this.

Reader feedback

Feedback from our readers is always welcome. Let us know what you think about this book—what you liked or may have disliked. Reader feedback is important for us to develop titles that you really get the most out of.

To send us general feedback, simply send an e-mail to `feedback@packtpub.com`, and mention the book title via the subject of your message.

If there is a topic that you have expertise in and you are interested in either writing or contributing to a book, see our author guide on `www.packtpub.com/authors`.

Customer support

Now that you are the proud owner of a Packt book, we have a number of things to help you to get the most from your purchase.

Errata

Although we have taken every care to ensure the accuracy of our content, mistakes do happen. If you find a mistake in one of our books—maybe a mistake in the text or the code—we would be grateful if you would report this to us. By doing so, you can save other readers from frustration and help us improve subsequent versions of this book. If you find any errata, please report them by visiting http://www.packtpub.com/support, selecting your book, clicking on the **errata submission form** link, and entering the details of your errata. Once your errata are verified, your submission will be accepted and the errata will be uploaded on our website, or added to any list of existing errata, under the Errata section of that title. Any existing errata can be viewed by selecting your title from http://www.packtpub.com/support.

Piracy

Piracy of copyright material on the Internet is an ongoing problem across all media. At Packt, we take the protection of our copyright and licenses very seriously. If you come across any illegal copies of our works, in any form, on the Internet, please provide us with the location address or website name immediately so that we can pursue a remedy.

Please contact us at copyright@packtpub.com with a link to the suspected pirated material.

We appreciate your help in protecting our authors, and our ability to bring you valuable content.

Questions

You can contact us at questions@packtpub.com if you are having a problem with any aspect of the book, and we will do our best to address it.

1

Installing and Managing Hyper-V in Full or Server Core Mode

In this chapter, we will cover the following topics:

- ▶ Verifying Hyper-V requirements
- ▶ Enabling the Hyper-V Role
- ▶ Installing Windows Server 2012 and Microsoft Hyper-V Server 2012
- ▶ Managing a Server Core installation using sconfig
- ▶ Enabling and disabling the graphical interface in Hyper-V
- ▶ Configuring post installation settings

Introduction

Microsoft has done a great job with Hyper-V. Since its first version in 2008, the enterprises noticed that it was a very good virtualization solution for a first release. The second version with Windows Server 2008 R2 brought a couple of new features that enable mobility such as **Live Migration** and **Dynamic Memory**. The third version in Windows Server 2012 goes beyond all expectations and brings all the components to allow IT administrators to have everything they need to build the base of their cloud. Almost everything in Hyper-V has been improved and it comes with lots of extraordinary features that will transform the way we manage and deploy our datacenters. All workloads can now be virtualized and new features deliver environments beyond virtualization as we know it. Hyper-V Replica, Shared Nothing Live Migration, Full PowerShell support, SMB 3.0, and new limits are some examples that makes Windows Server 2012 Hyper-V a key component with results like high availability, low cost, elasticity, reliability, and everything we need for our servers.

The Hyper-V journey starts with its installation. Even though the installation steps can be simple, it is crucial to take care of the server prerequisites and the post configuration tasks. It is also very important to verify all the hardware prerequisites, the installation, and the administration method that will be used to manage your server.

Having said that, Hyper-V installation should begin with one of the most important phases of virtual servers before even buying the server itself; it should begin with the planning phase. During this phase, you will identify the proper hardware configuration and all of the prerequisites based on your needs. By default, Hyper-V also needs some processor requirements and that's why these components must be present on every server that runs Hyper-V.

This chapter will provide all the information you need to know before, during, and after the Hyper-V installation to make sure that you can save time and solve any problems that you may face.

Verifying Hyper-V requirements

In order to install Hyper-V, you should make sure your server supports it by verifying the prerequisites. Failing with the Hyper-V requirements will result in an error while you install it.

Neither Windows nor Hyper-V offers a tool to verify the prerequisites, but the processor companies created tools such as **AMD-V System Compatibility Check** and **INTEL Processor Identification Utility**.

You will see in this recipe how to use them and also how to use the **Coreinfo** tool to facilitate the process.

Getting ready

To verify the prerequisites of your processor, you must download the Intel Processor Identification Utility. You can download it from the following link: `http://downloadcenter. intel.com/Detail_Desc.aspx?ProductID=1881&DwnldID=7838&lang=eng&iid= dc_rss`.

Based on the server processor, you can also download the AMD Virtualization Technology and Microsoft Hyper-V System Compatibility Check Utility from the following link: `http:// support.amd.com/us/Pages/dynamicDetails.aspx?ListID=c5cd2c08-1432- 4756-aafa-4d9dc646342f&ItemID=177&lang=us`.

To identify the processor brand, open the **Directx Diagnostic Tool** (**dxdiag**) and check the processor information.

You also need to download the Coreinfo tool at `http://technet.microsoft.com/en-us/sysinternals/cc835722` to verify advanced processor support such as **Second-Level Address Translation** (**SLAT**) to install Hyper-V in Windows 8.

How to do it...

In the following steps, you will see how to verify if your computer meets the requirements to install Hyper-V on Windows Server 2012 and Windows 8.

1. After downloading and installing the necessary tools as explained in the *Getting ready* section, install the utility based on your processor.

2. For AMD processors, the AMD-V System Compatibility Check provides the results for AMD processors, if it supports Hyper-V, as shown in the following screenshot:

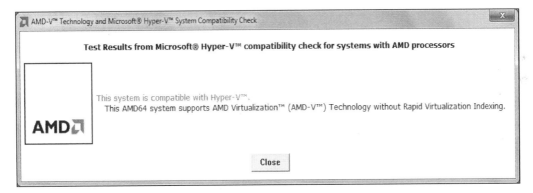

3. If you have an Intel processor, after the Intel Processor Identification Utility install, you will see three tabs once you run it.

4. Select the first tab named **Frequency Test** to show the highest frequency and speed that your processor can handle.

5. Select the second tab named **CPU Technologies** and check the results for the technologies supported by the processor model such as **Virtualization technology, Hyper-Threading** and other technologies.

6. Then, select the **CPUI Data** tab to see information such as the **Processor type, Family model, Cache sizes**, and **Data Execution Prevention (Execute Disable Bit)**.

7. For Intel processors, the result will be similar to the one shown in the following screenshot:

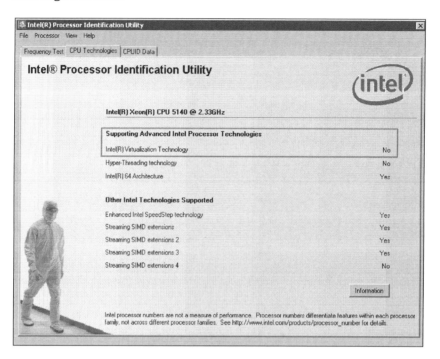

8. To verify whether the processor supports **Second-Level Address Translation (SLAT)** or not, use the free tool called **Coreinfo**.

9. After its download, copy it to the chosen directory, then access it through the command prompt and run the command `coreinfo -v`.

10. In the following screenshot, you can see an example of a computer running with an AMD processor, the SLAT support, the Hypervisor support, and it shows that the Hypervisor is not installed.

```
C:\>coreinfo -v

Coreinfo v3.0 - Dump information on system CPU and memory topology
Copyright (C) 2008-2011 Mark Russinovich
Sysinternals - www.sysinternals.com

AMD E-350 Processor
AMD64 Family 20 Model 1 Stepping 0, AuthenticAMD
HYPERVISOR      -       Hypervisor is present
SVM             *       Supports AMD hardware-assisted virtualization
NP              *       Supports AMD nested page tables

C:\>
```

11. With these steps, you have identified whether the computer you want to install Hyper-V on has all its prerequisites.

How it works...

The mentioned tools simply verify the processor properties to show if it has the necessary features to install Hyper-V. One of these features is the **Hardware-assisted virtualization**. This functionality allows Hyper-V to run under privileged access through a special layer in the processor. In some cases, this feature must be enabled through the **Basic Input-Output System (BIOS)**.

These three tools also check whether the **Data Execution Prevention (DEP)** is present. Intel calls this feature **Intel XD bit (Execute Disable Bit)**, and for AMD it is **AMD NX bit (no execute bit)**. This feature must be also enabled through the BIOS.

There is a particular prerequisite called **Second Level Address Translation (SLAT)** that is shown only by the Coreinfo tool. SLAT is the only requirement that is optional for Windows Server, but necessary for Windows 8 installations. It provides better performance by reducing the CPU time and improving the memory usage in virtual environments. The-v switch used by Coreinfo shows whether the Hypervisor is enabled, whether it supports virtualization, and whether your processor supports SLAT. For the last one you will see an asterisk (*) at Intel **Nested Page (NP)** tables on the AMD processor and **Extended Page Tables (EPT)** for Intel processors.

Coreinfo and both AMD and Intel utilities extract details about the processor information provided by the BIOS. Sometimes for security reasons these features can be enabled manually. It is also common in some cases for it to be necessary to update the BIOS in order to manage these features.

See also

▸ *Appendix A, Hyper-V Architecture and Components*

Enabling the Hyper-V role

By default, Windows Server does not come with Hyper-V installed. In order to start using the virtual environment, Hyper-V needs to be enabled. Even with its straightforward steps, it is important to understand how it works after the setup and what has changed in Windows architecture.

Getting ready

There are different methods to install Hyper-V. The most common one is through the graphical interface.

To get ready to enable Hyper-V you must be logged on with administrative privileges.

How to do it...

The following steps will demonstrate how to enable the Hyper-V Role for Windows Server and what is changed in the Windows architecture after its installation.

1. On the **Start Screen** select **Server Manager**.

2. In the Server Manager Dashboard, click on **Add roles and features**.

3. In the **Add Roles and Feature Wizard**, click on **Next** three times.

4. On the next screen, **Server Roles** page, select **Hyper-V,** as shown in the next screenshot, and click on **Next** three times.

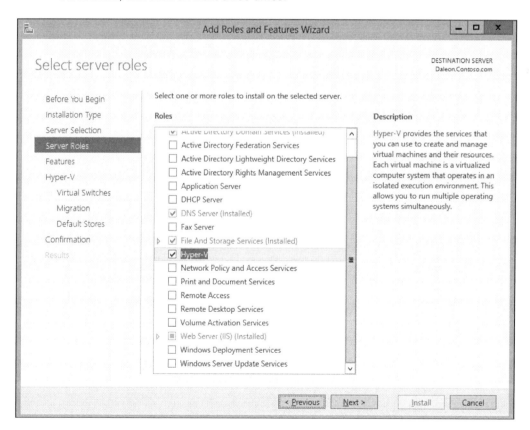

5. In the **Virtual Switches** window, select the network adapter you want to use on Hyper-V. You can add, remove, and modify the virtual switches after the Hyper-V installation through **Hyper-V Manager.**

6. On the **Virtual Machine Migration** page, check the **Allow this server to send and receive live migration of virtual machines** option if you want to enable live migration requests, then click on **Next**.

7. In the last Hyper-V installation page called **Default Stores**, specify the default location for virtual disks and virtual machine configuration files, click on **Next** and then **Install** to start the installation process.

8. Reboot the server after the installation.

How it works...

The process that you have performed to install Hyper-V is quite simple, but it changes the processor architecture by creating a new privileged layer called **ring -1** that runs under the normal layers. The setup process, completed in the previous task, installs the Microsoft Hypervisor on this layer to make sure that Hyper-V has more privilege than Windows itself. Basically, the host operating system runs above the Hypervisor together and at the same level as the virtual machines. The host turns into a special virtual machine containing the virtualization stack, responsible to manage all the virtual machines from it. The following diagram illustrates Hyper-V being installed in the ring -1 and all the partitions running under it.

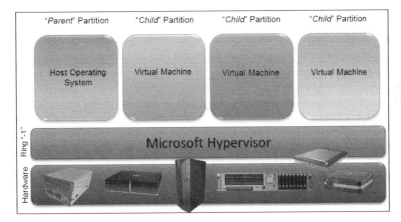

After the first reboot, the Windows boot (`winload.exe`) loads the driver (`hvboot.sys`) responsible to verify the processor that is running and if it supports virtualization. Then the Hypervisor image file is loaded. The host OS and the virtual machines are called **partitions**. Because they run at the same privileged access above the Hypervisor, the host OS is known as **parent partition** and the virtual machines are known as **child partitions**.

There's more...

For automation and fast installation, you can also enable Hyper-V using command lines. You can do that by using the command line `ocsetup`, `Servermanagercmd`, or Windows PowerShell.

Installing Hyper-V using Windows PowerShell

For a PowerShell installation, open Windows PowerShell and run the following command:

```
Add-WindowsFeature Hyper-V
```

See also

> ▸ The *Creating and managing virtual switches* recipe in *Chapter 3, Managing Disk and Network Settings*

> ▸ The *Hyper-V architecture components* recipe in *Appendix A*

Installing Windows Server 2012 and Microsoft Hyper-V Server 2012

After the prerequisites verification we are ready to install either Windows Server 2012 or Microsoft Hyper-V Server 2012. The basic installation is not so complicated and it's the same for both the products, but it takes time to be finished. It would be interesting to identify the needs of a server provisioning made by an automation task; in some companies it is common to have lots of physical and virtual machines being deployed, and automating the process could result in both cost and time saving.

In case you want to use the Windows Server 2012 installation, it offers two methods: Full Server and Server Core. The **Full Server** option provides a graphical interface to manage Hyper-V and Windows, including Hyper-V Manager, Server Manager, and all the other tools and services available on Windows. The problem with the Full Server option is that it comes with other components and services installed by default. That's why Windows Server 2008 introduced a new installation method called **Server Core** which is the default installation method in Windows Server 2012. This option does not come with the **Graphical User Interface** (**GUI**); instead, it has a command line interface. With Server Core, we have more security and better performance in the host computer because only the core components of Windows are installed and features such as the Internet and Windows Explorer are not present.

As a result, the command line interface from Server Core and Hyper-V Server provide the following:

- ▶ Reduced maintenance and management
- ▶ Less risk of bugs and failures
- ▶ Less disk and memory requirements
- ▶ Less updates requirements
- ▶ More security

Both these described options are available on Windows Server, which means that a Windows Server License has to be purchased, although there is a free version of Hyper-V called **Hyper-V Server**. This is a version very similar to Windows Server Core installation, but it comes with Hyper-V only and contains all the features of Windows Server 2012 Hyper-V.

In this task, you will see how to install Hyper-V Server.

Getting ready

Before you start, make sure you have the correct media file or DVD with the Windows Server 2012 installation image.

How to do it...

The following steps will walk you through the installation process of Windows Server 2012.

1. After the DVD boot process in the first screen, select your language, time and current format, keyboard or input method, and click on **Next**.

2. On the second screen, click on **Install now** and installation will automatically continue. If prompted, add the Windows **Product Key** and click on **Next** again.

3. Select the operating system to be installed and then click on **Next**.

4. In order to install Windows Server 2012, you will have to accept the license terms. Select the option **I accept the license terms** and click on **Next**.

5. For a new installation, select the option **Custom: Install Windows only (Advanced)**, as shown in the following screenshot. The upgrade option for this version has been disabled.

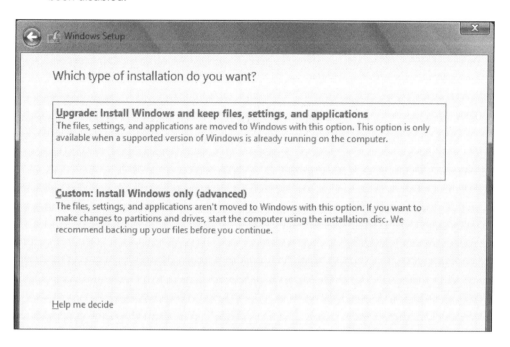

6. In the **Where do you want to install Windows** screen, select the hard drive you want to install Windows Server and click on **Next**. For advanced driver options click on **Drive options (advanced)**.

7. If you have an external storage device or a hard drive that needs a driver to be loaded, click on **Load Driver**, as shown in the next image, and install the proper drivers. Click on **Next**.

8. At this point, you need to wait for the installation to be completed. It can take from 10 to 30 minutes, based on your hardware.

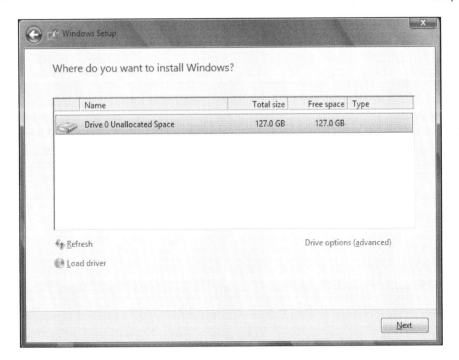

9. When it finishes, you will see the login screen, asking you to provide the username and password. The default user is `Administrator` with a blank password. By default, Windows creates a blank administrator password. For the first login, the system prompts you to insert a password.

How it works...

The process to install Hyper-V Server and Windows is the same. The setup will install all the necessary components, but only to run Hyper-V without any other services (or applications, in case of Hyper-V Server).The first step made by the installation is to load the setup image file `boot.wim` and after the process above the setup applies the `install.wim` image file containing the OS image.

After the installation, you will be prompted to change the administrator password and the system will be ready to be used.

See also

▸ The *Managing a Server Core installation using sconfig* recipe in this chapter

▸ The *Enabling remote management for Hyper-V in workgroup environments* recipe in *Chapter 5, Hyper-V Best Practices, Tips, and Tricks*

Managing a Server Core installation using sconfig

You read in the previous recipe about all the benefits of Server Core such as performance, security and so on. But without the GUI, it's not easy to do the daily management and maintenance of Hyper-V. If you want to change the computer name or the IP address, the GUI is always the easiest to use. But on the other hand, the command line can bring a fast and an automated process.

That's why in Windows Server 2012, the Server Core version of Windows and Microsoft Hyper-V Server 2012 comes with the **Server Configuration** (**sconfig**). This is a command line with a simple interface to reduce the time for doing the most common tasks in Windows. In the following screenshot, you can see an example of sconfig's first page:

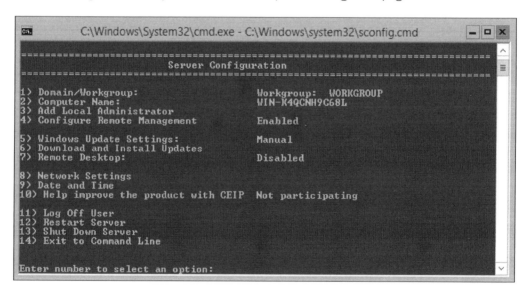

sconfig can do this via an intuitive numerical menu to facilitate the Windows configuration.

A simple example is when you have to change the IP address of your computer by using the command line. Have a look into the following command:

```
netsh interface ip set address "Local Area Connection" static
192.168.0.10 255.255.255.0 192.168.0.1 1
```

Sometimes it is hard to remember the exact command syntax and this can lead to server misconfiguration.

Using sconfig, the process would be simply to press the numbers *8*, *0*, and then *1* from the menu and simply specify the new IP configuration. That's it.

Besides IP configuration, the sconfig offers 13 other options:

- ▶ Domain/workgroup
- ▶ Computer name
- ▶ Adding local administrator
- ▶ Configuring remote management
- ▶ Windows update settings
- ▶ Downloading and installing updates
- ▶ Remote desktop
- ▶ Network settings
- ▶ Date and time
- ▶ Help in improving the product with CEIP
- ▶ Logging off the user
- ▶ Restarting the server
- ▶ Shutting down server

In this recipe, you will see how to set up the most common configurations in your server core without advanced command lines.

Getting ready

The Server Configuration tool is added by default on a Server Core installation or Hyper-V Server. Just type `sconfig` at the command line and the menu will be loaded.

How to do it...

In order to manage the server core installation using sconfig, carry out the following steps:

1. To change the domain/workgroup settings, press *1*.

2. Press *D* for domain or *W* for workgroup.

3. Specify the domain or workgroup name, the necessary username and the password, and press *Enter*.

4. To change the computer name, press *2* and specify the new computer name.

5. Select **Yes** to restart the computer.

6. To add a local administrator, press *3*.

7. Enter the account to join the local administrators group and type the user password.

8. To configure the remote management, press *4*.

9. Select one of the following options:
   - **Allow MMC Remote Management**
   - **Enable Windows PowerShell**
   - **Allow Server Manager Remote Management**
   - **Show Windows Firewall settings**

10. To change Windows update settings:
    1. Press *5*.
    2. Select *A* for automatic or *M* for manual.

11. To download and install updates:
    1. Press *6*.
    2. Select *A* for all updates or *R* for recommended updates only.

12. To enable remote desktop:
    1. Press *7*.
    2. Select *E* to enable or *D* to disable.

13. To configure network settings:
    1. Press *8*.
    2. Select the network adapter number you want to configure and then select one of the existing options:
       - **Set network adapter IP address**
       - **Set DNS Servers**
       - **Clear DNS Server Settings**

14. To change the date and time, press *9* and a graphical interface will show up with the date and time settings to be configured.

15. To restart and shut down the server:

    ❑ Press *1+0* to join Customer Experience Improvement Program

    ❑ Press *1+1* for logoff

    ❑ Press *1+2* to restart the computer

    ❑ Press *1+3* to shut down the server

    ❑ Press *1+4* to exit to command line

16. After these configurations using sconfig and with reduced command line interaction, your server will be ready for the production environment.

How it works...

Server Configuration basically runs scripts in the background for every option that has been selected through a numeric menu, making your life much easier. For every number you select, sconfig can run another script to show a submenu or just run the final script to apply the changes you have selected.

See also

▶ The *Enabling remote management for Hyper-V in workgroup environments* recipe in Chapter 5, *Hyper-V Best Practices, Tips, and Tricks*

Enabling and disabling the graphical interface in Hyper-V

Server Core has many installation benefits, but there are a few situations where the GUI is better and provides more options; for example, when we need to troubleshoot a problem on the server. Even with the handy tools from the previous task, nothing replaces the full server installation.

Windows Server 2012 allows the GUI installation and uninstallation; making our job easier when the GUI is necessary and providing all the benefits of a Server Core installation when you need it. It also allows a third option that enables the graphical management tools.

The three options available on Windows Server 2012 are as follows:

> ▸ **Server Core**: This option provides default installation with command line interface only
>
> ▸ **Minimal Server Interface**: This option comes with the Server Manager, **Microsoft Management Console** (**MMC**) and some Control Panel options
>
> ▸ **Server Graphical Shell**: This option allows for a full graphical interface server

By installing Windows Server with Server Core, you can save up to 3 GB of disk space, when the necessary components for the graphical interface are not present.

This recipe will show how to enable all the three options.

Getting ready

To follow the recipe make sure you have a Server Core installation of Windows with the installation media inserted onto the server.

How to do it...

The following steps will show you how to install the minimal server interface from a Server Core installation and how to enable the full graphical interface.

1. From the Server Core command line, type `PowerShell` to load PowerShell.

    To identify the index number that need to be used in order to enable the graphical interface, type the following command line, where `D:\` is the path for the Windows Server installation DVD drive.

    ```
    Get-WindowsImage -ImagePath D:\Sources\Install.wim
    ```

2. A list with the index number will be displayed, as shown in the following screenshot. Make a note of the number of the type of Windows Installation you want to enable in the next step. In this demonstration, the index number **2** will be used.

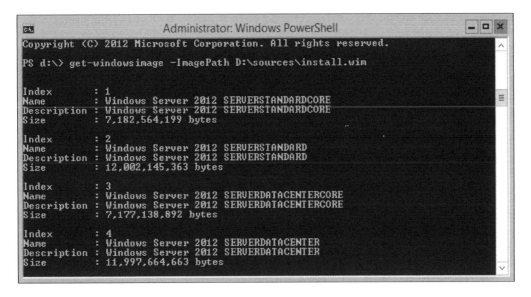

3. Create a new temporary folder to mount the WIM file with the following command:

   ```
   New-Item C:\Sources -Type Directory
   ```

4. To mount the image file in the directory created in the previous step, type the following command by specifying the index number obtained in *step 3*.

   ```
   Mount-WindowsImage -ImagePath D:\Sources\Install.wim -path C:\
   Sources -Index 2 -ReadyOnly
   ```

5. With the mounted image, type the following command to enable the Server Graphical Management Tool and the Infrastructure option.

   ```
   Install-WindowsFeature Server-Gui-Mgmt-Infra -Source C:\Sources\
   Windows\Winsxs
   ```

6. Restart the server and wait for the feature to be configured. It will take a couple of minutes.

7. To enable the full graphical interface, open Server Manager by typing `servermanager.exe`.

8. In the **Server manager dashboard**, click on **Add roles and features**.

9. In the **Add Roles and Features Wizard**, click on **Next** four times.

10. In **Features**, expand **User Interfaces and Infrastructure**, select the option **Server Graphical Shell** as shown in the following screenshot, and click on **Next**:

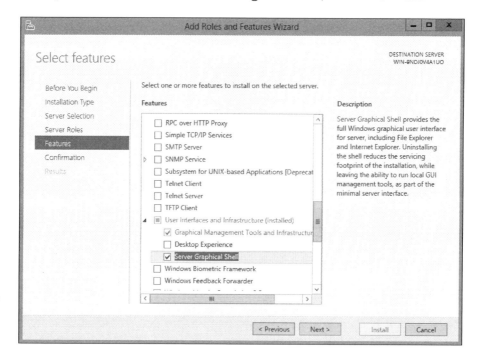

11. To complete the installation, in the **Confirm installation** selections page, click on **Install**.

You can also install the full graphical interface with the following PowerShell command:

```
Install-WindowsFeature Server-Gui-Shell
```

12. After the setup, you need to restart the server. You can check the **Restart each destination server automatically if required** option to automatically restart the server.

13. Having enabled the GUI, we can now see how to uninstall the GUI from the full server installation. In the **Server Manager** window, click on **Manage** and then **Remove Roles and Features**.

14. In the **Before You Begin** screen, click on **Next** four times.

15. Then, in **Features**, clear the check box for the **Server Graphical Shell** option and click on **Next**.
16. Confirm the uninstallation by clicking on **Remove** and wait for the server to be restarted.

How it works...

When Server Core is installed, it doesn't contain the necessary installation files to enable the graphical interface options. It helps to deploy your server core installations with much lesser disk space requirements. For environments where server deployment is done via OS deployment server, you can save a couple of gigabytes with Server Core. After the installation, you will be able to enable the graphical interface. But the installation files should be provided so that the operating system can install and configure the new features. You can use a local DVD drive or a shared folder containing the source folder of the Windows Server installation media.

With the minimal server interface, components such as Windows Explorer and Internet Explorer are not installed. However, Server Manager, **Microsoft Management Console** (**MMC**) and some control panel options that are available, which provide you the basic tools to manage your Server Core without the need to use command line.

The Server Graphical Shell installs all the graphical components, thus transforming your server into a full server installation.

With this new feature, it is now easier to allow the GUI only when needed, for example for a troubleshooting scenario or perhaps an installation of a new service.

Configuring post-installation settings

The Windows Server 2012 installation process is almost the same as Windows Server 2008. Some steps such as IP settings, computer name, and domain join have been removed (in comparison with older versions such as Windows Server 2003), to make it straightforward. That's why the post installation settings are more important than ever now because the setup just adds the default configurations like a random computer name in workgroup, the **Automatic Private IP Address** (**APIPA**) and some other settings.

A Windows Server installation with the default settings can lead to security risks, network access errors, and management problems.

Beyond that, Hyper-V also has some configurations that must be changed, such as default locations for new virtual machines, shortcuts, and other things that you will see in this task.

Getting ready

The only thing you need is a basic Windows Server installation with the Hyper-V role enabled.

How to do it...

The following steps will show how to configure the Windows and Hyper-V post installation settings:

1. First, you need to make sure the Windows Server post installation settings were completed. Before we start the Hyper-V post configuration, let's list the Windows Server post installation settings that you might need to change:

    ❑   Windows activation

    ❑   Configure the time, date, and time zone

    ❑   Network configuration such as IP address, default gateway, and DNS settings

    ❑   Computer name

    ❑   Workgroup or Domain settings

    ❑   Update and configure automatics updates

    ❑   Add the necessary roles and features

2. To guide you through the post configurations, the Windows setup opens the Server Manager tool during the first login, with some settings from the mentioned list for quick access and setup.

3. To see the list, click on **Local Server** in the pane on the left-hand side in Server Manager, as shown in the following screenshot:

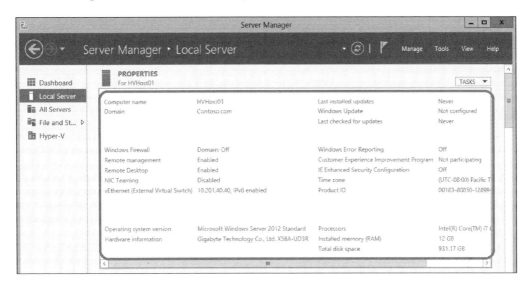

4. Using the list provided by Server Manager, you can make sure that your server is ready to be used with all the common post-installation settings. Select the components you want to change by clicking on the hyperlink in front of them and follow the configuration steps.

5. However, some other interesting settings are not provided by the Server Manager list because they are optional, but some of them you might want to consider are as follows:

   □ After using Server Manager, check the **Do not show me this console at logon** option

   □ Choose a wallpaper to show the system configuration using tools such as `bginfo` or `Backinfo` from **Sysinternals**

   □ From the Windows Explorer options, uncheck the **Hide extensions for known files type** option and check the **Show hidden files** option

   □ An antivirus installation that supports your Windows server version and the roles being executed on it

   □ Clients and agents for products such as backup, software deployment, monitoring systems, and so on

6. Now that your Windows Server is ready to go, you can open Hyper-V and change its default settings, if needed.

7. To open the Hyper-V settings, open the **Hyper-V Manager** tool and then click on **Hyper-V Settings** column on the right-hand side.

8. You'll then see the **Hyper-V Settings** window as you can see in the following screenshot:

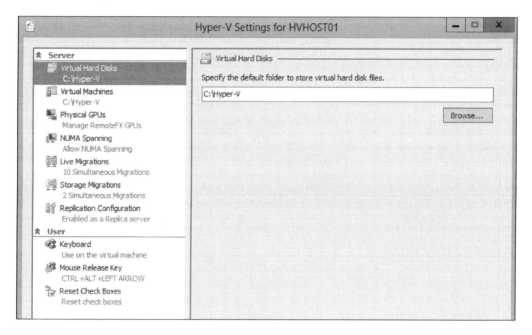

9. **Hyper-V Settings** allow you to manage the Hyper-V default settings divided in 10 components. To change the virtual hard disk's default location, click on **Virtual Hard Disks**.

10. To modify the default virtual machine location, click on **Virtual Machines** and specify the new location.

11. To manage and enable the **Remote FX** feature select **Physical GPUs**.

12. To allow the **Non-Uniform Memory Architecture** (**NUMA**) spanning, select **Numa Spanning**.

13. To enable and change the default values of virtual machine movement settings such as limits and networks that will be used, select **Live Migrations**, as shown in the following screenshot:

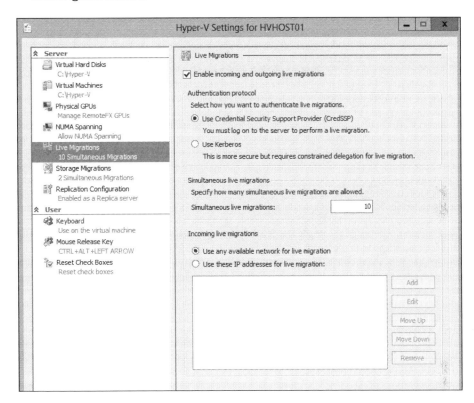

14. To change the maximum number of simultaneous storage migrations, click on **Storage Migrations**.

15. To set up your server as a replica server and change its configuration, click on **Replication Configuration**.

16. The next settings—**Keyboard**,**Mouse Release Key**, and **Reset Check Boxes**—can be changed as well, if needed. Change the settings that you want wherever necessary. After that, your Hyper-V Server will be ready with the specific server settings based on your needs.

How it works...

Changing these configurations might help in some cases when we need a different setting or when you don't want to change them manually every time you have to use them. The first steps showed the most common settings for every Windows server, no matter if it's a Hyper-V Server or not. You won't be able to access your network or access your Active Directory if you don't specify information such as the computer name, IP address, and the other components listed in the first step.

The settings showed between steps 6 through 16 are designed only for Hyper-V Servers and are optional, however most of them are not enabled by default, for example **Live Migration** and **Replication Configuration**. In this case, if you don't enable them, some tasks such as the **Hyper-V Replica** or the **Move** option will not work.

By completing all these steps, you will make sure your server was deployed with the correct and necessary configuration for Hyper-V and the operating system.

See also

▸   The *Migrating the Virtual Machine storage using Storage Migration* recipe in *Chapter 2, Migrating and Upgrading Physical and Virtual Servers*

▸   The *Installing and configuring anti-virus on host and virtual machines* recipe in *Chapter 5, Hyper-V Best Practices, Tips, and Tricks*

▸   The *Configuring Hyper-V Replica between two Hyper-V Hosts using HTTP authentication* recipe in *Chapter 8, Disaster Recovery for Hyper-V*

2
Migrating and Upgrading Physical and Virtual Servers

In this chapter, we will cover the following topics:

▶ Performing an in-place upgrade from Windows Server 2008 R2 to Windows Server 2012

▶ Exporting and importing virtual machines

▶ Migrating virtual machines and updating their integration services

▶ Converting VHD files to VHDX files

▶ Migrating Virtual Machine storage using storage migration

▶ Migrating virtual machines using Shared Nothing Live Migration

▶ Converting physical computers to virtual machines

Introduction

Microsoft has done a very good job with Windows 2012 and its new version of Hyper-V. Most of the new and cool features such as **Storage Migration**, **Hyper-V Replica**, **Hyper-V Extensible Switch**, and many more, focus on virtualization, increasing mobility, scalability, and reliability of your datacenters. With all of them together, we can now say that Windows Server 2012 provides the ultimate private cloud operating system. This means that you will have more flexibility, automation, and better management of virtual and physical servers, in creating your local private cloud infrastructure.

Having said that, the migration plan of the existing environment will still happen. You will probably want to start using all these features. However, the upgrade process needs attention, planning, and special configurations.

With Hyper-V 3 virtual machines, upgrades, and migrations are easier than never before. You can migrate the **Virtual Machine** (**VM**) from old Hyper-V versions using the **Export/Import** feature, move the VM storage of a running VM using Storage migration, or move the VMs on the fly using Shared Nothing Live migration between two Hyper-V servers and a network connection.

This chapter will show you everything you need in the following tasks to make sure you have an easy and a successful upgrade to the new Windows and Hyper-V versions.

Performing an in-place upgrade from Windows Server 2008 R2 to Windows Server 2012

One of the easiest ways to adopt Windows Server 2012 in an existing environment is the **in-place upgrade**. You might have a scenario with a fresh installation of Windows Server 2008 R2 with Hyper-V, where you want to update to Windows Server 2012 Hyper-V on the same hardware. In case you only have Hyper-V running with all the applications and drivers on the host computer being supported on Windows Server 2012, you can use the in-place upgrade option for upgrading. This will guarantee that your host computer will be easily upgraded to Windows Server 2012 with all the configuration and files preserved.

However, in other examples where applications or drivers might not work on Windows Server 2012 or the old installation of Windows Server 2008 R2 with lots of modifications caused by uninstalled applications, the best way would be migration to a new operating system.

It does not matter what your decision is, you need to make sure that you have a test and a rollback plan in place to check whether everything will work fine.

In-place upgrades offer an easy process to turn your Windows Server 2008 R2 installation into a Windows Server 2012 server with all the settings, configuration, files, and applications working as they were in the previous version.

In this recipe, you will see how to run an in-place installation of Windows Server 2012.

Getting ready

In-place upgrades require at least a Windows Server 2008 R2 of the same version as the one that will be installed.

Windows Server Core cannot be upgraded to Windows Server full installation and vice versa. However, after the upgrade, on Windows Server 2012, you can switch from one installation to another.

The setup wizard should be executed from the current Windows installation. Make sure that you are logged in as an administrator on the host computer.

All the virtual machines must be turned off before running the setup wizard. Open Hyper-V Manager and double check whether all the VMs are off.

Check whether you have the installation files on a folder or a DVD with the proper product key before you begin.

How to do it...

In the following steps, you will see how to upgrade your Windows Server 2008 R2 installation to Windows Server 2012, using the Windows installation process.

1. From the Windows Server 2008 R2 server, run the `Setup.exe` from the Windows Server 2012 installation folder.

2. In the **Windows Setup** window, click on **Install now**.

3. In the **Get important updates for Windows Setup**, select the update option you want to use. Select **Go online to install updates now (recommended)**, if your system is not up-to-date or **No thanks** to continue the update process.

4. If prompted, insert the Windows Server 2012 product key and click on **Next**.

5. In the **Select the operating system you want to install**, select the OS you want to install and click on **Next**.

6. In **License Terms**, check the **I accept the license terms** option and click on **Next**.

7. In the **Which type of installation do you want?** window, select the **Upgrade: Install Windows and keep files, settings and applications** option as shown in the following screenshot:

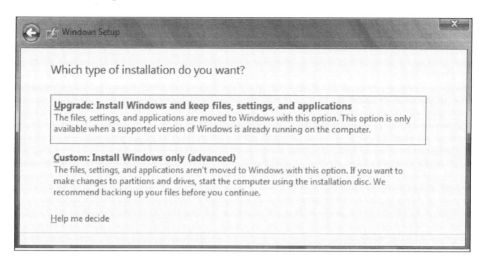

8. In the **Compatibility report**, which is also saved on your desktop for further reference, check and solve all the dependencies and identify the potential errors that the installation might find, before you continue, as shown in the next screenshot.

9. Click on **Next** to start the upgrade process and wait for it to be finished. It will take about 10 to 30 minutes, based on the number of roles, applications, and settings that will be upgraded.

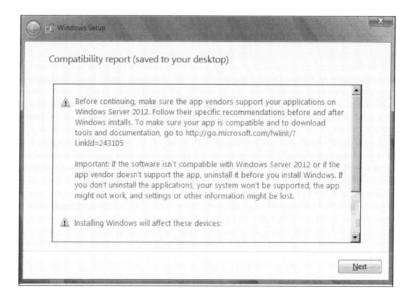

10. When the upgrading is finished, log in with an administrator account, open Hyper-V Manager, and update the integration components of all the virtual machines.

How it works...

In-place upgrades are an easier way to migrate your current Windows Server 2008 R2 servers to Windows Server 2012, but it is also the most risky option. It is important to verify whether all the applications, roles, features, and configurations will work on Windows Server 2012.

In some scenarios, where an old server installation is present, administrators prefer to install a fresh Windows installation and move the roles using tools such as Windows Server Migration Tools or the Hyper-V import option for virtual machines. The benefit of the two last options is that you will make sure that the old configuration or settings that could be a problem for both old and new installations will not be on the new servers.

If you are comfortable with running an in-place upgrade after checking all the compatibility issues and running a backup, you will need to run the installation setup from the running server and walk through the wizard. For the **Which installation type you want?** option you just need to select **Upgrade** and the wizard will start a compatibility report to check whether everything will work fine with the new Windows installation. After checking and addressing any problems that you may have, just click on **Next** and wait for the upgrade to be completed.

With five or six easy steps, your current server running Hyper-V will be upgraded with the new Windows version.

After the upgrade, on the Hyper-V Manager of Windows Server 2012, you will need to upgrade the Integration Components on every existing virtual machine.

See also

▶ The *Exporting and importing virtual machines* recipe in this chapter

▶ The *Migrating virtual machines and updating their integration services* recipe in this chapter

For more information about the **Windows Server Migration tools**, visit the following link: http://technet.microsoft.com/en-us/library/jj134202.

For more information about migrating a **Failover Cluster** environment, visit the following link: http://blogs.msdn.com/b/clustering/archive/2012/06/25/10323434.aspx.

Exporting and importing virtual machines

If you don't want to perform an in-place upgrade from Windows Server 2008 R2 to Windows Server 2012, the migration from an old Hyper-V version to Windows 2012 is not so complicated either. You need to install a new server with Windows 2012, enable Hyper-V, export the virtual machine from the old server, and import them back to your new server. That's it! This is the same process that we have been using since the first version of Hyper-V in Windows Server 2008. However, the previous versions of Hyper-V had some limitations; for example, you could import only a virtual machine that had been exported before and lots of other issues regarding different configurations in the source and destination host.

The next few steps will guide you through the new process and options to import and export virtual machines introduced in Hyper-V 3.0.

Getting ready

Before you start to export your virtual machines, make sure they are turned off or in save state. You can't export a virtual machine with it running or in pause state.

How to do it...

The following steps will show you how to export and then import a VM back in Windows Server 2012. The export process can also be used in Windows Server 2008 and 2008 R2, so that you can import the VMs in Windows Server 2012.

1. Open the **Start screen** and select **Hyper-V Manager**.
2. Select the virtual machines you want to export, right-click on them, and select **Export**, as you can see in the following screenshot:

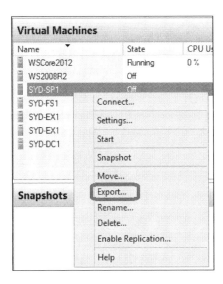

3. In the **Export Virtual Machine** window, enter the path you want to export the virtual machines to and click on **Export**.

4. Copy the exported virtual machine files to the destination host.

Also, you can import and export VMs using the PowerShell commands `Import-VM` and `Export-VM` respectively. For more information, open PowerShell and type `Help Import-VM` for import and `Help Export-VM` for export.

5. Open **Hyper-V Manager** on the destination host and select **Import Virtual Machine** from the pane on the right-hand side.

6. On the **Before You Begin** screen, click on **Next**.

7. On the **Locate Folder** screen, specify the folder from which you want to import the virtual machine files and click on **Next**.

8. In the **Select Virtual Machine** window, select the virtual machines to be imported and click on **Next**.

9. In the **Choose Import Type** window, select the type of import, as shown in the next screenshot, and click on **Next**.

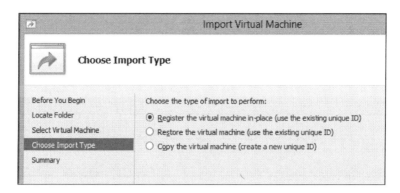

10. If the source virtual machine has different virtual switches attached to it or different configurations that the destination host will not support, new windows can be displayed asking you to address the problem. The next screenshot shows an example of a VM with a different virtual switch name. Address all the problems or conflicts that the VMs have and click on **Next**.

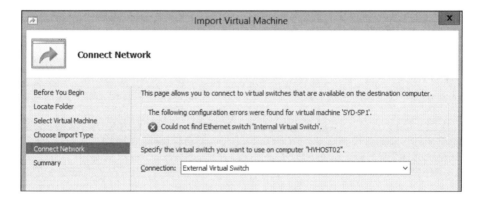

11. If prompted, specify the folders that you want the virtual machine files and disks in, and click on **Next**.

12. Click on **Finish** when it is done and you will see the imported virtual machine in the Hyper-V console.

How it works...

The process to export the **Virtual Machine** (**VM**) collects its entire configuration file, snapshots, the **Virtual Hard Drive** (**VHD**), and puts all of them together in a new folder with the virtual machine name in the specified path during the export process. It's also possible to select more than one virtual machine and export them in just one go, in case you are migrating from old Hyper-V versions.

 Hyper-V 3.0 now allows a VM to be imported without requiring the export process. You can copy all the virtual machine files to a new host and during the importation, you just need to select the VM configuration file (.xml) and continue the steps as shown in the previous section.

Windows Server 2012 Hyper-V introduces an improved and new process to import virtual machines. Firstly, you need to specify the folders where the virtual machine files sit. It does not matter if the virtual machines were exported or not. You can simply copy and paste the VM files and the result will be the same.

After that, the wizard shows a list of virtual machines that you want to import. The good news here is that Hyper-V lists the VMs as per their names and not by using the **Global Unique Identifier** (**GUID**). It makes the process easier.

The wizard provides three different types of import. The first type of import—**Register the virtual machine in-place (use the existing unique ID)**—assumes that all the files of the imported VM are in a single place and you have to just register the VM. It can be used to register VMs in a new host using the same VM path. The second one—**Restore the virtual machine (use the existing unique ID)**—is almost the same as the previous option, except that it allows you to specify the path of the VM files. Also, it copies the files to the new destination path. The last option—**Copy the virtual machine (create a new unique ID)**—creates new VMs with new IDs and can be very helpful when you just want to use the VM files as a template to create new VMs.

The problem with the previous versions of Hyper-V is when the VM has a different configuration in the source host. For example, if the VM has a different virtual switch or a hardware setting that is not present in the destination host, the import process would fail. Now the import is clever enough to identify whether the VM has conflicted or has different settings. Memory, processor, disk, networks, and file paths are checked and in case of problems, the wizard will prompt you to make changes, based on the destination limits and configuration.

When finished, your virtual machine will be ready to be started on the new server, making your migration much simpler.

See also

▸ The *Migrating virtual machines and updating their integration services* recipe in this chapter

Migrating virtual machines and updating their integration services

Most people think that the process to migrate the virtual machine from one host with a previous Hyper-V version, to another one with a newer version, is simply done by the export and import process shown in the previous task. You will probably notice some strange behavior in the VMs such as mouse integration, slow performance, and some other issues. You will understand with the next steps why this problem occurs and how to migrate the virtual machine without such problems.

Getting ready

For virtual machines with a supported Linux operating system, you need to download the latest Linux integration components. You can download the current version from here: `http://www.microsoft.com/en-us/download/details.aspx?id=34603`.

To know which Linux operating systems have the Hyper-V support, access the website `http://technet.microsoft.com/library/hh831531.aspx`.

For instructions about the Linux integration components' installation, refer to the following documentation: `http://www.microsoft.com/downloads/info.aspx?na=41&srcfamilyid=216de3c4-f598-4dff-8a4e-257d4b7a1c12&srcdisplaylang=en&u=http%3a%2f%2fdownload.microsoft.com%2fdownload%2fA%2f5%2fE%2fA5EEAE8B-570D-4882-8215-21EE3C0CABAF%2fLinux%20Integration%20Services%20v3.2%20Read%20Me.pdf`.

How to do it...

The following steps will demonstrate how to upgrade the Integration Components of Windows virtual machines and some details about Linux VMs:

1. For Linux virtual machines, you should uninstall the integration components manually before the export process; for Windows virtual machine, proceed with the following process.

2. Using **Hyper-V Manager**, export the virtual machine to a temporary location.

3. In the new Hyper-V server, open the **Hyper-V Manager** again and import the virtual machine.

4. Start the virtual machine and after logging in, navigate to the **Virtual Machine Connection**, click on **Action | Insert Integration Services Setup Disk**, as shown in the following screenshot:

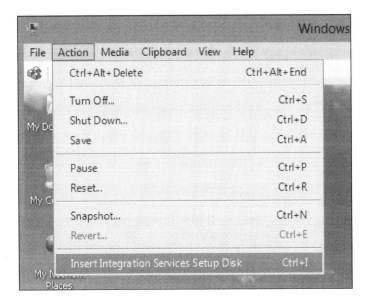

5. Install the integration components for the Linux operating system manually. You can refer to the documentation provided at the beginning of this recipe.

6. In the **Upgrade Hyper-V Integration Services** window, click on **OK**. Wait until the **Integration Services** installation has finished and click on **Yes** to restart your virtual machine. The VM will start normally after the installation, loading the new integration services and providing all the necessary components to allow communication between the virtual machine and Hyper-V.

How it works...

Every virtual machine running on Hyper-V needs a set of services called **Integration Components** for Windows VMs, and **Integration Services** for Linux VMs. These components allow complete integration between the VM and the virtualization stack. The services are enabled when the correct integration components are installed. These are as follows:

- ▶ Operating system shutdown
- ▶ Time synchronization
- ▶ Data exchange
- ▶ Heartbeat
- ▶ Backup (volume snapshot)

To check whether these services are available, you can open the **Virtual Machine Settings** and click on **Integration Services**, as in the following example:

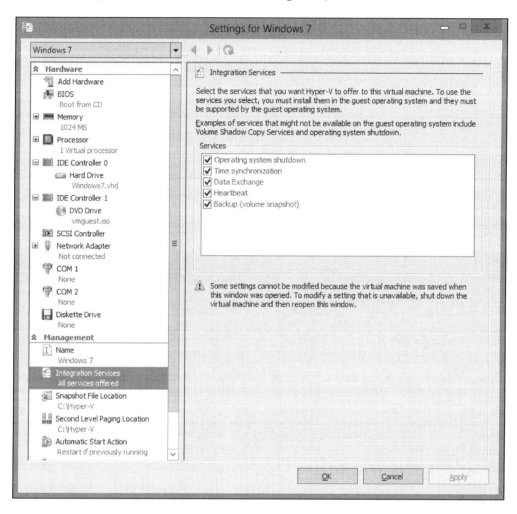

Failing to install or having an older version of the Integration Components can lead to poor performance, mouse issues, and other problems with the integration services.

Some operating systems that run as a virtual machine have Integration Components in their kernel by default—for example, in Windows 7, Windows Server 2008, 2008 R2, and some Linux distributions. But because the Integration Components are based on the Hyper-V version, when moving the virtual machine to a Hyper-V 3.0 host you need to update it as shown in the previous steps.

Following this task, you will ensure that every virtual machine has the latest Integration Service, thus providing more reliability and better performance.

There's more...

To check the Integration Services version on all the virtual machines from your host computer, you can use the following commandlet:

```
Get-VM | Format-Table Name, IntegrationServicesVersion
```

All the virtual machines and the Integration Services versions will be listed in the result pane.

See also

▶ The *Exporting and importing virtual machines* recipe in this chapter

Converting VHD files to VHDX files

Microsoft has been using the same **Virtual Hard Disk** (**VHD**) format since the one created by Connectix in 1995. That was created to allow Windows 3.1 to run on Mac computers. It has been improved, but as with any other product's lifecycle, its life ended. On Windows Server 2012, the default format is **VHDX** and provides lots of features and enhancements compared to its previous version.

It has been designed to work well with all the new modern storage options and has capabilities to provide reliability and store large scenarios. VHDX now supports 64 TB against 2 TB of VHD. Also, it supports larger logical sector sizes up to 4 KB, and large block sizes up to 256 MB, to optimize the virtual disk performance.

Another interesting feature is the use of the log in order to ensure the security and resiliency against corruptions that can occur in power failures, for example.

With all these excellent features, it will be very good practice to convert the existing virtual machines running on VHD files for much better performance, security, and reliability.

Getting ready

Copy your existing VHD file to another location or run a backup to assure you will be able to recover it in case of any problems.

Make sure that you also have enough disk space and that the virtual machine is turned off.

How to do it...

You will see in the following steps how to convert a VHD to a VHDX, and attach it to a virtual machine.

1. In order to convert a VHD file to VHDX, open Hyper-V Manager and click on **Edit Disk**, on the column on the right-hand side.

2. On the **Before You Begin** page, click on **Next**.

3. For the **Locate Virtual Hard Disk** option, specify the path where your VHD file is and click on **Next**.

4. For **Choose Action**, select **Convert**, as shown in the following screenshot, and click on **Next**:

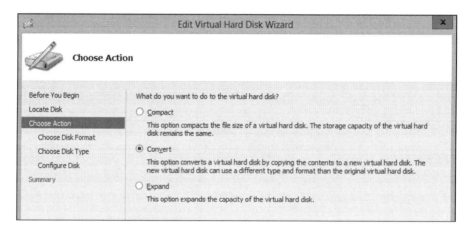

5. In the **Convert Virtual Hard Disk** window, select **VHDX**, and click on **Next**.

6. On the next screen, select either **Fixed size** or **Dynamically expanding** as the disk type and click on **Next**, as shown in the following screenshot:

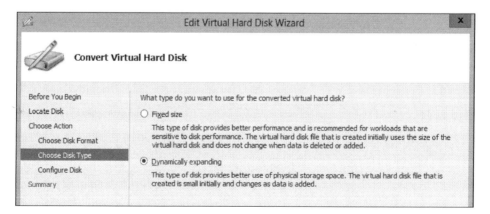

7. For the **Configure Disk** option, specify the VHDX file path and click on **Finish** to start the conversion.

8. When finished, open the virtual machine properties where the disk is attached to, select the **Hard Drive** option, and specify the new VHDX path. When finished, turn the virtual machine on.

How it works...

Converting VHD files to VHDX is quite easy, but it can take some time, based on the VHD file size. The convert wizard just asks for the VHD path of the file that needs to be converted, the disk type, and the destination path.

After completing the conversion, the virtual machine settings must be changed and the new file should be replaced.

It is important to know that everything that works on VHD works on VHDX too. Given all the benefits and improvements, there is no reason why you should not convert these disks. In case you need, for some reason, to roll back to a VHD, that is possible too. You only need to run the conversion wizard again, select the VHDX, and convert back to a VHD.

With all the virtual machines running with VHDX files, you can be sure that they will give better performance and consistency.

There's more...

For large-scale migration scenarios or in case you just need to facilitate the conversion process, you can also use the commandlet `Convert-VHD` on PowerShell.

The only thing you need to specify is the destination VHD.

```
Convert-VHD –Path C:\Hyper-V\Win.vhd –DestinationPath c:\Hyper-V\NewWin.vhdx
```

See also

▶ The *Creating and adding virtual hard disks* recipe in *Chapter 3, Managing Disk and Network Settings*

Migrating Virtual Machine storage using Storage Migration

In a virtual environment, with thousands of physical and virtual servers, it is normal to face some problems or limitations that require reallocating a virtual machine to another location. Let's list some examples of the issues you might encounter:

- ▸ Hardware limitation
- ▸ Storage upgrade and maintenance
- ▸ Poor VM Performance (I/O)
- ▸ Fix configuration mistakes

Windows Server 2012 Hyper-V introduces a new feature to help you in these scenarios called **storage migration**, providing the ability to reallocate the virtual machine storage while it's running.

This recipe will walk through all the details and steps to show you how to move the virtual machine storage using the storage migration.

Getting ready

The storage migration feature copies the current storage to the destination location, but it keeps the source files until the migration completion. Make sure that you have enough disk space when reallocating the VM storage within the same partition.

How to do it...

The following steps will guide you through the wizard to migrate the virtual machine storage to another location while the VM is still running.

1. Open the **Start** screen and select **Hyper-V Manager** from the available list.
2. Right-click on the virtual machine that you want to move and click on **Move**, as shown in the following screenshot:

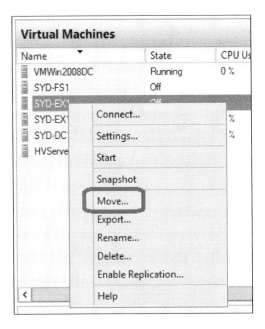

3. In the **Before You Begin** page click on **Next**.

4. In the **Choose Move Type** window, select **Move the virtual machine's storage** and click on **Next**, as shown in the following screenshot:

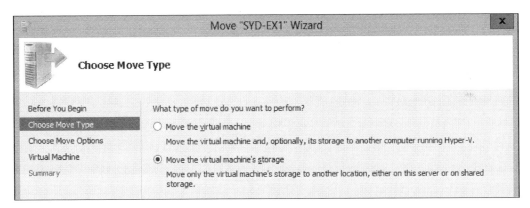

5. In the next window, **Choose Options for Moving Storage**, you can select to move the virtual machine's data to different locations with the option **Move Virtual Machine's data to different locations**. If you want to move the data to a single location, you can select the **Move Virtual Machine's data to a single location** or **Move only the virtual machine's virtual hard disks** options as shown in the following screenshot. Select the option you want and click on **Next**.

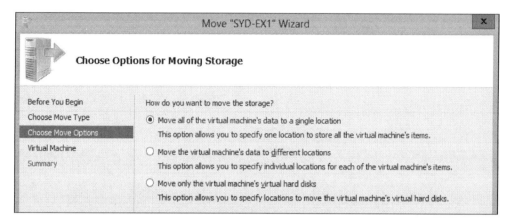

6. In the **Choose new location for virtual machine** window, select the new location path in the **Folder** option in which the virtual machine will be moved and click on **Next**.

7. Review the options you have chosen in the **Completing Move Wizard** screen and click on **Finish** to start the move process.

8. Wait for the move process to finish and verify if the virtual machine is running under the new path.

How it works...

The storage migration is an out-of-the-box feature that can be used without any prerequisites for a local move request, allowing you to move the VM storage to another path in the local storage or a shared folder on the network using the new SMB 3.0 protocol. It is independent of hardware vendors and more than one migration can occur simultaneously.

The Storage Migration wizard offers three options to move the virtual machine storage. The **Move all of the virtual machine's data to a single location**, the simplest and the default option, moves all the VM storage and configuration files to a single location. The **Move the virtual machine's data to different locations** option allows you to specify different paths for every virtual machine storage and configuration files. The last one, **Move only the virtual machine's virtual hard disks**, allows you to specify different locations to move only the virtual machine's hard disks.

Hyper-V starts the process of copying the virtual machine configuration files and its virtual hard disk to the new location while the VM is still running and the disk is still being used. Then, after a certain amount of copied data, Hyper-V starts to mirror the source and the destination hard drive. By completing the copying and mirroring, the system switches the reads and writes to the new virtual hard drive and deletes the source files.

During all these processes, the virtual machine might have a poor disk performance, but this all happens with no downtime. Once this is finished, you will see the virtual machine up and running in the new path.

There's more...

You can create a script to automate the process using PowerShell with the `Move-VMStorage` command to move a virtual machine to another location at the same server.

```
Move-VMStorage –VMName "Windows 7" –DestinationStoragePath "E:\Windows 7\"
```

The previous command line moves a virtual machine called `Windows 7` to the destination path `E:\Windows 7\`.

Moving all the virtual machines to a new storage location

Using PowerShell, you can migrate all the local virtual machines to a new location using a single command line:

```
Get-VM * | Move-VMStorage –DestinationStoragePath "E:\Virtual Machines\"
```

With this command, PowerShell gets all the virtual machines from the local host and moves them to the new path on the `E` drive.

Migrating virtual machines using Shared Nothing Live Migration

Mobility! That's the word that comes up when talking about Windows Server 2012 Hyper-V. On previous versions of Hyper-V, the Live Migration was introduced as a feature that allows you to move virtual machines from one node to another in a cluster with no downtime. It basically moves the virtual machine memory and the VM configuration from one node to another and switches the server access to the storage. It is handy when you need to run any maintenance task on the host server or in case of scalability, for example. The only problem was the dependency of a shared storage in a cluster environment.

Although Live Migration still exists on Windows Server 2012 with lots of improvements, Hyper-V 2012 can now move any running virtual machine from one server to another and the only requirement is a network connection, simple as that. There is no need for clustered environments to move your VMs across your servers. For a cloud infrastructure, the scalability and mobility provided by Shared Nothing Live Migration allows you to move the whole VM storage, configuration files, and memory on the fly to another server with only one limit for concurrent migrations: your hardware.

Getting ready

Shared Nothing Live Migration is available only on Windows Server 2012 Hyper-V and Microsoft Hyper-V Server 2012. You cannot migrate VMs from (or to) old Hyper-V versions.

Make sure that you have enough disk space on the destination server to move your VMs. Also make sure that the network configuration for, and the communication between, the host servers is working properly.

How to do it...

In the following steps, you will see how to enable live migrations and how to perform a Shared Nothing Live Migration to migrate a VM from one host to another.

1. To enable Live Migrations on the host server, open **Hyper-V Manager** and click on **Hyper-V Settings** on the right column.

2. In **Hyper-V Settings**, click on **Live Migrations** and check the **Enable incoming and outgoing live migrations** option.

3. For the **Authentication protocol** option, select **Use Credential Security Support Provider (CredSSP)** or **Use Kerberos**.

4. For the **Simultaneous live migrations** option, specify the number of concurrent live migrations that will be allowed.

5. In **Incoming live migrations**, specify a particular network for live migration by selecting **Use these IP addresses for live migration** or select **Use any available network for live migration** to use any local network adapter available to move the VMs. The following screenshot shows an example of the existing options described in the previous steps. When finished, click on **OK**.

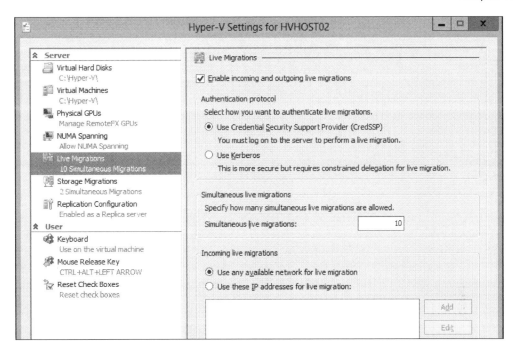

6. To move your virtual machine using Shared Nothing Live Migration, open **Hyper-V Manager**, right-click on the VM you want to move, and select **Move**.

7. In the **Before You Begin** page, click on **Next**.

8. In the **Choose Move Type** window, select **Move the Virtual Machine**, as shown in the following screenshot, and click on **Next**.

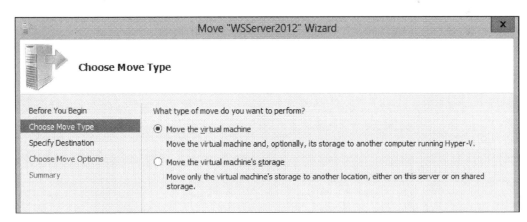

9. In **Specify Destination Computer**, type the destination server where you want to move your VM and click on **Next**.

10. In **Choose Move Options**, select **Move the virtual machine's data to a single location** to move all configuration files and virtual disks to the same location. Select **Move the virtual machine's data by selecting where to move the items** to select the location of each item to be moved, or select **Move only the virtual machine** to move the VM only and keep the VHD files on the same location and click on **Next**, as shown in the following screenshot:

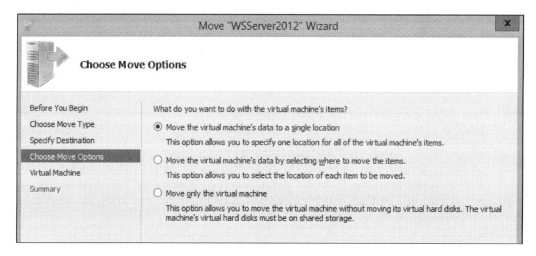

11. In **Choose a new location for virtual machine**, select the destination folder where the VM will be moved and click on **Next**.

12. In the **Summary** page, verify the selected options and click on **Finish** to start the moving process. Wait until completion and check the virtual machine on the destination host.

How it works...

Shared Nothing Live Migration has an easy and intuitive wizard to move your VMs across your host servers. Different to Storage Migration, by default live migrations are disabled on Hyper-V. To enable it you must specify some options such as authentication protocol, simultaneous live migration, and incoming live migration.

The first configuration, authentication protocol, let you choose two options to specify the way Hyper-V will authenticate to start the live migrations. By selecting **Credential Security Support Provider** (**CredSSP**) you can live migrate virtual machines only if you are logged on to the source computer to start it, so that CredSSP can be used to authenticate the migration. This option does not require any prerequisites, but you will not be allowed to perform a live migration using other remote management tools such as Hyper-V Manager from another server or PowerShell sessions. The migration will be initiated only when you are logged on the source server.

If you also want to start live migrations using these remote management tools, you can select **Kerberos** for authentication. When starting a live migration, either locally on the server or remotely, a constrained delegation will be used to authenticate and start the migration. This is the best option due to the flexibility to start the migration from remote tools. It requires pre-configuration on Active Directory. Kerberos authentication will be demonstrated in the *There's more...* section.

The next option provides a field to specify the number of simultaneous live migrations that Hyper-V will support. In this option, the only limit is the hardware and the network connection between the servers.

The last option, incoming live migrations, allows you to configure the network that will be used for live migrations. For better performance and resilience, it is recommended to use a specific network for live migration, but if you have only one network adapter on the host computer or it doesn't have a particular adapter for live migration, you can use any available network. After enabling live migrations and setting up these three options, you are ready to move your VMs.

The wizard is launched with a simple right-click on the VM. Shared Nothing Live Migration and Storage Migration use the same wizard, which improves the user experience and reduces the number of windows and options on Hyper-V. The first window, **Choose Move Type**, has the Shared Nothing Live Migration option (**Move the virtual Machine**) and the Storage Migration option (**Move the virtual machine's storage**).

After selecting to move the VM and specifying the destination server where the VM will be moved, you can select one of the three move options to move the VMs to a single location, select different locations per VM item or move only the VM. The option to move only the VM works when you are storing the VM in a shared folder on the network or any other type of shared storage.

When the migration starts, Hyper-V authenticates the connection on the destination host and starts the process by migrating the VM disks. After moving all the disk data, it migrates the virtual machine memory.

When finished, your VM will be up and running on the destination host. All the migration process happens with no downtime.

There's more...

The PowerShell commandlet to move a VM can be considered one of the easiest options on Hyper-V, because the entire process happens with just one line of command. The whole configuration and migration process described in this recipe can be automated using PowerShell.

To enable live migrations of virtual machines, type the following command line:

```
Enable-VMMigration | Set-VMMigrationNetwork Any | Set-VMHost –
VirtualMachineMigrationAuthenticationType CredSSP
```

You can also change the migration network from any to a specific network by adding the IP address or the authentication type by changing **CredSSP** to **Kerberos**.

After the live migration is enabled, type the following commandlet to move VMs. In this example, a VM called SYD-FS1 will be moved to the server HVHost02 and the storage will be located at D:\Hyper-V. For more information about Move-VM, type Help Move-VM.

```
Move-VM SYD-FS1 HVHost02 –IncludeStorage –DestinationStoragePath D:\
Hyper-V\
```

Configuring constrained delegation to authenticate live migrations

Constrained delegation allows live migrations to be started using any remote management tool and might help in providing more flexibility to move your VMs.

To enable it, open **Active Directory Users and Computers** from one of the Domain Controllers where the host servers sit, right-click on the host computer account and click on **Properties**. In the **Properties** window, click on the **Delegation** tab, select **Trust this computer for delegation to the specified services only** and select **Use Kerberos**, as shown in the next screenshot.

Click on **Add** and then **Users or Computers**. In the **Select Users or Computers box**, type the destination host server name and click **OK**.

In the **Add Services** dialog box, select **cifs** and **Microsoft Virtual System Migration Service** and click on **OK**. The two services will be listed in the service type, as shown in the next screenshot:

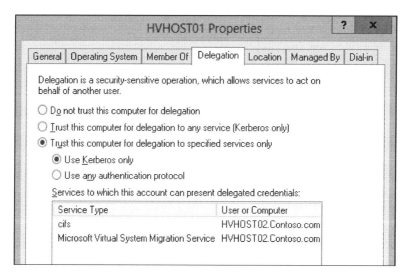

Click on **OK** to close the computer properties window and repeat the same process on the destination server computer account.

After that, you can change the live migration authentication type to use Kerberos.

See also

▸ The *Migrating virtual machines storage using Storage Migration* recipe in this chapter

▸ The *Using Live Migration in a Cluster environment* recipe in *Chapter 7, Configuring High Availability in Hyper-V*

Converting physical computers to virtual machines

Every day we can see companies implementing virtual servers to explore the virtualization benefits such as cost reduction, flexibility, automation, and so on.

That's why physical to virtual migration is still very common and it's important to make sure that the existing servers running under old and unnecessary hardware can be converted into virtual machines.

In this recipe, you will see how to convert a physical server into a virtual machine using the tool **Disk2vhd**.

Getting ready

Disk2vhd is not a default Windows tool and it has to be downloaded from the following link: `http://technet.microsoft.com/en-us/sysinternals/ee656415`.

The minimal operating system for client conversions is Windows XP SP2 and for server versions is Windows Server 2003. Also, you need to pay attention to the implications caused by licensed software applications such as OEM OSes.

How to do it...

In order to convert physical computers to virtual machines, carry out the following steps:

1. Download and extract the Disk2vhd tool to a temporary folder in the computer you want to convert.

2. Double click on the `disk2vhd.exe` file and click on **Yes** if you receive a message from **User Account Control**. Click on **OK** on the EULA page.

3. After opening Disk2vhd, select the path in which you want to save the virtual hard drive in **VHD File Name**, as shown in the following screenshot:

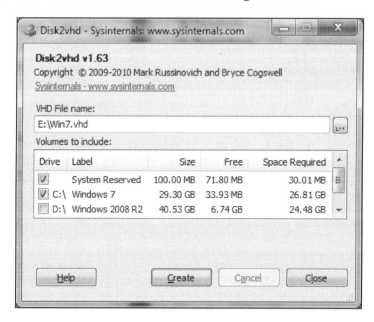

4. Under **Volumes to Include**, select the volumes you want to convert and click on **Create**.

5. Disk2vhd will start to convert the online system, without the need for a shutdown or restart. The time to complete this is based on the disk performance and the volume size you selected.

6. After the conversion, copy the output vhd file to the Hyper-V server you want to import the virtual machine to.

7. In Hyper-V, create a virtual machine with the configuration you want and under **Connect Virtual Hard Disk**, select the VHD file created from the previous steps.

8. After you've finished creating the virtual machine using the converted virtual hard disk, start it through the Hyper-V console.

 To prevent name and IP conflicts, make sure the old physical computer is not connected on the same network as the new virtual machine.

9. Start the converted virtual machine and after the logon process, using the **Virtual Machine Connection**, click on **Action** and **Insert Integration Services Setup Disk**.

10. An **AutoPlay** window will open. Select **Install Hyper-V Integration Components** and wait until the setup finishes installing the components.

11. After installing the integration components your converted virtual machine is ready to be used.

How it works...

Disk2vhd is a free Microsoft tool that creates a virtual hard disk file from a physical computer. After specifying the destination path and the volumes you want to convert, as shown in the third and the fourth step, the tool uses the **Windows Volume Snapshot** functionality to create a point-in-time snapshot of the volumes you included in the third step. One of the benefits of Disk2vhd is the ability to convert the physical computer while it's running.

The seventh step showed a virtual machine being created using the output file from the conversion. After that, it is also important to install the Hyper-V Integration Components. By completing the installation you have finished the conversion, allowing you to start your physical computer decommission.

There's more...

Disk2vhd is very handy for simple conversions, but if you want to convert lots of physical computers, the best solution is to use System Center Virtual Machine Manager 2012 with the option **Physical to Virtual** (**P2V**) conversion, providing a centralized console and with advanced options and configurations.

Converting physical computers to virtual machines using a command line

Disk2vhd also supports the command line interface, allowing you to create scripts to automate both tasks and the conversion.

The command line usage is as follows: `disk2vhd <drive:> <vhdfile>`.

To convert the `C` partition into a VHD file in the `D` partition, the command line is as follows:

```
Disk2vhd C: D:\ConvertedVM.vhd
```

3
Managing Disk and Network Settings

In this chapter, we will cover the following:

- ▸ Creating and adding virtual hard disks
- ▸ Configuring IDE and SCSI controllers for virtual machines
- ▸ Creating resource pools
- ▸ Creating and managing virtual switches
- ▸ Using advanced settings for virtual networks
- ▸ Enabling and adding NIC Teaming to a virtual machine
- ▸ Configuring and adding Hyper-V Virtual Fibre Channel to virtual machines

Introduction

Every virtual machine has its own hardware profile, based on the system and applications that you run. Having said that, we need to identify the best hardware options to improve performance, reliability, high availability, and other resources available for every scenario that may arise. Normally, the principal hardware components are the disks and the network being used on these virtual machines.

In some examples, you need more disk performance for a database, or maybe a high network connection using a dedicated fibre channel connection for storage access. You also may require protection against hardware failure or advanced security protection to your virtual machine network. That's why we created a whole section in this book to go deep into the various configuration and options for virtual machine disks and networks that Hyper-V offers so that you can select the best setting based on the workload you need.

Creating and adding virtual hard disks

When creating a virtual machine, you also need to specify its disk configuration. Hyper-V has a set of options and advanced settings for different scenarios when the matter is virtual hard disks.

On a daily basis, the administration of the virtual machine and virtual disk configuration will be one of the most common tasks you do. This recipe will show you how to create a Virtual Hard Disk (VHD) and the new VHDX format for a virtual machine (VM), explaining all the details and options you need to know to make sure you can select the correct configuration for the correct scenario.

Getting ready

Some of the virtual hard disks require the same amount of physical disk for their size. Make sure that you have enough disk space on your host server before you start.

How to do it...

The following steps demonstrate how to create and attach a virtual hard disk to a virtual machine:

1. To create a new VHDX file, open **Hyper-V Manager**, click on **New** in the pane on the right-hand side, and select **Hard Disk**.

2. On the **Before you Begin** page, click on **Next**.

3. Select the disk format from the given formats—VHD and VHDX—on the **Choose Disk Format** page and click on **Next**.

4. In **Choose Disk Type**, select the disk you want to create, as shown in the following screenshot, and click on **Next** again:

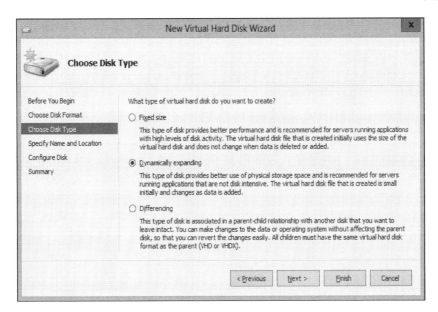

5. On the next page, specify the disk name and location, and click on **Next**.

6. In the **Configure Disk** page, select the option you want to create your disk, the disk size, and click on **Finish**.

7. After creating the VHDX file, open the virtual machine settings of the VM you want to add the disk, select the **IDE** or **SCSI Controller** you want and add the virtual hard disk you created, as shown in the following screenshot:

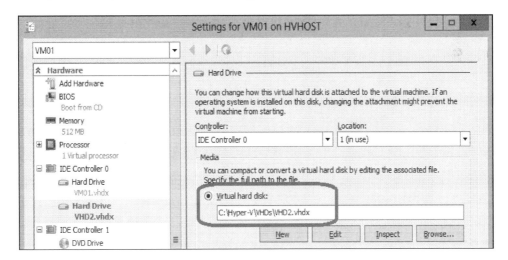

8. Now you can open the disk configuration from your virtual machine and the new hard drive will be available to be managed.

How it works...

The previous process showed how to create a virtual hard disk file, or the VHD file, as we call it. This format is almost the same since the first virtualization product released by Microsoft—**Microsoft Virtual PC 2004**. Essentially, a VHD contains a file system and partition as a normal physical hard drive. However, these are represented as a file that is to be added into the virtual machines. The maximum size of a VHD file is 2 TB. Also, the format is vulnerable for corruption in cases of power failure.

Windows Server 2012 Hyper-V introduces a new format named VHDX. This format has a limit of 64 TB and has better protection against data corruption in cases of power failure or unplanned shutdown in the host server. It's also efficient in representing data (also known as **trim**) and improved alignment of the virtual disk format. The method that the virtual machine uses to write the data into a VHDX file has been improved as well, by allocating the data in larger block sizes, thus providing more performance.

With this new format's benefits and increased limit, there is no reason why you should select the VHD format. However, it is not available in old Hyper-V versions, and you can still convert to VHDX without losing any data, in case you have to.

The most important option when creating a VHD file is that of the disk type. The first one, called **fixed size**, creates a file with the same size as specified during the wizard. That's why it takes longer to be created and also requires the necessary disk space on the destination location. It is not that much, but fixed disks provide a little better performance compared with other disk types.

The second and the default option, **dynamically expanding**, creates a file with a couple of MB, no matter the size you specified during the wizard. The disk size will increase based on the data you store on that disk. That's why this disk type requires the physical disk to be monitored. The performance difference between fixed and dynamic disks is quite similar on Windows Server 2012, but dynamic disks have more disk fragmentation when compared with fixed disks.

The last and least used option is the **differencing disk**. While you create it, the system asks you to specify an existing parent disk to be used as a base disk. All the writes operations will be made only in the differencing disk. A common example of this disk is when a read-only parent disk is used, with an installed operating system and lots of virtual machines using a differencing disk linked to this parent disk. This saves disk space in the host server. As this option has a single point of failure and a poor performance, the best practice is to use this only for test and development scenarios.

On the **Configure Disk** page, you have the option to create a blank virtual hard disk, copy the contents of a physical disk, or copy the content of an existing virtual hard disk, which is interesting in case you have an existing VHDX that can be used as a template.

By clicking on **Finish**, the system creates the virtual hard drive file in the specified location. You can open the virtual machine you want and then add the created disk to it.

There's more...

PowerShell lovers can create a virtual hard disk with the `New-VHD` command let and add a virtual hard drive to a virtual machine with the `Add-VMHardDiskDrive` command, as shown next.

This example shows how to create a dynamic virtual hard disk with 10TB on the local `D` partition:

```
New-VHD -Path D:\VHD\NewDisk.vhdx -SizeBytes 10TB -Dynamic
```

In this next example, the command adds the NewDisk VHDX file to a virtual machine called `VM01`.

```
Add-VMHardDiskDrive -VMName VM01 -Path 'D:\Hyper-V\Virtual Hard Disks\
NewDisk.vhdx'
```

Mounting a virtual hard disk on the host computer

If you need to open a virtual hard disk on the host computer, on Windows Server 2012 it is much easier than for the older versions of Windows. The only thing you have to do is to select the VHD file you want to mount and double click on it. That's all. After that, the disk will be listed on **Windows Explorer**, under **Computer**.

To mount a VHD via PowerShell you can also use the command let `Mount-VHD` specifying its path, as shown in the following example:

```
Mount-VHD -Path C:\Hyper-V\VHDs\VM01.vhdx -ReadOnly
```

To make sure the disk will not be changed you can use `-ReadOnly` at the end of the Mount-VHD to protect it against any writes activities. If you don't use it the disk will be mounted and changes will be saved to it.

The process to dismount a virtual disk is similar. All you have to do is type the same example as above, but changing the first command to `Dismount-VHD` with`-path` and the VHD path.

Adding a pass-through disk for a virtual machine

Although VHDX supports up to 64 TB disks, you can still attach a physical disk to your virtual machines. You will also not be able to move your virtual machine to another host, use snapshots, or use host-based backups. It performs better and its limitations do not bog it down. To add a pass-through disk, make sure that the physical disk is seen as offline in the host computer. Open the virtual machine settings, select the controller you want to add the disk, select the physical hard disk option in the drop-down list in the **Media** section under **Settings**, and click on **OK**. After that, the disk will be exclusively used by the VM.

You can also use PowerShell with the `Get-VMScsiController` and `Add-VMHardDiskDrive` commandlets to add a physical disk to a VM, as shown in the next example:

```
Get-VMScsiController –VMName VM01 –Number 0 | Add-VMHardDiskDrive –
DiskNumber 1
```

Creating virtual machines on file servers

Thanks to SMB 3.0, now you can create virtual machines and put their virtual disks on the file servers. You can copy the VHDs on shared folders and simply create the VM using the network path.

In the example in the next image, a VHD has been created and placed on a network share that has been set up with all the control permissions to the user and a computer account of the Hyper-V Server. When creating the virtual machine, all you have to do is specify the **Unique Naming Conversion** (**UNC**) path of the VHD on the shared folder.

To store the virtual machines on Shared Folders using SMB 3.0, you need to make sure that the user account used to create the VM and the host computer account have full access on the share and NTFS permissions.

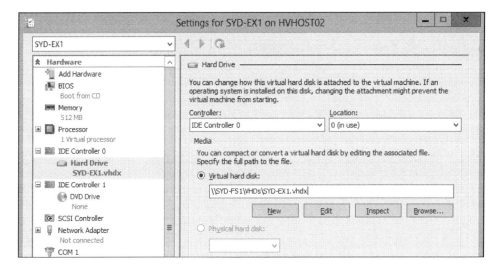

▸ The *Converting VHD files to VHDX* files recipe in *Chapter 2, Migrating and Upgrading Physical and Virtual Servers*

▸ The *Configuring IDE and SCSI controllers for virtual machines* recipe in this chapter

Configuring IDE and SCSI controllers for virtual machines

Every virtual machine on Hyper-V supports IDE and SCSI disks, each one having its own set of benefits, limits, and its own configuration.

It is important to identify when they are necessary, what their limitations are, and (most importantly) how to add and manage them, as you will see in the following tasks.

Getting ready

By default, every virtual machine has default IDEs and one SCSI controller that can be used instead of adding new ones. You can use these steps to change the existing controllers as well, rather than adding new ones.

How to do it...

The following steps show how to add and attach IDE and SCSI controllers for virtual machines.

1. To add a new controller for a virtual machine, open **Hyper-V Manager**, select the virtual machine on which you want to add a new controller and click **Settings** in the pane on the right-hand side (or with a right-click on the VM).

2. By default, you can see the two IDE controllers on the virtual machine settings. To add a hard drive or a DVD drive, select **IDE Controller 0** or **1**, the drive type, and click on **Add**.

3. When adding a new hard drive, you can specify the VHD path under **Virtual Hard Disk** or use the button **New** to open the **Virtual Hard Disk Wizard**.

4. If you prefer to add an SCSI controller for a virtual machine, select **Add Hardware** on the left, select **SCSI Controller** and click on **Add** as shown in the following screenshot:

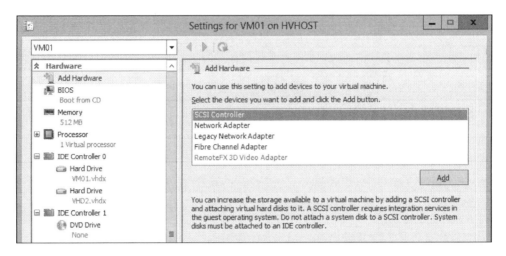

5. Select the new or the existing SCSI controller on the pane on the left-hand side and click on **Add** to insert a new hard drive.

6. Specify the hard drive path or use the **New** button to create a new VHDX file.

7. By clicking on **OK**, your virtual machine will be configured with the new controller and its disks attached to it.

How it works...

On Hyper-V, all the virtual machines by default come with two IDE controllers and one SCSI controller as explained, with the ability to add or remove them, based on the limits that each one has.

The IDE disk has to be used by default because it is the only supported method to boot an operating system. You can mix IDE and SCSI controller for the same VM, but the startup disk used to boot the operating system of your VM must be on an IDE controller. You can add up to two IDE controllers per virtual machine and two disks per IDE controller.

If you have a virtual machine that requires more than four disks, the best option is the SCSI controller. It has a limitation with respect to large environments supports for up to 256 disks divided in four SCSI devices (64 disks per SCSI controller). Another benefit is its ability to add disks while the virtual machine is running, without the need to shut it down. SCSI controllers are loaded through the virtual machine integration services and that's why it can't be used for booting disks.

For instance, you can use IDE controllers for the boot disk containing the operating system and SCSI controllers for additional disks with the benefit of adding them on the fly.

There's more...

PowerShell also provides a few commandlets for managing IDE and SCSI controllers, such as `Get-VMScsiController`, `Get-VMIdeController`, `Add-VMScsiController`, and `Remove-VMScsiController`.

In this handy example, we get every virtual machine with the name that starts with **VMExc** and add a new SCSI controller:

```
Get-VM –Name VMExc*  |  Add-VMScsiController
```

Thanks to the new PowerShell version, you can specify the virtual machine to which you want to add the SCSI controller using a single command, without the need to use the `Get-VM` first:

```
Add-VMScsiController –VMName VMExc*
```

These two commands do the same thing—adding a new SCSI controller to every VM with their names starting with VMExc. This is a good option to demonstrate how easy it is to use PowerShell.

See also

▸ The *Adding a pass-through disk for a virtual machine* recipe in this chapter.

Creating resource pools

In a private cloud environment, it is common to have different servers as per department, location, areas, or even clients, as services providers, say.

To aggregate resources and make them easier to be allocated and metered, Hyper-V 3.0 introduces the **resource pools**.

The idea of resource pools is to put physical resources allocated to virtual systems in a pool. The resources types that can be used in Hyper-V are as follows:

▸ Memory

▸ Processor

▸ Ethernet

▸ VHD

▸ ISO

▸ Virtual Floppy Disks (VFD)

▸ Fibre Channel Ports

▸ Fibre Channel Connections

In this recipe, you will see some examples of the most common resource pools, such as storage and Ethernet pools.

Getting ready

The option to create resource pools is not enabled through the graphical interface, only via PowerShell. However, you should open PowerShell as an administrator before you start.

How to do it...

The following steps will walk you through the process of creating disk and Ethernet resource pools:

1. Before we start to create our storage resource pool, we need to aggregate some virtual hard disks together. In this example, four VHDs are created in a folder called **StoragePool1**, as shown in the following screenshot:

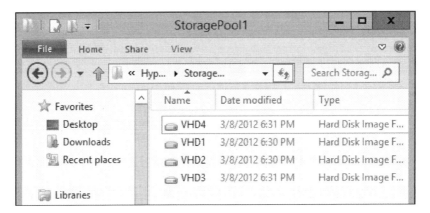

2. Open PowerShell and type the `New-VMResourcePool` command specifying the disk's path after the `-path` option.

   New-VMResourcePool –Name StoragePool1 –ResourcePoolType VHD –Paths C:\ Hyper-V\StoragePool1

3. After creating the resource pool, select the virtual machine you want to add the new storage resource pool to from **Hyper-V Manager** and open its settings.

4. In the **Virtual Machine Settings,** select the hard drive that you want to add a disk to, select the resource pool in the drop-down list in the pane on the right-hand side, and then select the virtual hard disk from the selected resource pool, as shown in the next image. Click on **OK** to confirm and add the disk from the resource pool.

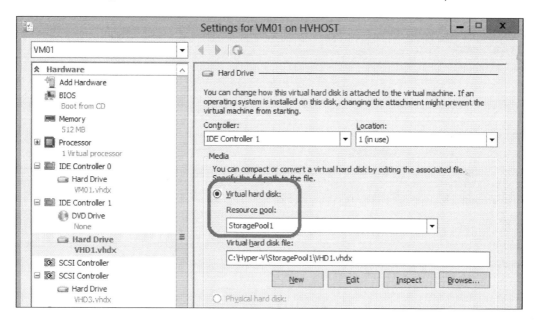

5. To create an Ethernet resource pool, open up PowerShell again and type the `New-VMResourcePool` commandlet using **Ethernet** after `ResourcePoolType`:

```
New-VMResourcePool -Name EthernetResourcePool1 -ResourcePoolType
Ethernet
```

6. Now open the virtual machine settings for which you want to use the new Ethernet resource pool.

7. Select the network adapter you want to add the resource pool to and select the new resource pool. Select the virtual switch in the pane on the right-hand side, as shown in the following screenshot:

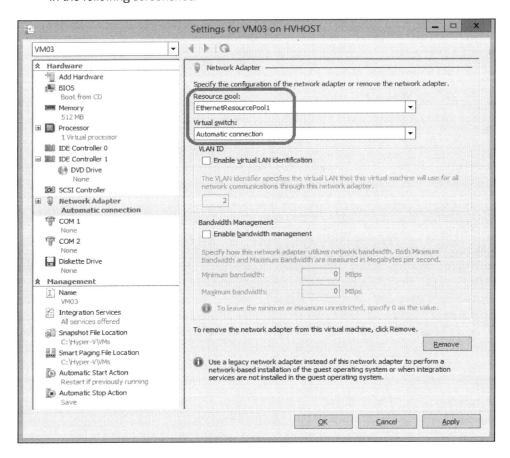

8. Click on **OK** and after that, your virtual machine will be configured with the new resource pool.

How it works...

The first steps walked you through an example of storage resource pools, one of the most common ones.

Using the `New-VMResourcePool` command, we created a resource pool called **StoragePool1** using every available disk from the path `C:\Hyper-V\StoragePool1`. In this example, all the four disks are available in the new resource pool.

It is possible to create a resource pool containing VHDs from different paths. To do that, you need to add a comma after the first path, as shown in this example:

```
New-VMResourcePool "Resource Pool Name" -ResourcePoolType
VHD -Paths "C:\Hyper-V\StoragePool1", "D:\Hyper-V\
StoragePool1"
```

Although the steps have shown only two examples of resource pools, you can create other types as well. The available resource types that can be created are memory, processor, ethernet, vhd, iso, vfd, fibrechannelport, and fibrechannelconnection.

Some of the existing resource pools don't have a graphical interface option when created, for example the memory and processor resource pool. But customers can use the Hyper-V Msvm_ResourcePool WMI class to create an advanced option or to integrate resource pools to other management solutions.

Another handy scenario of resource pools is their usages in conjunction with the resource metering feature. With both, you can measure the usage and the workload per resource pools basis, creating a cost report for a customer using all their resource pools' metering data, for example.

There's more...

Because of the lack of graphical interface, it is interesting to know that PowerShell has a command to list more information about the resource pools—Get-VMResourcePool. By typing the Get-VMResourcePool commandlet, PowerShell shows all the existing pools and information such as name, type, computer name, and so on. To list the resource pools by type, you can use a simple filter such as Get-VMResourcePool -ResourcePoolType Ethernet and then get an all Ethernet resources pool, for example.

See also

▶ The *Using Resource Metering* recipe in *Chapter 9*

Creating and managing virtual switches

Virtual switches are the components on Hyper-V that are responsible for controlling the network traffic between the virtual machine, the host, and the physical network. Their supporting features and advanced management capabilities limit, secure, isolate, protect, and control the way the VMs send and receive the network data.

The virtual switches on Hyper-V 3.0 come with some interesting features such as private VLANs, bandwidth management, spoofing protection, and other components that we will cover in this recipe.

Before we start with advanced components, you will see the basic switch options, and how to create and add a virtual switch to a virtual machine.

Getting ready

To use the external switches on Hyper-V, make sure that the network drives are installed and the network adapter is enabled on the host computer.

How to do it...

The following steps cover the process of creating a new virtual switch and configuring its common settings.

1. To create a new virtual switch, open the **Hyper-V Manager**, and click on **Virtual Switch Manager** in the action pane.

2. Select the option between **External, Internal,** or **Private** and click on **Create Virtual Switch**, as shown in the following screenshot:

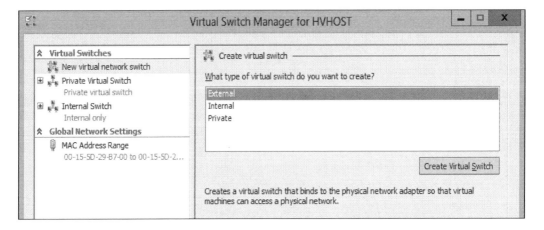

3. A new virtual switch will be available on the left-hand side. Specify a name and a description for your virtual switch in the pane on the right-hand side.

4. For the **Connection type** option, you can select **External, Internal**, or a **Private network**. For external networks, you have two options—**Allow management operating system to share this network adapter** and **Enable single-root I/O virtualization (SR-IOV)**. For external networks, select the network adapter from the host computer that will be bound to the virtual switch in the drop-down list. In the following screenshot, a virtual switch has been created using the external network option:

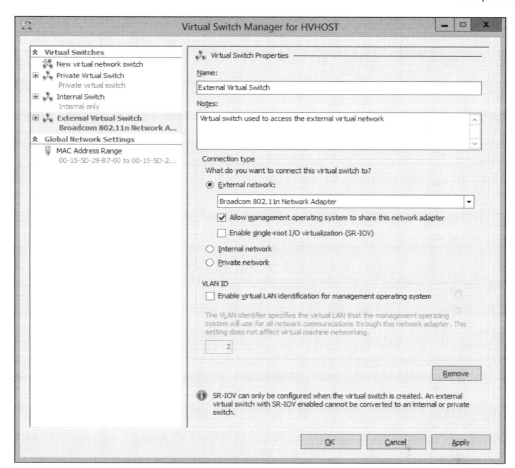

 When creating an external network option, the network connectivity in the host computer is temporary disrupted.

5. If necessary, enable the **VLAN ID** by clicking on **Enable virtual LAN identification for management operating system** and specify an ID for it under **VLAN ID**.

6. To confirm the options that have been chosen and to create your new virtual switch, click on **OK**.

7. To add the new virtual switch to a virtual machine, open **Hyper-V Manager**, select the virtual machine you want to change, and click on **Settings** in the action pane.

8. In the virtual machine settings, select an existing network adapter or add a new one, using the **Add Hardware** option in the pane on the left-hand side.

9. In the network adapter, under **Virtual switch**, from the the drop-down list, select the virtual switch that you want to add to your VM. In the following screenshot, the virtual switch created in the previous task—**External Virtual Switch**—has been added.

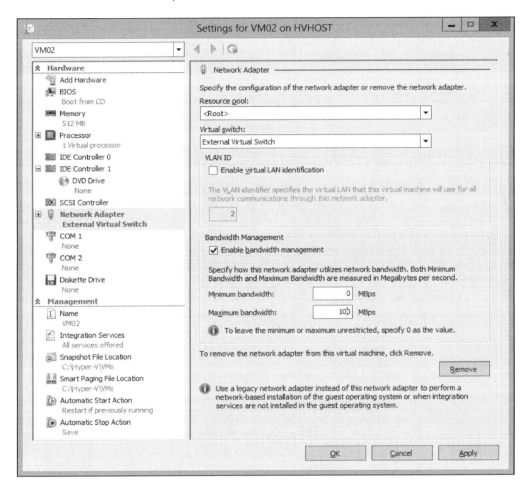

10. To create a network bandwidth limit for your VM, check the **Enable bandwidth management** option, specify the minimum and maximum bandwidth, as shown in the previous image, and click on **OK**.

11. After that, your virtual machine will use the created virtual switch and you will be able to change the network settings within the VM.

How it works...

As with the previous versions, Hyper-V still has the same three network types when creating a new virtual switch: external, internal and private network.

The external network is used when you want to allow the virtual machine to access the physical network. Essentially, a physical network adapter is bound to the virtual switch, and Hyper-V takes over the control and the access between the virtual machines using the virtual network and the network adapter on the host computer.

 Windows Server 2012 Hyper-V now supports wireless network adapters being used when creating an external virtual network

While creating an external network, you can specify to share the external network adapter with the host computer by selecting **Allow management operating system to share this network adapter**. Although this option is good for test environments and examples when there's only one physical network adapter, it is recommended to use a dedicated physical network adapter for the host computer and a different physical network adapter per external network, based on the workload needed per VM.

The second network called **internal network** allows the communication between all the virtual machines amongst themselves, as well as with the host computer. This network doesn't have a physical network adapter attached to it. It's very common for test and development scenarios when the VMs need a local and restricted network access. It also creates a NIC in the parent partition, allowing the administrator to configure the network for accessing VMs connected to the same internal network.

Private networks don't have a physical network adapter bound to a physical network adapter either. It limits all the communication to the virtual machines only. They don't have access to the host and the physical network when using the private networks. The only network traffic within a private network is between its virtual machines.

When adding the same virtual switch for multiple virtual machines, you may require some isolation between them. For example, when you have an internal network being used for 20 VMs, you can isolate them in two groups of 10 virtual machines. In a physical network this is known as **Virtual Local Area Networks** (**VLAN**). If your physical network adapter has support, you can do the same via Hyper-V by setting up all the virtual machines with the same VLAN ID.

When you specify a virtual switch into a VM, there is another new feature that can create a **Quality of Services** (**QoS**) policy called **bandwidth management**. With this, you can limit the network usage per virtual machine by setting up the minimum and the maximum values, so that Hyper-V can block the bandwidth usage when it reaches the specified limits, or the inverse by putting a high reservation to make sure that your VM has a dedicated workload on that network adapter.

Using legacy network adapters

The virtual switch drivers are loaded when the virtual machines and their integration components start. If you have VMs with no support for integration components, or if you need to boot the VM via the network, the normal virtual switch will not work. In these cases you can add the legacy network adapter. To add this adapter, open the virtual machine settings, click on **Add Hardware** in the top-left pane, select **Legacy Network Adapter**, and click on **Add**.

A new legacy network adapter will show up in the pane on the left-hand side, as shown in the following screenshot:

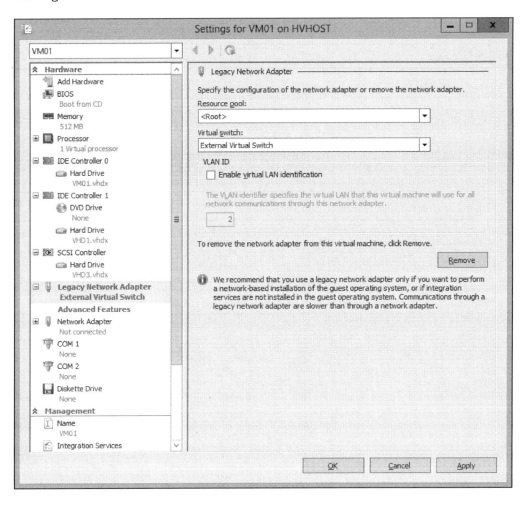

Under **Virtual Switch**, select the switch you want to use on the virtual machine and click on **OK**. Your virtual machine will start and will automatically recognize the new network adapter, allowing you to boot over the network, or in VMs that are without the integration components.

See also

▶   The *Using advanced settings for virtual networks* recipe in this chapter.

Using advanced settings for virtual networks

Creating and adding a virtual switch to a virtual machine is not the end of the story in Windows Server 2012 Hyper-V. Many of the features and settings were introduced in this new version, which can be configured using the graphical interface, such as DHCP Guard, Router Guard, port mirroring, and other options that require PowerShell such as **Port ACLs**, for example.

If you think this is not enough, no problem! Hyper-V introduced extensible switches, allowing you to write your own code, creating new capabilities for monitoring, forwarding, and filtering virtual switch traffic.

This recipe will cover these advanced networking features and explain how they work.

Getting ready

This recipe shows the advanced options of a virtual switch, but note that it doesn't show how to create one. Use the previous recipe to create a virtual switch before you start the next steps.

How to do it...

The following steps will demonstrate all the advanced virtual switch options such as VMQ, IPSec Task Offload, SR-IOV, DHPC Guard, Router Guard, and Port Mirroring.

1. To modify the advanced network settings, select the virtual machine you want to change and open its settings, as shown in the following screenshot:

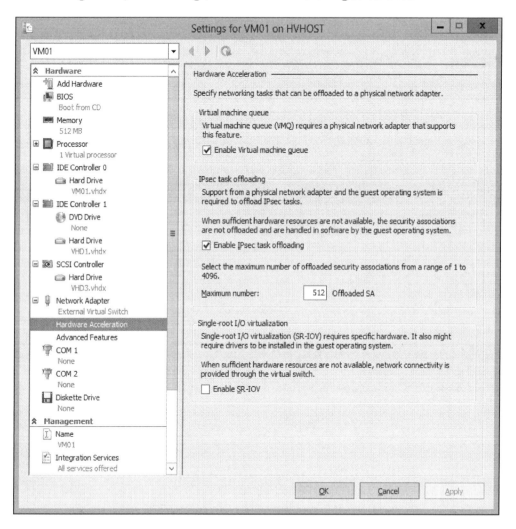

2. Select the network adapter that you want to manage and click on the plus icon (**+**) to open the options **Hardware Acceleration** and **Advanced Features**, as shown in the previous image.

3. To disable **Virtual Machine Queue (VMQ)**, uncheck the **Enable Virtual machine queue** option.

 It is best to enable the VMQ to save the CPU workloads.

4. To disable **IPSec task offloading**, uncheck the option **Enable IPSec task offloading**.

5. To enable the SR-IOV feature, check the **Enable SR-IOV** box.

 SR-IOV can only be enabled when creating the virtual switch.

6. Now, select the **Advanced Feature** under the network adapter to change the advanced network adapter settings, as shown in the following screenshot:

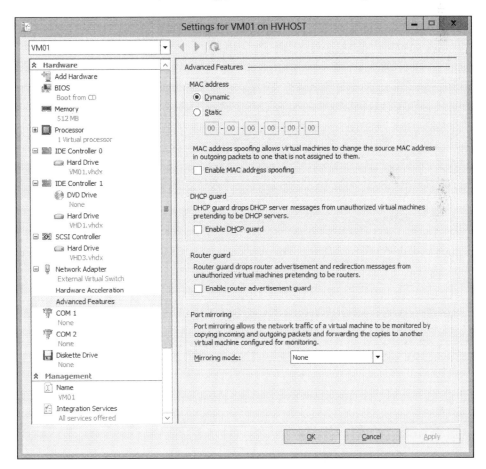

7. To change the **MAC address** to static, select **Static** and specify the static MAC address.

8. To enable the MAC address spoofing option, select the checkbox **Enable MAC address spoofing**.

9. To enable the DHCP guard, check the **Enable DHCP guard** option.

10. To enable the router guard, check the **Enable router advertisement guard** option.

11. To enable **Port mirroring**, select the mirroring mode from the drop-down list.

12. After selecting and modifying the advanced options that you've chosen, click on **OK** and the virtual machine will start getting all the configurations that have been modified.

How it works...

Now that you have seen how to enable the advanced features in the virtual network adapter, let's see the explanation for all of them.

The first one, called **Virtual Machine Queue** (**VMQ**), spreads the physical network adapter processing dynamically across all the available CPUs in the host server. This decreases the CPU utilization when network utilization is being used in large numbers. If this feature is disabled, the CPU in the host computer will be stressed while processing multiple network I/Os.

IPSec task offloading can also reduce the CPU utilization when large IPSec packets are used by the network, thus saving the CPU performance and making a better use of the bandwidth. In this new version of Hyper-V, the IPSec task offloading uses a new version (V2) that supports additional cryptography algorithms and IPv6.

Another interesting configuration available now on Hyper-V 3 is the **Single-root I/O virtualization (SR-IOV)**. This feature allows a network adapter to be bound directly to a virtual machine. In other words, Hyper-V doesn't manage the network adapter as it does in other network types. It simply passes through all the traffic between the virtual machine and the physical network adapter. This feature is perfect when the virtual machine requires a large network workload, thus reducing the network latency and the CPU utilization on the host server. Another interesting point is that you can still use all the other features such as snapshots, save, pause, storage, and live migration, making it easier to adopt, but you can't use Hyper-V extensible switch features and NIC teaming.

In the **MAC address** setting, you can specify a static MAC address instead of a dynamic address. With the dynamic MACs the VM gets a different MAC every time you turn it on. If the VM requires the MAC to always be the same, you can set up a static one through this option.

 Please note that SR-IOV and VMQ need to be supported in the host server.

The **MAC Spoofing** checkbox can be enabled in cases when the virtual machine needs to send and receive traffic using different MAC addresses, flooded unicasts packets, or when it needs to override on their MAC. This option is common when **Network Load Balancing** is used within the VM.

The last configuration, **Port mirroring,** allows the network traffic to be mirrored with another virtual machine so that you can use it to monitor all the incoming and outgoing traffic to the destination VM. You have to select the source and the destination virtual machine in order to use port mirroring.

There's more...

Every setting for network adapters and virtual switches can also be configured via PowerShell using the command let `Set-VMNetworkAdapter`.

In this example, we'll be using the `Get-VM` command to get all the VMs, and turning on at the same time the **DHCP Guard**, **MAC address spoofing**, and the **Router guard** for all of them.

```
Get-VM * | Set-VMNetworkAdapter –DhcpGuard On –MacAddressSpoofing On –
RouterGuard On
```

See also

> ► The Configuring Port ACLs recipe in *Chapter 6, Security and Delegation of Control*

Enabling and adding NIC teaming to a virtual machine

In case of failure, high availability is always needed in important services to make sure they are running. A highly available environment has various components such as servers, failover cluster, storage replication, and so on. Of course, all these components need to be connected amongst themselves and that's why the network adapters need high availability in cases of failures. 75 percent of companies use highly available solutions, using solutions to aggregate two or more network adapters into a single one. This provides for load balancing and high availability. This solution is called **Load Balance and Failover** (**LBFO**), or **NIC teaming** and it's normally made via hardware. By using NIC teaming, you can have traffic failover and load balancing made via Windows. This prevents loss of connectivity in case of a network adapter failure, without the need for a third-party solution or a hardware component for it.

This recipe will walk through the details to enable NIC teaming and will explain the various options as well.

Getting ready

The best practice is to use the same network adapters with the same configurations such as speed, drives, and functionalities. Having said that, make sure that you have network adapters with the same settings before you start.

How to do it...

The following steps show how to create, configure, and add NIC teaming to a virtual machine.

1. Open **Server Manager**, click on **All Servers** or **Hyper-V** in the pane on the left-hand side, right-click on the server for which you want to enable NIC teaming and click on **Configure Network Adapter Teaming**, as shown in the following screenshot:

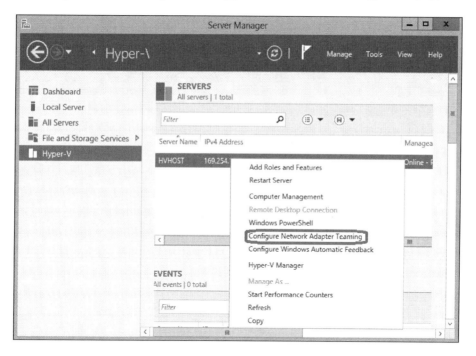

2. In the **NIC Teaming** window, click on **TASKS** and **New Team**, as shown in the following screenshot:

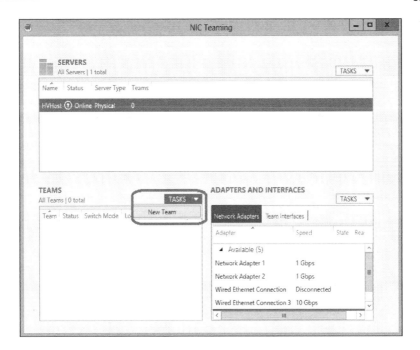

3. In the **New team** window, specify the team name at the top and select the network adapter that you want to add to the NIC teaming.

4. Under **Additional properties**, select the **Teaming mode**, the **Load distribution mode**, and the **Primary team interface**. Click on **OK**, as shown in the following screenshot:

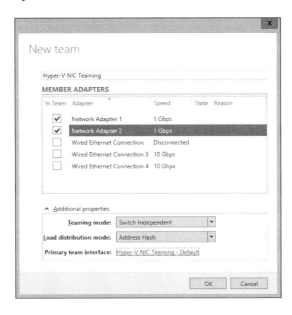

5. Now, when you open the network settings on your Windows server, you will see the new NIC teaming and you can start setting up the network configuration, IP settings, and so on, as with any other normal network adapter.

6. To add the new NIC team to a virtual machine, open **PowerShell** and run the following command specifying the virtual machine name under <VMName>:

```
Get-VM <VMName> | Set-VMNetworkAdapter -AllowTeaming On
```

7. Open the virtual machine settings for which you have enabled teaming, select **External network** and select NIC teaming from the drop-down list.

8. Click on **OK** and the network adapter in teaming will be available to be used in the virtual machine.

How it works...

Although you can add team network adapters to a virtual machine on Hyper-V, it's not a Hyper-V feature. NIC teaming is a functionality of Windows Server and can be used for any network workload, including those generated by virtual machines.

By default, Windows Server NIC teaming supports up to 32 network adapters in a single team.

 Hyper-V supports only two network adapters in teaming to be assigned to a virtual machine.

There are three modes for NIC teaming. The default one is **switch independent**. In this option, the switch will not know that the network adapter is in a team, thus allowing it to be connected to different switches. The other one is **static teaming**. This requires the switch and the computer to be configured in order to be able to identify problems with the network adapters. The last option is the **Link Aggregation Control Protocol** (**LACP**). LACP identifies the links dynamically. In most cases, the LACP needs a manual configuration to enable the protocol utilization on the port.

Enable the virtual machine in order to use NIC team by using the PowerShell command and add the NIC to the virtual machine. You will have the same environment as a physical server being used in the virtual machine, with no additional tools or third-party solutions.

Although this is possible, it's important to mention that NIC teams can only be formed between homogenous NICs. For instance, there can be two 1 GB or two 10 GB NICs in a team, but there cannot be a 1 GB and a 10 GB in the same team.

Configuring and adding Hyper-V Virtual Fibre Channel to virtual machines

Fibre Channel (**FC**) is one of the best and the fastest network technologies used primarily for storage connections. It's the perfect choice for high-speed connections between the servers and the storage, and it's common in physical server scenarios.

Now in Hyper-V 3.0, we can add fibre channel network adapters to virtual machines, providing the same capabilities and high performance as a physical server, allowing the guest operating system to be used in clustered environments, for example.

This recipe will show how to create the fibre channel SANs and add them to a VM.

Getting ready

Before you create the Fibre Channel SANs, make sure that the Fibre Channel port's HBAs are installed and enabled in the physical computer.

How to do it...

In the following steps, you will see how to add and configure a new Fibre Channel SAN for a virtual machine.

1. To create a new Fibre Channel SAN, open the **Hyper-V Manager** and click on **Virtual SAN Manager** in the pane on the right-hand side.

2. In the **Virtual SAN Manager** window, click on **New Fibre Channel SAN** in the pane on the left-hand side. Specify the virtual SAN name and write the additional notes in the pane.

3. Select the checkbox for the physical HBAs you want to link to your virtual SAN and click on **Ok** to create your virtual SAN, as shown in the following screenshot:

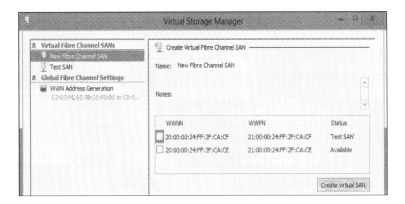

4. Open the settings of the virtual machine if you want to add the Fibre Channel adapter to, click on **Add Hardware** in the left, select **Fibre Channel Adapter,** and then **Add**.

5. In the new Fibre Channel adapter, select the virtual SAN from the drop down list that you want to add to your VM.

6. If you want to edit the port addresses, click on **Edit Addresses**, as shown in the following screenshot:

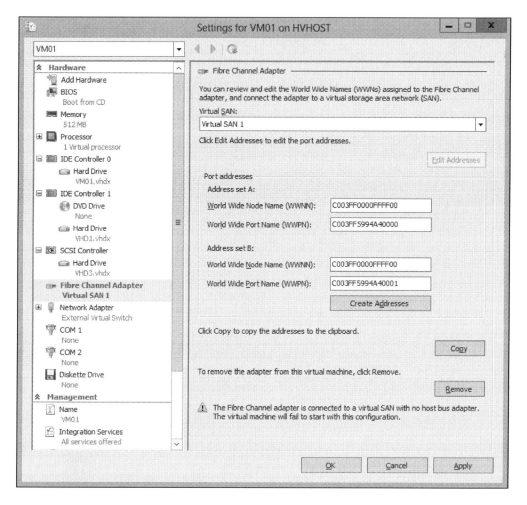

7. Click on **Copy** if you want to copy the edited port addresses to the clipboard to make it easier in case you need to use it for reverence to change some storage configuration.

8. Click on **Ok** to confirm and create the new Fibre Channel adapter.

How it works...

In the new Hyper-V version, it's easy to connect the virtual machine to storages using fibre channels. All you need to do is create a virtual SAN. After that, you need to add a new fibre channel adapter to the VM and change the **World Wide Names** (**WWNs**) if necessary. You can add up to four fibre channel adapters per virtual machine. Every fibre channel adapter has a set WWN and they are used to identify storage targets and initiators. These addresses are generated automatically, based on the configuration in the **Global Fibre Channel Settings**, which can be changed via the virtual storage manager. Also, you can change the auto-generated addresses by clicking on **Edit Addresses**.

Finally, you can open the virtual machine disk configuration and initiate the storage disks within the VM.

 Fibre channels can only be used for data volumes, not as the boot disk.

4

Saving Time and Cost with Hyper-V Automation

In this chapter, we will cover the following topics:

- ▸ Installing and running Hyper-V from a USB stick
- ▸ Creating virtual machine templates
- ▸ Learning and utilizing basic commands in PowerShell
- ▸ Using small PowerShell commands for daily tasks
- ▸ Enabling and working with a remote connection and administration through PowerShell

Introduction

In today's cloud world, it's very important to work more effectively and to be able to automate processes to act more like a service provider. In daily administration, tasks such as creating a new virtual machine or changing their settings, can take time and resources that could be used in other tasks. With Windows Server 2012 and PowerShell together, you can do almost everything using automated tasks, commandlets, and scripts to save time, thus making them your allies in cutting manual processes and costs. However, people think that scripts and command lines are complex and difficult to be adopted.

PowerShell is necessary for the IT professional today. You should invest in learning it to advance in your career, as more and more Microsoft products will be managed by PowerShell in the future. PowerShell is here to stay and is your friend who will help you to achieve automation in your environment.

The main idea of this recipe is to show how easy and user-friendly PowerShell Version 3 is, and how to create simple steps to make sure that your tasks will be done faster and with lesser work.

Installing and running Hyper-V from a USB stick

Hyper-V Server is the free version of Hyper-V and it offers almost all the components and features that are available in Windows Server with Hyper-V. It is a Windows version containing only the Hyper-V Failover Cluster and it has to be installed as any other Windows Server on the local hard disk. What if you could run Hyper-V Server from a USB stick, allowing you to take it wherever you go in your pocket, making your Hyper-V available on any computer through a USB boot? It will come in very handy when you need a Hyper-V ready for a test environment or even just to run your virtual machines and bring all of them with you on a USB stick. In this recipe, you will see what you need and how to enable the Hyper-V Server to be installed and made available from the USB stick.

Getting ready

To run Hyper-V from the USB stick, you need at least an 8 GB flash drive. The computer which is to run the Hyper-V needs to support boot from USB and the Hyper-V pre-requisites, as described in the *Verifying Hyper-V requirements* recipe in *Chapter 1, Installing and Managing Hyper-V in Full or Server Core Mode*.

To create the USB stick with Hyper-V on it, you need to download and install the **Windows Automated Installation Kit** (**WAIK**) for Windows 7 or a newer version, on the computer that will be used to perform this recipe. The WAIK for Windows 7 can be downloaded from the following link:

```
http://www.microsoft.com/download/en/details.
aspx?displaylang=en&id=5753
```

You will also need to install .NET Framework 3.5 or a newer version, and download Microsoft Hyper-V Server 2012 from the Microsoft website. Open the Hyper-V Server image file that you downloaded, navigate to the `Sources` folder, and copy the `Install.wim` file to a local folder on your computer.

How to do it...

The following steps will show how to prepare a USB flash drive to create a bootable version of Microsoft Hyper-V Server 2012.

1. Open the command prompt as an administrator to create the VHD file that will be used to add the Hyper-V image on the USB stick.

2. Run the following commands to create a folder named hvboot and the VHD file named HyperV.vhd with 6 GB capacity. The command will also attach the VHD as the local letter R.

```
mkdir c:\hvboot
diskpart
create vdisk file=c:\hvboot\hyperV.vhd maximum=6000 type=fixed
select vdisk file=c:\hvboot\hyperV.vhd
attach vdisk
create partition primary
assign letter=r
format quick fs=ntfs label=hyperV
exit
```

3. After creating the VHD file, you can apply the Hyper-V Server image using the Install.wim file. From the following command change <architecture> to AMD64 or IA64, based on the architecture you want to create and then boot your USB stick. Change <path to wim > to the install.wim file path.

```
cd /d "c:\program files\Windows AIK\tools\<architecture>\"
imagex /apply <path to wim> 1 r:\
```

4. Using the diskpart tool you have to detach the virtual disk from your computer using the following command lines:

```
diskpart
select vdisk file=c:\hvboot\hyperV.vhd
detach vdisk
exit
```

5. Now you can attach the USB stick you want to use to be formatted and to receive the VHD file created in the previous steps.

6. Use the diskpart tool again to identify the USB stick disk number.

```
diskpart
list disk
```

7. Use the following commands to create and format a new partition and assign the letter Z to the USB stick. Replace <USB Stick number> with the number identified in the previous task.

```
select disk <USB stick number>
clean
create partition primary
select partition 1
active
```

```
format quick fs=ntfs
assign letter=z
exit
```

8. Copy the VHD file created in *step 2* to the `z:` drive where the USB stick is attached.

9. Use the `Bootsect` tool to update the master boot code. From the following command, change `<architecture>` to `AMD64` or `IA64`, based on the architecture that you want to create. Boot your USB stick.

```
cd /d "c:\program files\Windows AIK\tools\PETools\<architecture>\"
bootsect /nt60 z: /force /mbr
```

10. Use the `diskpart` tool again to attach the VHD file to the `z` drive.

```
diskpart
select vdisk file=z:\HyperV.vhd
attach vdisk
exit
```

11. Use the `BCDBoot` tool to copy the necessary boot files so that you can boot your USB stick.

```
bcdboot r:\windows /s z:
```

12. As you are installing Hyper-V Server on a USB flash drive rather than a normal hard drive, you have to disable the paging file. Use the following command to load the registry from the VHD file:

```
reg load HKLM\HyperVTemp r:\windows\system32\config\system
```

13. Remove the page file value from the registry with the following command:

```
reg add "HKLM\HyperVTemp\ControlSet001\Control\Session Manager\
Memory Management" /v PagingFiles /t REG_MULTI_SZ /d "" /f
```

14. Delete the page file entry with the following command:

```
reg delete "HKLM\HyperVTemp\ControlSet001\Control\Session Manager\
Memory Management" /v ExistingPageFiles /f
```

15. Unload the temporary registry with the following command line:

```
reg unload HKLM\HyperVTemp
```

16. Type the following commands to detach the VHD file from the `z` drive:

```
diskpart
select vdisk file=z:\hyperV.vhd
detach vdisk
exit
```

17. Now you can remove the USB stick from your computer and attach it onto another computer to boot Hyper-V Server.

 You may need to change the boot order or the boot configuration from your computer BIOS to allow it to boot from USB.

18. At the first bootup, your bootable Hyper-V will be loaded and the system will prompt you to add the new administrator password. Type the new password twice and click on **OK**.

19. After the first login, Hyper-V will load the SConfig tool, allowing you to change the most common settings using a friendly command-line interface.

20. Now you can set up your Hyper-V Server and enable remote administration to manage it, using Hyper-V Manager from another computer.

How it works...

Almost the whole process to create the USB stick with Hyper-V is done via commands.

The first thing was to create a new VHD file and enable it to receive the Hyper-V image by creating a primary partition and formatting it using NTFS.

Then, by using the ImageX tool, you actually apply the Hyper-V Server image that is in the Install.wim file to the VHD file mounted on the R drive.

After that, the USB flash drive was prepared and formatted via Diskpart. The VHD file containing the Hyper-V image was copied onto it and it was configured with the boot configuration using the BCDBoot tool.

The last commands removed the paging file to improve the USB stick performance.

That's it. In the first USB boot, you will have to finish the Hyper-V Server installation process. After that, you will have your Hyper-V Server running from the USB stick wherever you go.

See also

▶ The recipes *Installing Hyper-V Server* and *Using sconfig in Server Core* from *Chapter 1, Installing and managing Hyper-V in Full or Server Core Mode*

▶ The *Enabling Hyper-V Remote Management* recipe from *Chapter 5, Hyper-V Best Practices, Tips, and Tricks*

Creating virtual machine templates

The time spent to create a virtual machine is quite small, but the problem is that it doesn't have an operating system on it. Also, it is time consuming if you have to install and prepare the operating system on every new virtual machine.

If you consider the time taken to install the operating system, the updates configuration, and all the other components of a server, it can take hours. But using templates, you will be able to create new virtual machines with the operating system ready to be used, in less than 5 minutes.

Enterprises will most likely consider System Center for managing their environment, and **Virtual Machine Manager** will handle this automatically. It will also combine several different profiles to give you a more flexible solution to mix and match templates, based on needs and specifications.

In case you don't have the **System Center Virtual Machine Manager**, you can use simpler templates on Hyper-V with a pre-configured operating system to save time during the virtual machine creation.

Given that some system attributes are required to be unique, simply copying virtual hard drive files and building another virtual machine around them will not work. That's why this recipe will show you how to create and prepare a virtual machine that can be used as a template in an environment without System Center.

Getting ready

To save time and steps in this recipe, make sure that you already have a virtual machine created with the operating system that you want to use as a template, and that all the other software applications and components that you need are available as well. The process shown in this recipe applies to Windows Server 2008, Windows Vista, and newer versions. For other versions, make sure that you run Sysprep to reset computer name, SID, and the license details.

Some applications such as Active Directory Domain Services, SQL Server, among others, don't support imaging using Sysprep. Make sure that your application can be used in conjunction with Sysprep.

How to do it...

The following steps demonstrate how to prepare an existing operating system to be used as an image and how to create a base VHD for VM template.

1. After creating a virtual machine with the operating system and other software applications, clients, automatic IP configuration, and so on, open Windows Explorer and navigate to the following path: `C:\Windows\System32\Sysprep`.

2. Right-click on `Sysprep.exe` and select **Run as Administrator**.

3. Click on the drop-down list under **System Cleanup Action** and then select **Enter System Out-of-Box Experience (OOBE)**.

4. Check the **Generalize** checkbox and in **Shutdown Options** select **Shutdown**, as shown in the following screenshot:

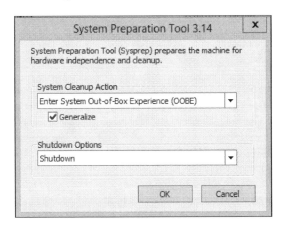

5. Click on **OK** and wait for the system to be turned off.

6. After the shutdown process, open the virtual machine VHD path and rename it to identify your template.

7. In the example shown in the following screenshot, you can see different virtual hard disks being used as templates.

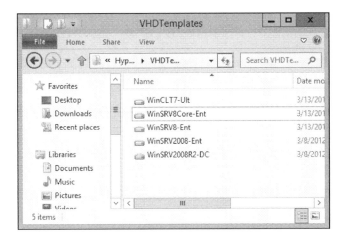

8. To create a virtual machine from the template, copy one of the VHD used as template to another location.

9. Create a new virtual machine using the template virtual hard disk. The system will reboot and the `sysprep` process will continue, prompting the product key and the administrator's password.

10. Specify the installation information and after the first login, you may change the computer name and any other necessary configuration, such as network settings and client options.

11. After these changes, your new virtual machine created from a template will be ready to be used.

How it works...

The process to create a virtual machine from a template consists of two steps.

The first one is to install a virtual machine with the **Operating System (OS)**, software, clients, updates, and all the configuration settings needed for the template. Then, to reset the computer name and the computer **Security IDentifier (SID)** to be used on any new VM, you should run the **System Preparation (Sysprep)** tool. This will mean that you can use the same operating system with existing settings, but with a new name and SID. It is important not to turn on the template VM again to prevent Sysprep from finishing the process to reset the OS settings.

After that, you can rename the VHD used to create the template VM so that it can be identified.

The second step, which is used for every VM created from the template, consists of the VHD being copied to the location where the new VM will sit and the new VM creation using the existing VHD.

By using VHD as templates, you can save hours of installing, updating, and configuring the OS and all its software.

See also

The *Creating and adding virtual hard disks to virtual machines* recipe from *Chapter 3, Managing Disk and Network Settings*

Learning and utilizing basic commands in PowerShell

Windows Server 2012 introduced the full PowerShell support with over 2300 commandlets, including the Hyper-V module that comes with 164 commands at the time of writing. It is true that the **Graphical User Interface** (**GUI**) is easier than almost all the other options. But PowerShell Version 3 proved that it can be handy in most of the common scenarios.

This recipe will demonstrate how easy PowerShell is and provide you with some helpful information with examples to guide you in using the commandlets with no advanced knowledge or a lot of effort.

Getting ready

To get ready, you just need to open a PowerShell window as administrator, from the taskbar, and run the command `Update-Help` to update all the existing help content. To update the `Help` command, you will need Internet connection.

How to do it...

The following steps will walk through the commandlets to identify the existing Hyper-V commands and how to get more information about how to use them:

1. PowerShell divides the commands as per components such as `AppLocker`, `Server Manager`, and also Hyper-V. These divisions are called **modules**. To see the current commands that exist in the Hyper-V Module, you need to use the `Get-Command` commandlet, specifying the module that you want to see, as shown in the next example. A list of all the 164 commandlets for Hyper-V will show up, as shown in the following screenshot:

    `Get-Command -Module Hyper-V`

2. To find a command using a particular word such as New, Start, Add, VHD, VM, Switch and so on, you can use the Get-Command with the Name switch. Using the next example as a reference, you can change the term between the asterisks at the end of the command to find the word that you are looking for. In the example, PowerShell shows every command from the Hyper-V module that contains the word vhd.

```
Get-Command –Module Hyper-V –Name *vhd*
```

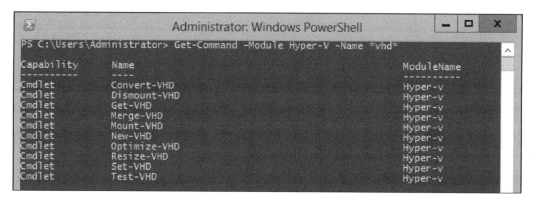

3. You can also use the switches Noun and Verb to find a command with a particular noun or a verb, as shown in the following examples, to find commands with the noun VM and the verb Start.

```
Get-Command -noun VM
```

```
Get-Command –Verb Start
```

4. Now that you know the existing Hyper-V commands, you can move on to one of the most important commands in Hyper-V—the Help command. By using the Get-Help command, you can understand what you can do with the commandlet and how to do it. For example, if you want to see what you can do with the New-VM command, you can type the following Help commands, the last one being the handy one to show examples of the usages of New-VM:

```
Get-Help New-VM
```

```
Get-Help New-VM –Detailed
```

```
Get-Help New-VM –Full
```

```
Get-Help New-VM –Examples
```

5. By referring to the previous example of New-VM, you can use the following command to create a virtual machine named NewVM with 512 MB of memory at the path C:\ Hyper-V\VMs:

```
New-VM –Name NewVM –MemoryStartupBytes 512MB –path C:\Hyper-V\VMs
```

6. One of the problems with these commands is trying to remember the switches that can be used. That's why in this new version of PowerShell, you can type the command and when executed, it can continue processing your command even if you forget a switch. To make it simple, the next example shows a VM being created in three different ways, but with almost the same results—a new VM called NewVM with 512 MB of memory.

    ```
    New-VM –Name NewVM –MemoryStartupBytes 512MB –path C:\Hyper-V\VMs

    New-VM –Name NewVM

    New-VM
    ```

7. If you don't think this is easy, you can use a GUI interface to guide you to type a command. To use the GUI window, type Show-Command.

8. In the **Commands** window, select the Hyper-V module in the first drop-down list and then the command that you want to use. The following screenshot shows an example of using the New-VM command:

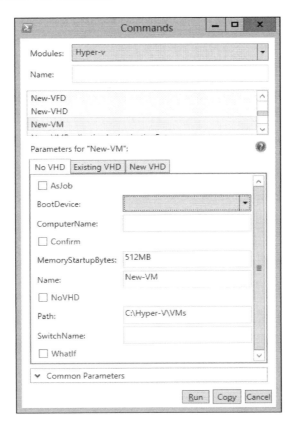

9. Use the other tabs such as **Existing VHD** and **New VHD,** as shown in the previous screenshot, to insert more options for your new VM. These tabs will be different based on the command you chose. To see advanced options, click on **Common Parameters** in the **Commands** window.

10. Now you can use the previous task from this recipe to see how to use the other commands on PowerShell.

How it works...

PowerShell offers different commands, each one with lots of switches and options that are difficult to remember. The purpose of this recipe was to show how simple it can be know more about the commands in PowerShell by using some commands. We used Get-Command to find other commands, the helpful Get-Help command using the –Examples switch to show some nice examples, and the GUI provided by the Show-Command to help IT admins who don't like the commandline interface.

After these steps, you can identify and learn how to use the Hyper-V commands on PowerShell.

There's more...

Using PowerShell to create multiple VMs in a single command line

Keeping the the previous example in mind, create some new virtual machines with the New-VM command, and then you can explore some other advanced options using loops and variables to create lots of VMs in just one command line. In the following command, there is a variable called $CreateVM and a loop from one to ten which will create VMs with the name starting with NewVM followed by the loop number.

```
$CreateVM = @(); (1..10) | %{ $CreateVM += New-VM -Name "NewVM$_"
}"NewVM$_" }
```

The next screenshot shows the 10 virtual machines which were created after running the command line.

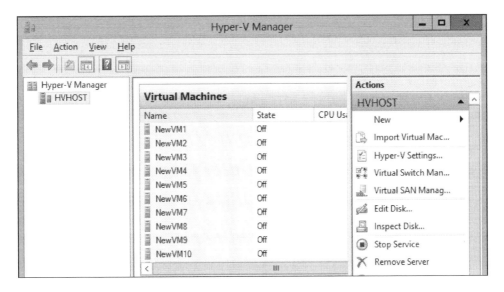

See also

▶ The *Using small PowerShell commands for daily tasks* recipe in this chapter

▶ The *Enabling PowerShell remote administration* recipe in this chapter

Using small PowerShell commands for daily tasks

As a virtualization administrator, you will come across a lot of scenarios where you will need to create, modify, move, export, and other tasks to manage your virtual machines every day. In some examples, you will need to change a few small and easy settings, which can be done via a graphical interface. However, you will also get cases where lots of virtual machines will need some advanced configuration or some settings that take a long time to complete.

It's a fact that PowerShell is a handy and strong ally in all these examples, and this recipe will show some examplesof how to perform daily tasks such as disk, network, memory, export, and virtual machine manipulation using a couple of small and simple PowerShell commandlets.

Getting ready

Make sure that you have a PowerShell window opened as administrator before you start.

How to do it...

These tasks show lots of handy examples of daily tasks that can be used to help you administer your Hyper-V servers, such as creating and changing VHDs, virtual switches, VM tasks, migrations, and much more.

1. Let's start with a simple command `New-VHD`, to create a virtual hard disk for a VM. Type the following command to create a `20GB` `VHDX` file named `NewDisk` on the `D:\` partition.

    ```
    New-VHD -SizeBytes 20GB -Path D:\NewDisk.vhdx
    ```

2. To add the created VHDX file to a VM, use the command `Add-VMHardDiskDrive`, as shown here:

    ```
    Add-VMHardDiskDrive -VMName NewVM -Path D:\Hyper-V\NewDisk.vhdx
    ```

3. To create a new virtual switch, you can use the `New-VMSwitch` command. The following example creates an external switch and binds it to a network adapter called **Wired Ethernet Connection**.

    ```
    New-VMSwitch "External Switch" -NetAdapterName "Wired Ethernet
    Connection" -AllowManagementOS $true
    ```

4. To add a network adapter to a VM, use the `Add-VMNetworkAdapter` command. The next command adds a network adapter named `Prod NIC` to all the virtual machines that start with `Prod`.

    ```
    Add-VMNetworkAdapter -VMName Prod* -Name "Prod NIC"
    ```

5. Use the `Connect-VMNetworkAdapter` to add VMs to a virtual switch. The following command gets all the VMs starting with `TestVM` and adds to a switch called **Private Switch**.

    ```
    Connect-VMNetworkAdapter -VMName TestVM* -SwitchName 'Private
    Switch'
    ```

6. To add a legacy network adapter to a virtual machine, you can also use the `Add-VMNetworkAdapter` with the `IsLegacy` switch. The following example shows the usage of this command. This gets all the VMs starting with `NewVM` and adds a legacy network named **BootableNIC.**

    ```
    Get-VM NewVM* | Add-VMNetworkAdapter -IsLegacy $true -Name
    BootableNIC
    ```

7. You can use the `Set-VMNetworkAdapter` to change the virtual machine network adapter settings. The first command below is changing the maximum and minimum bandwidth configuration to all virtual machine starting with `VMTest`. The second command enables Mac address spoofing to all VMs that end with `NLB`.

```
Set-VMNetworkAdapter -VMName VMTest* -MaximumBandwidth 100MB
-MinimumBandwidthAbsolute 20MB

Set-VMNetworkAdapter -VMName *NLB -MacAddressSpoofing On
```

8. To add Fibre Channel HBAs to virtual machines you can use the `Add-VMFibreChannelHBA` as the next example:

```
Add-VMFibreChannelHba -VMName NewVM -SanName VMProd
```

9. You can also use basic tasks such as starting and stopping virtual machines using the `Start-VM` and `Stop-VM` commands, as shown in the following two examples:

```
Start-VM -Name SPVM*

Stop-VM -Name TestVM -TurnOff
```

10. To create virtual machine snapshots you can use the tricky command `Checkpoint-VM`. The next example creates a snapshot called `PreMigrationSnapshot` to all the VMs starting with `ProdServer`.

```
Checkpoint-VM -Name ProdServer* -SnapshotName PreMigrationSnapshot
```

11. To create a virtual machine from a snapshot you can use the `Export-VMSnapshot` command as follows:

```
Export-VMSnapshot -Name 'PosUpdates' -VMName NewVM -Path E:\
NewVMfromSnapshot
```

12. In the case of a server migration, you can use the `Export-VM` command to export VMs to a local folder. The following command shows a handy example of all the virtual machines being exported to a local drive in their own folders.

```
Get-VM | Export-VM -Path E:\ExportedVMs\
```

13. To move the virtual machine storage, use the `Move-VMStorage` command, specifying the destination path that you want to move the VM storage to, as shown in the following example:

```
Move-VMStorage NewVM -DestinationStoragePath D:\NewVM\
```

14. For moving all the storage from local VMs to a new storage, by creating a folder for each migrated VM, you can use the next example:

```
Get-VM | %{ Move-VMStorage $_.Name "D:\Hyper-V\$($_.Name)" }
```

15. Use the `Set-VM` to change the VM settings. In the next example, all servers starting with `VMExchange` are having their dynamic memory enabled with the minimum, maximum, and startup values being configured. There's also a command which only changes the memory settings, called `Set-VMMemory`. The second example does exactly the same thing as the first, just using different commands.

```
Set-VM -Name VMExchange* -DynamicMemory -MemoryMinimumBytes 8GB
-MemoryMaximumBytes 12GB -MemoryStartupBytes 10GB

Set-VMMemory -VMName VMExchange* -DynamicMemoryEnabled $true
-MaximumBytes 12GB -MinimumBytes 8GB -StartupBytes 10GB
```

How it works...

From simple tasks, such as starting a VM, to advanced ones, such as moving all virtual machine storage to a new location, it is much easier to use PowerShell rather than the GUI interface. From the 164 Hyper-V commandlets, you have seen examples of the following type:

- ▶ `Add-VMFibreChannelHba`
- ▶ `Add-VMHardDiskDrive`
- ▶ `Add-VMNetworkAdapter`
- ▶ `New-VMSwitch`
- ▶ `Connect-VMNetworkAdapter`
- ▶ `New-VHD`
- ▶ `Checkpoint-VM`
- ▶ `Export-VMSnapshot`
- ▶ `Move-VMStorage`
- ▶ `Set-VM`
- ▶ `Set-VMMemory`
- ▶ `Set-VMNetworkAdapter`
- ▶ `Start-VM`
- ▶ `Stop-VM`

These are the normal commands used day-to-day in order to create disks and networks, change VM settings, start VMs, add fibre channels adapters, create snapshots, migrate VMs, and other tasks that can be easily done via PowerShell.

You might encounter other tasks that will require different commands, but with this start, you can have an idea of commands and the things you can do via PowerShell.

There's more...

If you are not sure whether a commandlet will work or what the result will be, you can test it before you run it. The new switch Whatif added at the end of the command PowerShell can tell you whether it's going to work or not.

The following screenshot shows a command that uses the whatif option and when executed, PowerShell explains that it will not work and why. After fixing it, you can try using the whatif command again. For the Export-VM command, you will see the What if: Export-VM will export the virtual machine "NewVM1" message.

Using PowerShell ISE for advanced script editing

For advanced and big scripts, you can use a very interesting tool named **PowerShell ISE**. It offers a GUI PowerShell window with colors, line count, command predict, error verification, and a debugging option, making your scripting experience easier and faster.

The next screenshot shows an example of a script being written by PowerShell ISE with a window showing the command prediction feature, and the command column in the pane on the right-hand side.

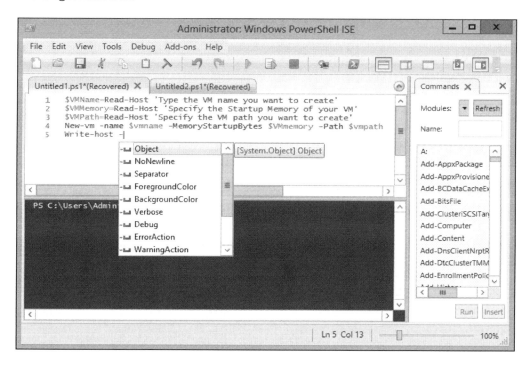

Enabling scripts to be executed in PowerShell

By default, the scripts execution is disabled in PowerShell for security reasons. However, there is a commandlet to enable or change the default settings. This commandlet is called `Set-ExecutionPolicy`. This command can change the script execution policy to `unrestricted` for running every script, remote signed to run remote, signed scripts, or all signed to run only signed scripts, and other options. To change the policy, run the `Set-ExecutionPolicy` command with the policy that you want to add. In the next example, the command being used enables all the scripts to be executed by changing the policy to `unrestricted`. You can also use `RemoteSigned`, `AllSigned`, `Restricted` and other options as the policy.

```
Set-ExecutionPolicy Unrestricted
```

After this command, you will have changed the script execution policy to `unrestricted` and all the scripts will run without any limitation.

▶ The *Creating and adding virtual hard disks to virtual machines* and
   Creating and managing virtual switches recipes in *Chapter 3, Managing Disk
   and Network Settings*

▶ The *Configuring PowerShell for remote administration* recipe in this chapter

Enabling and working with remote connection and administration through PowerShell

Working with PowerShell can be very common for daily tasks and server management.
However, as there is more than one server to be managed, sometimes it can be difficult to
log on and run the PowerShell scripts (most of the time the same one) on different computers.

One of the benefits that PowerShell offers is the remote option that allows you to connect
to multiple servers, enabling a single PowerShell window to administer as many servers as
you need.

This recipe will show how to enable PowerShell to be managed remotely and some commands
to connect to different computers.

Getting ready

The PowerShell remote connection uses port 80, HTTP. Although the local firewall exception
is created by default when it's enabled, make sure that any other firewall has the exception
to allow communication between your servers.

How to do it...

These tasks will show you how to enable the **PowerShell Remoting** feature to manage your
Hyper-V Servers remotely using PowerShell.

1. Open a PowerShell window as an administrator from the server for which you want to
   enable the PowerShell Remoting.

2. Type the `Enable-PSRemoting` commandlet to enable PowerShell Remoting.

3. The system will prompt you to confirm some settings during the setup. Select A for
   `Yes to All` to confirm all of them. Run the `Enable-PSRemoting` command on all
   the servers that you want to connect to remotely via PowerShell.

4. In order to connect to another computer in which the PowerShell Remoting is already enabled, type `Connect-PSSession HostName`, where `hostname` is the computer name to which you want to connect.

5. To identify all the commands used to manage the PowerShell sessions, you can create a filter with the command `Get-Command *PSSession*`. A list of all the `PSSession` commands will appear, showing you all the available remote connection commands.

6. To identify which command lines from Hyper-V can be used with the remote option `computername`, use the `Get-Command` with the following parameter:

```
Get-Command –Module Hyper-V –ParameterName Computername
```

7. To use the remote PowerShell connection from PowerShell ISE, click on **File** and select **New Remote PowerShell Tab**. A window will prompt you for the computer name to which you want to connect and the username, as shown in the following screenshot. Type the computer name and the username to create the connection and click on **Connect**. Make sure that the destination computer also has the remoting settings enabled.

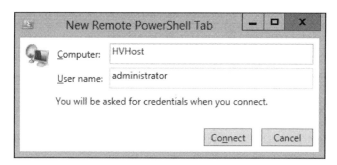

8. A new tab with the computer name to which you have connected will appear at the top, identifying all the remote connections that you have through PowerShell ISE. The following screenshot shows an example of a PowerShell ISE window with two tabs. The first one to identify the local connection called PowerShell 1 and the remote computer tab called `HVHost`.

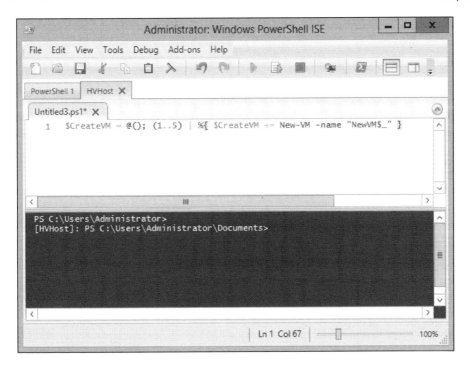

How it works...

The process to enable PowerShell involves the creation of a firewall exception, WinRM service configuration, and the creation of a new listener to accept requests from any IP address. PowerShell configures all these settings through a single and easy command—Enable-PSRemoting. By running this command, you will make sure that your computer has all the components enabled and configured to accept and create new remote connections using PowerShell.

Then, we identified the commands which can be used to manage the remote connections. Basically, all the commands that contain PSSession in them.

Some examples are as follows:

- ▶ Connect-PSSession to create and connect to a remote connection
- ▶ Enter-PSSession to connect to an existing remote connection
- ▶ Exit-PSSession to leave the current connection
- ▶ Get-PSSession to show all existing connections
- ▶ New-PSSession to create a new session

Another interesting option that is very important, is to identify which commands support remote connections. All of them use the `ComputerName` switch. To show how this switch works, see the following example; a command to create a new VM is being used to create a VM on a remote computer named `HVHost`.

```
New-VM -Name VM01 -ComputerName HVHost
```

To identify which commands support the `Computername` switch, you saw the `Get-Command` being used with a filter to find all the commandlets.

After these steps, your servers will be ready to receive and create remote connections through PowerShell.

5

Hyper-V Best Practices, Tips, and Tricks

In this chapter, we will cover the following topics:

- ► Using the Hyper-V Best Practices Analyzer
- ► Setting up dynamic memory for virtual machines
- ► Enabling remote management for Hyper-V in workgroup environments
- ► Installing and configuring anti-virus for the host and virtual machines

Introduction

The new version of Hyper-V comes with lots of improvements and new features that will make your job easier when working with virtual environments. However, you have to make sure that you are using the appropriate options and configurations the virtual machines, the operating system, the system configuration, and other components that you have deployed.

One methods that will ensure that you use the correct settings and apply the best configuration is to use the best practices for Hyper-V. **Best practices** are a set of rules and tips created by Microsoft to help you identify problems, misconfiguration issues, and anything else that is generally not recommended.

By applying these rules, you can enhance performance, increase the security, and improve the Hyper-V administration.

This chapter will show you some of these best practices and how they can easily be identified and implemented.

Using the Hyper-V Best Practices Analyzer

Microsoft has created a few rules to help you improve your environments— these are referred to as best practices. However, it is not easy to know all of them and to make sure your Hyper-V servers are compliant with all of these practices.

To make this job easier, Windows Server comes with the **Best Practices Analyzer** (**BPA**). It has a set of best practices and rules which it will compare against all the components of your server and it will then generate a report with all the problems that are found during the scan. The report will provide helpful details such as problems, impact, and resolutions for possible issues.

Windows Server comes with best practices for almost all the roles as well as a specific one only for Hyper-V with all the practices to analyze your host server, configuration, and virtual machines.

This recipe will show you how to use the Hyper-V Best Practices Analyzer (BPA) to analyze your systems.

Getting ready

The Hyper-V Best Practices Analyzer works only with the pre-installed Hyper-V Role. Make sure that Hyper-V is installed and as a best practice, run the BPA after every server installation and configuration is performed.

How to do it...

By following these steps, you will see how to run the best practices analyzer for Hyper-V and explore its results:

1. Open the **Server Manager** from the Windows **Taskbar**.
2. From the **Server Manager** window, click on **Hyper-V** on the pane on the left-hand side. Then use the scroll bar on the right-hand side to scroll down until the best practices analyzer option can be seen.
3. Under **Best Practices Analyzer**, navigate to **Tasks | Start BPA Scan**, as shown in the following screenshot:

4. In the **Select Servers** window, select the Hyper-V servers that you want to scan and click on **Start Scan**.

5. The scan will start on all the selected servers. When the scan has finished, the BPA results will be shown in **Server Manager**, under **Best Practices Analyzer**.

6. When completed, the scan results will be listed in three columns—**Server Name**, **Severity**, and **Title**. Use the filters above each column to organize the information based on your queries.

7. Click on one of the results to see the information provided by BPA. The following screenshot shows an example of a warning scan result and its description:

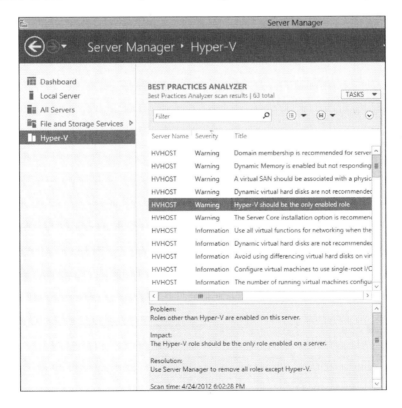

8. Open the results and analyze the problem, impact, and resolution for each server.

9. Use the filter at the top to find only warnings and errors.

10. After identifying the results, you can apply the resolutions provided by the Hyper-V BPA.

How it works...

The Best Practice Analyzer for Hyper-V has 74 scans to identify which settings are not configured, based on the Microsoft documentation and practices. It is enabled automatically when the Hyper-V role is installed.

When BPA scans the servers, it shows the results for every scan, providing helpful details about what was scanned, the impact, and even how to resolve any problems it finds. It will also give you the option to apply the necessary changes for your server in compliance with the best practices.

BPA is available through Server Manager and can be used at any time. The recommendation is to scan every server after their final configurations and also on a monthly basis after that.

Hyper-V BPA will also display information about Microsoft Support. If the server has a configuration that is not supported by Microsoft, it will inform you of this through the reports.

After running and applying the recommended settings, you can then be sure that your servers have all the best practices, currently recommended by Microsoft.

There's more...

All of Windows Best Practices are available through PowerShell as well. You can scan, filter, get the results, and extract reports using the PowerShell commandlets.

To start a scan using the Hyper-V BPA, type the following command:

```
Invoke-BpaModel -BestPracticesModelId Microsoft/Windows/Hyper-V
```

After invoking the Hyper-V BPA, you can use the `Get-BPAResult` command to analyze the results. The following command shows the BPA scan results:

```
Get-BpaResult -BestPracticesModelId Microsoft/Windows/Hyper-V
```

The following screenshot is an example of how the `Get-BPAResult` output could look:

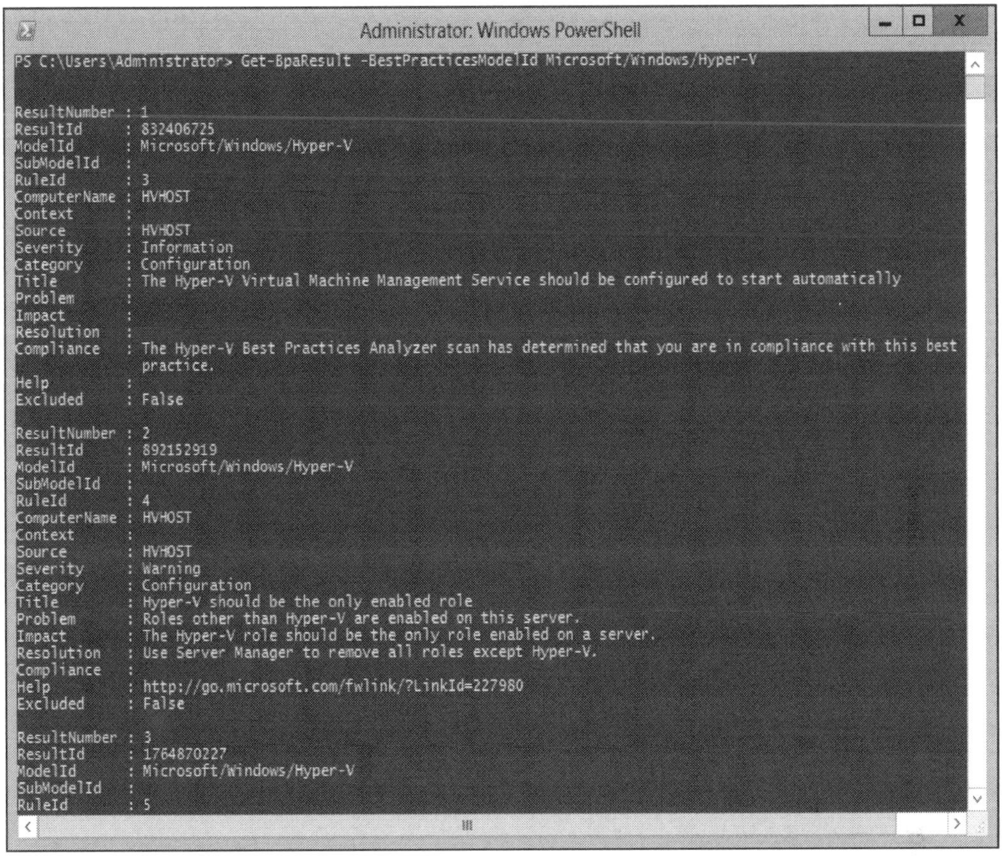

If you want to filter only the warnings and the errors by using PowerShell, you can also use the following command:

```
Get-BpaResult -BestPracticesModelId Microsoft/Windows/Hyper-V | Where-
Object {$_.Severity -eq "Warning" -or $_.Severity -eq "Error"}
```

Using PowerShell to create HTML reports with the BPA results

To improve the PowerShell results it is possible to produce a BPA HTML report using the following command. This following script uses the previous `Get-BpaResult` filter example to show only the warning and the error results:

```
$head = '<style>
BODY{font-family:Verdana; background-color:lightblue;}
TABLE{border-width: 1px;border-style: solid;border-color: black;border-
collapse: collapse;}
```

```
TH{font-size:1.3em; border-width: 1px;padding: 2px;border-style:
solid;border-color: black;background-color:#FFCCCC}
```

```
TD{border-width: 1px;padding: 2px;border-style: solid;border-color:
black;background-color:yellow}
```

```
</style>'
```

```
$header = "<H1>Hyper-V BPA Errors and Warnings Results</H1>"
```

```
$title = "Hyper-V BPA"
```

```
Get-BpaResult -BestPracticesModelId Microsoft/Windows/Hyper-V |
```

```
Where-Object {$_.Severity -eq "Error" -or $_.Severity -eq "Warning" } |
```

```
 ConvertTo-HTML -head $head -body $header -title $title |
```

```
 Out-File report.htm
```

```
.\report.htm
```

The following screenshot shows the output file that is created after running the script:

Title	Problem	Impact	Resolution
Hyper-V should be the only enabled role	Roles other than Hyper-V are enabled on this server.	The Hyper-V role should be the only role enabled on a server.	Use Server Manager to remove all roles except Hyper-V.
The Server Core installation option is recommended for servers running Hyper-V	This server is running a full installation instead of a Server Core installation.	Running a full installation exposes a larger attack surface and may require more maintenance, such as installing updates.	Reconfigure the server to run a Server Core installation by using Server Manager to remove the features under the User Interfaces and Infrastructure category.
Domain membership is recommended for servers running Hyper-V	This server is a member of a workgroup.	There is no central management for this server.	If you have a domain environment available, join this server to that domain.

Setting up dynamic memory for virtual machines

Sometimes, it is hard to know how much memory a virtual machine needs. Even when capacity planning is performed, the Virtual Machine (VM) will never use the full memory specification, resulting in poor memory utilization and a loss of resources.

Windows Server 2008 R2 SP1 introduced a new feature **Dynamic Memory** (**DM**) that allows the memory on the host server to be shared with the virtual machines using a method called **Ballooning**. Ballooning ensures that the VMs use only the memory that they need and releases it back to the host if another VM requires more memory. This allows the memory in the parent partition to be reallocated automatically through the VMs, increasing or decreasing it, based on the current workload.

Let's use an example of a VM with a database server that was installed and configured to use 16 GB of memory. That is the value that you got from the planning phase. The problem is that the database server will only use 16 GB when a huge workload is created. This stipulation represents less than 10 percent of the server lifetime. What if you could use the unused memory from its 16 GB, let's say 4 GB, for another VM that requires more memory? In the case of an unexpected workload on the database server, Hyper-V could automatically reallocate the memory back to the database server. Likewise, it could borrow more memory from other unused VMs.

In this scenario, it is possible to understand how DM can save and make better use of the memory on the servers.

In this recipe, you will see all the settings and necessary configurations to use DM among your VMs.

Getting ready

To make sure that the dynamic memory will work on your VMs, check if the latest version of integration services has been installed. To use DM, the virtual machine needs to be installed with any of the following operating systems:

- Windows Vista Enterprise and Ultimate editions installed with SP1
- Windows 7 Enterprise and Ultimate editions
- Windows 8
- Windows Server 2003 and 2003 R2 Enterprise or Datacenter with Service Pack (SP) 2
- Windows Server 2008 and 2008 R2 Enterprise or Datacenter with SP2
- Windows Server 2012

How to do it...

The following steps will demonstrate how to enable and monitor dynamic memory your virtual machines:

1. Open **Hyper-V Manager** and select the virtual machine you want to configure the dynamic memory for.

2. Right-click on the virtual machine and click on **Settings**.

3. In the **Virtual Machine Settings** window, click on **Memory** in the pane on the left-hand side.

4. In the **Startup RAM field**, specify the capacity of the memory to be used when the virtual machine is started.

5. To enable dynamic memory, select the checkbox **Enable Dynamic Memory**.

6. Specify the limits for maximum and minimum memory to be used by the VM under **Minimum RAM** and **Maximum RAM**.

7. Specify the percentage value of the memory that will be reserved for the buffer in **Memory buffer**.

8. In **Memory weight**, you can change the way that Hyper-V prioritizes the availability of memory for this VM compared with the other local VMs. The following screenshot shows all the DM settings, which were explained earlier.

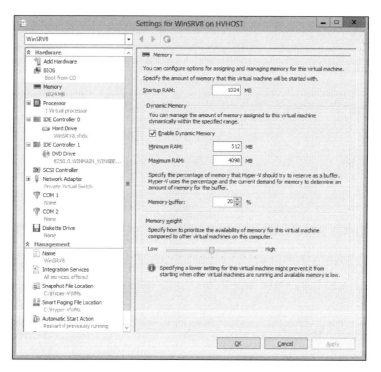

9. Click on **OK** and close the **VM Settings window**.

10. To monitor the dynamic memory settings being used by your started VMs, select the VM and click on the **Memory** tab at the bottom of Hyper-V Manager, as shown in the following screenshot:

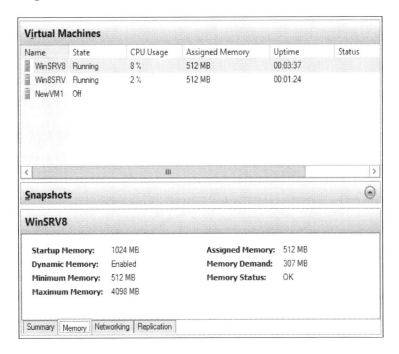

How it works...

By default, the dynamic memory configuration is disabled on every virtual machine. It can be enabled and configured as shown in the preceding steps by using the GUI through PowerShell, or when the VM is created.

The three most important settings for DM are **Minimum, Maximum**, and the new option—**Startup**. Every time the VM starts, the value in the **Startup RAM** will be allocated only for that VM. Once Windows and the integration services are loaded, Hyper-V begins to change the VM memory based on its workload, the configured settings, and the other VMs.

A problem that can arise with the **Startup RAM** setting is when you need to restart a VM that has less memory than what is specified in the startup RAM field and there is no available memory from other VMs. The new version of Hyper-V introduces **Smart Paging** that allows the missing value per VM—necessary for the VM memory—to be written in the page file on the host server, providing a reliable restart process and therefore not causing errors during the VM restart. If the VM needs 1 GB of memory to be started, Hyper-V can use the paging file on the host computer to allow the VM to startup. The Smart Paging option can be used only when the virtual machine is restarted, when the physical memory is not available, or when the memory cannot be reclaimed from other virtual machines which are also running on the host. Having said that, it is a best practice to add the page file onto a fast hard drive to avoid performance issues.

The **Memory buffer** option allows you to specify the percentage of memory that will be available for buffer when moving memory to other VMs. This value is reserved if no other VM has a higher priority and if there is available physical memory on the host. For example, if a VM has 10 GB of memory and the buffer is configured to 20 percent, the host computer will allocate an additional 20 percent, which in this case is 2 GB of physical memory to the VM. The end result will mean that, the VM will have 12 GB of physical memory allocated to it on the host computer. The default value is 20 percent, but it can be changed based on the VMs priority.

Another new feature that has been added in the new Hyper-V version is that the **Maximum RAM** value can be increased and the **Minimum RAM** value can be decreased while the virtual machine is running.

The last option—**Memory weight**—lets you prioritize the availability of memory for the selected VM compared to other virtual machines. If you have one VM with a low value and one VM with a high value and both need more memory, Hyper-V will prioritize the VM with the higher value; except if the memory was already allocated to the VM. In this case, Hyper-V will not reclaim the allocated memory, as this could cause a problem on the running the VM.

For monitoring purposes, to see the DM utilization currently being used, you can also use the new **Memory** tab in the Hyper-V Manager. Hyper-V Manager offers information such as:

- ▶ Startup memory
- ▶ Dynamic memory
- ▶ Minimum memory
- ▶ Maximum memory
- ▶ Assigned memory
- ▶ Memory demand
- ▶ Memory status

Hyper-V extracts the memory details from the VM using the integration services and shows them using the **Memory** tab, allowing the administrator to check the memory information in real time.

After enabling dynamic memory for your VMs, you can save hardware resources, use memory more efficiently, and ensure that each VM will get the necessary memory depending upon their workload.

There's more...

Using PowerShell to manage dynamic memory for virtual machines

For bulk configuration and automation, you can also use a commandlet—Set-VMMemory—that is designed only to manage the Dynamic Memory settings. All the configurations such as maximum bytes, minimum bytes, and startup bytes can be specified using this command line. In the following example, all the VMs starting with **SP** had the Dynamic Memory option enabled, with the other values configured as well. A new PowerShell feature that helps is that you can use abbreviations such **MB** for megabytes, **GB** for gigabytes, and **TB** for terabytes.

```
Set-VMMemory -VMName SP* -DynamicMemoryEnabled $true -MaximumBytes 6GB
-MinimumBytes 4GB -StartupBytes 5GB
```

Also, you can use the Set-VM commandlet to change the same settings as shown in the following example:

```
Set-VM -Name SP* -DynamicMemory -MemoryMinimumBytes 4GB
-MemoryMaximumBytes 6GB -MemoryStartupBytes 5GB
```

Enabling remote management for Hyper-V in workgroup environments

Hyper-V Manager allows the administrators to manage the Hyper-V server and the virtual machine, using a GUI interface, which is installed automatically on the Hyper-V servers. The Hyper-V Manager supports remote management, in case you have Hyper-V Server or Windows Server 2012 with Hyper-V to use the same tool. This provides the same functionality as the one used in the server. This tool can be used from another Windows Server 2012 or a Windows 8 client with the Hyper-V Manager tool installed.

In workgroup scenarios, there is no single sign on available and additional permissions and configurations have to be enabled to allow remote connections using Hyper-V Manager.

This recipe will guide you through the steps to setup both computers to have the Hyper-V Manager enabled remotely in workgroup scenarios.

Getting ready

To make the process easier, we will need the `HVRemote` script which can be downloaded from the following link: `http://archive.msdn.microsoft.com/HVRemote`. Copy the script in a folder on both of the computers.

The supported client to manage the new version of Hyper-V must be Windows 8 only.

To save some time and unnecessary complications, make sure the two computers have their network configurations already set, such as IP address, computer name, and so on.

How to do it...

The following steps will walk you through the details to enable and configure Hyper-V remote management using the HVRemote tool.

1. From the server to which you want to connect, open **PowerShell** and type `sconfig`.

2. In the **Server Configuration** options, press number *4* to select the **4) Configure Remote Management** option.

3. In the **Configure Remote Management** options, press the number *1* to select the option **1) Enable Remote Management**, as shown in the following screenshot:

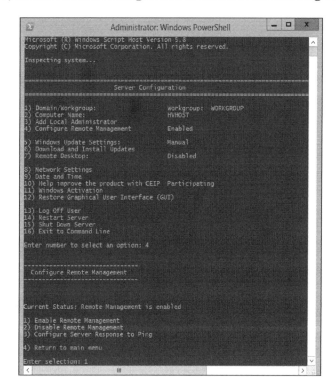

4. Click **OK** on the pop-up message that confirms the operation.

5. Press the number *3* to select option **3) Configure Server Response to Ping**. Press *Y* in the **Configure Remote Management** pop-up message to confirm the operation.

6. Press the number *4* to return to the main menu and press the number *3* to select option) **Add Local Administrator**.

7. Type the username, ensuring that it is the same user name as the client computer that you want to use Hyper-V Manager from. Confirm the user password twice by using the same username and password as the client computer.

8. Press *1+6* to exit the **sconfig** interface.

9. Using PowerShell, open the folder where the HVRemote script is. For example, if the script is in a folder named HVRemote on the C partition, type the command CD C:\HVRemote to open the folder.

10. Type the following script and at the end, specify the username you will use from the client computer. In the following example, the username used was Leandro:

```
cscript hvremote.wsf /add:Leandro
```

11. Log in to the client computer using an administrator account to configure the remote settings. For a quick reference, the username should be the same as the one created in the *step 6*.

 If you change the username or the password on one computer, you will also need to change it on the other computer(s) as well.

12. From the client computer, open **Control Panel** and click on the **Program and Features** option.

13. In the **Programs and Features** window, click on **Turn Windows Features on or off** in the pane on the left-hand side.

14. From the **Windows Features** window, open **Hyper-V** and select **Hyper-V Management Tools**, as shown in the following screenshot:

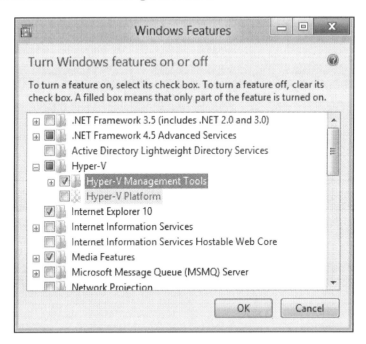

15. Click on **OK** and wait the installation to be completed.

16. Click on **Start**, type notepad, select **Notepad** from the search list with the right-click of the mouse and click on the **Run as Administrator** option.

17. From Notepad, click on the **File** menu and then click on **Open**.

18. Navigate to the C:\Windows\System32\Drivers\etc folder.

19. In the **Text Document (*.txt)** option in Notepad, select **All Files** to show the files within the **etc** folder.

20. Select the **Hosts** file and click on **Open**.

21. At the end of the file, add an entry for your server with the IP address followed by the server name, as shown in the following example, with the IP **10.10.0.1** and server name **HVHost**.

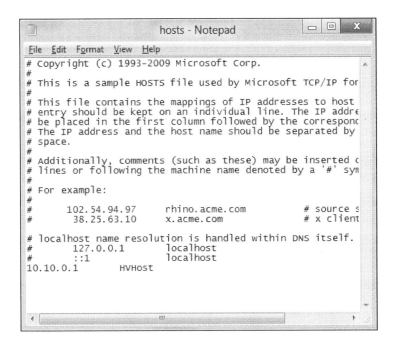

22. Open the command prompt as an administrator, access the folder with the HVRemote script on it, and then type the following command line:

```
cscript hvremote.wsf /AnonDCOM:grant
```

23. Type **Hyper-V** in the **Start** menu and select the **Hyper-V Manager**.

24. Right click on **Hyper-V Manager** and then click on **Connect to a Server...**.

25. In the **Select Computer** window, specify the Hyper-V server you want to connect in **Another computer** and then click on **OK**.

26. The connection will be established and you will be ready to manage your server remotely.

How it works...

When the client and the server that you want to manage remotely are members of a domain environment, the process is much simpler than the one explained in the previous task. The only things that you need to do are configure the firewall, install the Hyper-V Management Tools from the client or server you want to use to connect, open Hyper-V Manager, and connect to the server using an account with administrative privileges on the destination Hyper-V server.

However, in the case of non-domain joined computers, a couple of other settings must be configured. The first thing that had to be done was to allow the Hyper-V server to receive remote connections using the Hyper-V manager. After that, an administrator account was added using the same user name as the one on the client computer. If both the computers are using the same username and password, you can just ignore this setting. However, as the administrator account is disabled by default on the client computer, the method to create a user with the same user name and password on both computers is the best one. The method used to set up the firewall and the local user was performed in **sconfig,** to help with the advanced firewall configurations.

We also used the `HVRemote` script and the command `cscript hvremote.wsf add:Username` on the server to add the user in to the **DCOM Users** group, the **AZMan** role administrator, and the necessary permissions in some WMI namespaces.

Most of the configurations that we have looked at used command lines, so that you can use the same process for all the Hyper-V versions, such as Hyper-V Server, Hyper-V full installation, and core installation.

From a client computer with Windows 8 installed, the Hyper-V Management Tools were installed and to allow the connection using the computer name, we added an entry in the host file. Finally, `HVRemote` script was used to allow anonymous access to the Distributed COM.

After these configurations you will be able to open Hyper-V Manager on the client computer, connect to the Hyper-V Server, and manage it remotely.

See also

The *Enabling and working with remote connection and administration through PowerShell* recipe *Chapter 4, Saving Time and Cost with Hyper-V Automation*.

Installing and configuring an anti-virus on host and virtual machines

This is one of the most common discussions with Hyper-V. Lots of IT professionals struggle with the option of whether or not to install **Anti-Virus** (**AV**) on the host and the virtual machines.

Security is the prime concern in all scenarios and as a Hyper-V administrator, you need to make sure that there are no compromises on your servers, either physical or virtual. This recipe will show you first how to configure the Hyper-V exceptions, when using an AV system in the parent partition, and then discuss in the *How it works* section when and where the AV is necessary.

Getting ready

Due to the vast number of anti-virus products, this recipe will only focus on configurations that have to be done and not actually how to do them. Make sure that you are familiar with your AV settings so that you are able to apply the same configuration demonstrated in the AV itself.

Before you begin, make sure that your AV software supports Windows Server 2012 Hyper-V.

How to do it...

The following steps will show you how to identify the default path used for virtual machines and virtual disks, and how to configure the exceptions for your AV system:

1. Before creating the anti-virus exceptions, you need to identify which paths are in use by Hyper-V.

2. To identify the default virtual machine and virtual hard disk configuration path, open **Hyper-V Manager** and click on **Hyper-V Settings** in the pane on the right-hand side.

3. The **Hyper-V Settings** window will open as shown in the following screenshot:

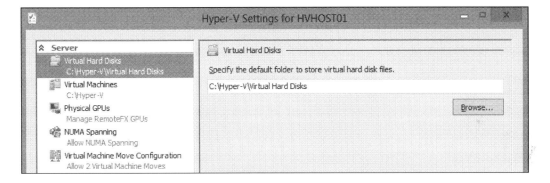

4. Click on **Virtual Hard Disks** to identify the default folder being used for virtual hard disks.

5. Click on **Virtual Machines** to identify the default folder used to store the virtual machines configuration files.

 Even for specifying the default location, you can change it during the virtual machine creation. It's also important to verify any other virtual machine that's not using the default location settings.

6. The exclusions are made based on the Hyper-V file locations. The default location for virtual machine configuration files is `C:\ProgramData\Microsoft\Windows\Hyper-V` and for virtual hard disks is `C:\Users\Public\Documents\Hyper-V\Virtual Hard Disks`. Take a note of the current locations.

7. Open your anti-virus software on the host computer and add an exception for the following directories and files based on the current location of the files:

   ❑ Directories used for machine configuration files

   ❑ Directories used for virtual hard disk files

   ❑ Snapshot directories

   ❑ `Vmms.exe` and `Vmwp.exe` processes

   ❑ Any other custom configuration directories

   ❑ CSV Directory `C:\ClusterStorage` (for cluster environments)

8. After these steps, your anti-virus will be configured with the proper exception settings for Hyper-V.

How it works...

Before we dig in to the details of the previous steps, it is important to discuss the pros and cons of AV on the host computer. This discussion does not change the necessity of having AV on the virtual machines. Because of the Hyper-V architecture, the parent partition cannot see the read memory information being used by the VMs. Having said that, every virtual machine needs AV; depending upon the operating system, roles, access, and other components present on it.

If you follow the best practices for Hyper-V such as running it using the server core installation, no Internet access nor any other programs or roles installed, you probably don't need any AV installed on the host computer. These best practices already have all the security needed for the parent partition, excluding the requirement to install AV on it. However, you can still install it in case of security compliance or for any other reason.

For servers with the full Windows version, with people browsing on the Internet, and using other software or roles, AV has to be installed with the Hyper-V exclusions configured.

6
Security and Delegation of Control

In this chapter we will cover:

- ▶ Configuring Windows Update for Hyper-V
- ▶ Configuring Cluster-Aware Updating for cluster nodes
- ▶ Delegating control in Hyper-V
- ▶ Configuring Port ACLs
- ▶ Installing and configuring BitLocker for data protection
- ▶ Configuring Hyper-V auditing

Introduction

In general, security is very important in infrastructure, and this applies to virtualization as well. In a highly virtual environment, and also in a private cloud, you must ensure that security is met on all layers. The new Hyper-V version comes with lots of configuration options to allow you to protect your host and virtual machines. The core security areas for virtual environments involve settings and options such as software and hardware updates, backup, high availability, access control, network protection, and auditing. In this chapter, you will see some of them, such as how to configure **Windows Update** for the Full and Server Core installations, access control using **Authorization Manager** and **Simple Authorization**, network protection with **Port ACLs**, disk encryption with **BitLocker**, and Hyper-V auditing.

By using these configuration options, you can enforce a safer environment for virtual and host computers.

Configuring Windows Update for Hyper-V

During Windows development, Microsoft tries to find every risk and vulnerability to security breaches that can cause problems or downtime such as external access, buffer overflows, blue screens, and system crashes. Even after the final version release, it is common to find these errors and bad functions in Windows. That's why Microsoft has a service named **Windows Update**, which provides update packages for all these problems that may arise in Hyper-V or any other component of Windows. It is also important to note that Microsoft has security teams that try to find security breaches before someone with bad intentions does. To make sure your servers are safe against all these threats, you need to make sure that they are up-to-date with all updates installed.

The Server Core installation is a good option to reduce the number of updates to be installed once only the core components are used, but this doesn't mean that you don't need to install updates for it. Some of these updates are designed to modify or improve the core components of Windows, whether Server Core or Full Windows installation.

This recipe will show you how to configure Windows Update settings in Full and Server Core installations.

Getting ready

The Microsoft software update services can be accessed via the Internet or through an internal server named **Microsoft Server Update Services** (**WSUS**). Make sure you have your internal WSUS server up and running; you can also download the updates directly from the Internet onto your server or copy downloaded updates from another computer.

How to do it...

The following steps show how to configure Windows Update for both graphical and command-line interfaces:

1. To enable and configure Windows Update in a Full Windows installation, launch the Start menu, type `control`, and open **Control Panel**.

2. Click on **System and Security**, and then click on **Windows Update**.

3. Click on **Change settings** in the left-hand pane.

4. In the **Change settings** window, click on the drop-down list to see the available options, as shown in the following screenshot:

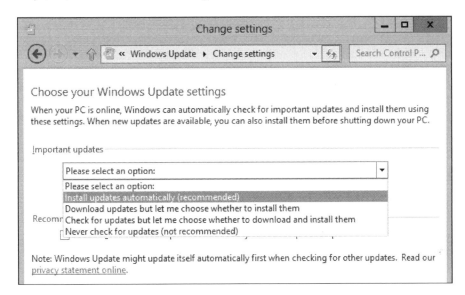

5. To use the recommended setting, select **Install updates automatically (recommended)**. You can also select one of the other three available options.

6. To get the recommended updates for your server, check the checkbox for **Give me recommended updates the same way I receive important updates**, under **Recommended updates**, and click on **OK** to confirm.

7. To verify and install available updates, click on **Check for updates** in the left-hand pane.

8. To view the history of installed updates, click on **View Update history**.

9. To enable automatic update settings using the Server Core installation of Windows, log in to the server as an administrator and type `sconfig` in the command prompt.

10. In the **Server Configuration** window, type 5 to select the option **Windows Update Settings**, as shown in the following screenshot:

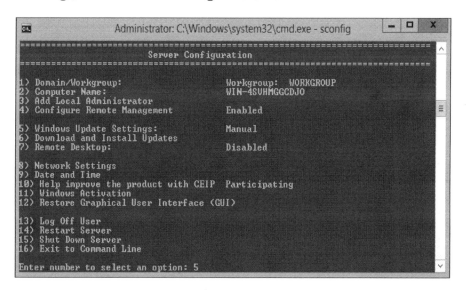

11. Type A for automatic or M for manual updates. If you choose manual updates, the system will never check for updates, and they will have to be installed manually, but if you choose automatic updates, the system will check for updates at 3:00 A.M. every day, by default; you can change this later by using Group Policy. Click on **OK** in the **Update Settings** pop up.

 You can also run the command `cscript scregedit.wsf /AU 4` from the path `C:\Windows\System32`, to enable automatic updates without the need to use `sconfig`.

12. To check, download, and install updates, type 6 in the **Server Configuration** window to select **Download and Install Updates**.

13. Type A to search for all updates, or type R for recommended updates only.

14. After checking for updates, available updates will be listed. Type A to install all updates, N to quit without installing, or S to select a single update. If you elect to update the system, click on **Yes** to restart the computer and apply the updates.

15. When finished, type 16 to quit **sconfig**.

16. You can alternatively use Group Policy to configure Windows Update. To use Local Group Policy Editor to set the Windows Update configuration, type `gpedit.msc` in the Start menu or at the command prompt.

17. In the **Local Group Policy Editor** window, under **Computer Configuration**, navigate through **Administrative Templates | Windows Components | Windows Update**.

18. On the right-hand panel, double-click on the **Configure Automatic Updates** policy.

19. In the **Configure Automatic Updates** window, select **Enabled**.

20. Under **Options** in **Configure Automatic Updating**, select the option you want.

21. In **Scheduled install day**, select the option for the day(s) on which you want to install the updates.

22. In **Scheduled install time**, select the time at which you want to install the updates. When finished, your configuration screen should look as shown in the following screenshot:

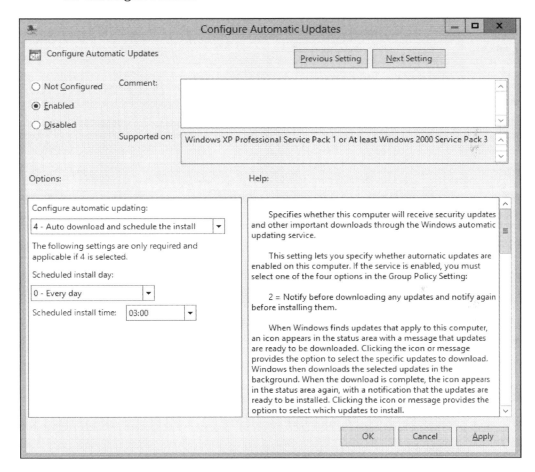

23. If you have a WSUS server, click on **Next Setting**. Otherwise, click on **OK**.

24. To specify a WSUS server, select **Enabled** under **Specify intranet Microsoft update service location**.

25. Under **Options**, specify your WSUS server URL in both options.

26. In the following screenshot, a server named `WSUSServer` has been used. Click on **OK** when finished.

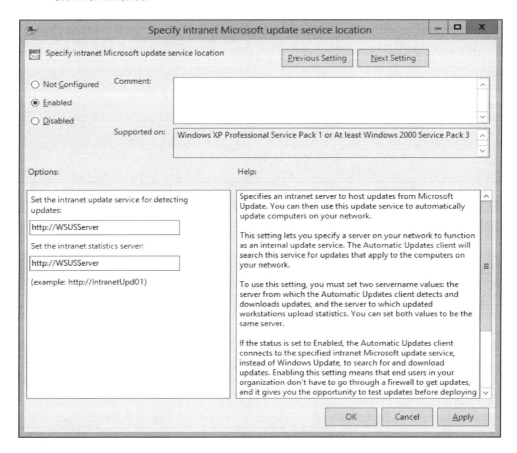

How it works...

The Windows Update service can be configured using the Control Panel, command lines, and `sconfig`, for Server Core scenarios.

For a single server installation or standalone servers, the command-line and Control Panel options are the most effective. With `sconfig`, you don't even need to know how to use the configuration commands to set up Windows updates.

For domain-joined servers or standalone servers that require WSUS configuration, you have to use group policies. In the previous steps, you saw how to use the group policy. However, using **Active Directory**, you can also apply policies using **Group Policy Objects** (**GPOs**), which can be linked to an **Organizational Unit** with multiple servers.

It is important to remember that Windows updates have to be applied to every computer; it doesn't matter whether they are physical or virtual, or clients or servers. Make sure that the Windows Update policy for the Hyper-V servers is aligned to your business requirements, as some updates require a reboot. Also, for production environments, the use of WSUS is strongly recommended.

To save time and Internet bandwidth, it is also a best practice to install the WSUS server, so that you can download, manage, and install updates, from a single console.

With this configuration on every computer, you will make sure your servers are protected with the latest updates.

Configuring Cluster-Aware Updating for cluster nodes

One of the most complicated tasks in previous Windows versions, regarding Windows Updates, is the process of updating a cluster. The whole procedure is manual and requires a lot of effort to guarantee that all nodes within the clusters are up-to-date.

Windows Server 2012 introduces **Cluster-Aware Updating** (**CAU**), which automatically installs updates for all node members of a cluster in a synchronized and orchestrated way. Once CAU is able to do all the jobs with no user interaction, it allows enterprises to update their clusters in a dynamic and automated process, saving costs, time, and resources otherwise spent on running updates on clusters. As a result, it will reduce outages in clusters when running updates and reduces your tasks for manual updates.

CAU will be responsible for checking, downloading, and installing all available Windows updates packages and installing with minimum or no downtime for the services running in the cluster environment. For virtual machines in a cluster, CAU will start live migration tasks to move the VM across the other nodes while the update occurs and move it back when it is finished.

This recipe will guide you through the steps to make sure your Windows Server 2012 clusters are updated automatically using CAU.

Getting ready

Once configured, CAU can download updates from either the Windows Update website or an internal Windows Update service, such as Windows Server Update Services (WSUS). Before you begin, make sure an update service is configured.

Another thing to note is that CAU can only be used in Windows Server 2012 clusters.

If you want to use CAU from a remote server, you will need to install Failover Clustering Tools, using Server Manager. If you are using one of the nodes to configure and install the updates, Failover Clustering Tools is already installed.

How to do it...

The following steps will demonstrate how to configure CAU for automatic updates by using the self-updating option, how to preview updates, and how to manually apply updates to a cluster:

1. To configure Cluster-Aware Updating using the self-updating option for automatic updates, type `Cluster` in the Start menu, and click on **Cluster-Aware Update**.

2. In the **Cluster-Aware Updating** window, under **Connect to a failover cluster**, type the name of the cluster you want to update and click on **Connect**.

3. In the same window, click on **Configure cluster self-updating options**, as shown in the following screenshot.

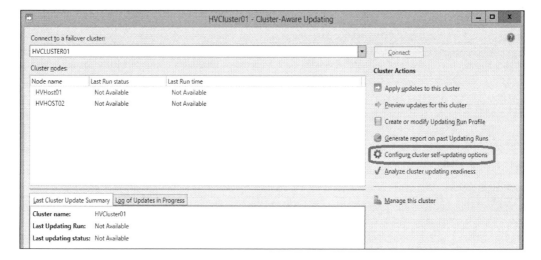

4. In the **Getting Started** window, click on **Next**.

5. In **Add Clustered Role**, check the **Add the CAU clustered role, with self-updating mode enabled, to this cluster** checkbox, if the cluster is not configured with CAU yet. If you want to prestage a computer account in Active Directory for the CAU clustered role, check the **I have a prestaged computer object for the CAU clustered role** checkbox and click on **Next**.

6. In **Self-updating schedule**, select the frequency for self updating, the start date, and the other options (based on the frequency that you selected), and click on **Next**.

7. In **Advanced Options**, select the advanced configuration for the self-updating policy, as shown in the following screenshot, and click on **Next**:

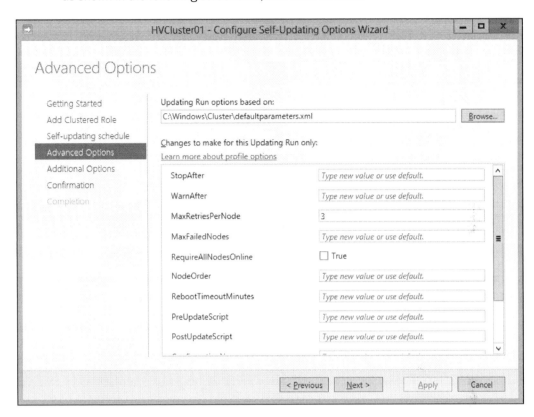

8. In **Additional Options**, select **Give me recommended updates the same way that I receive important updates**, to also have recommended updates installed beside important ones, and click on **Next**.

9. In the confirmation window, click on **Apply** to confirm the new configuration; a task is created to automatically update the cluster.

10. To preview the updates that have to be installed, open the **Cluster-Aware Updating** console again and click on **Preview updates for this cluster**.

11. In the **Preview Updates** window, click on **Generate Update Preview List** and wait for the list to be created. A list with the node names and the updates to be installed will be listed, as shown in the following screenshot:

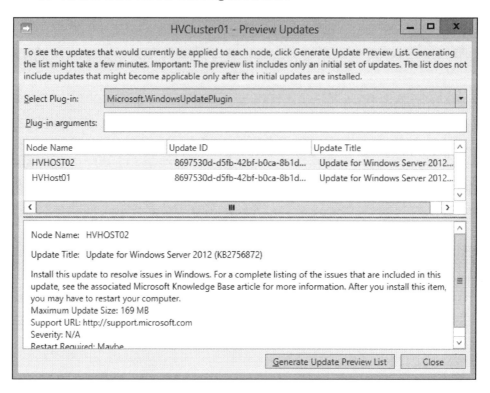

12. To manually apply updates to a cluster, click on **Apply updates to this cluster** in the **Cluster-Aware Updating** console.

13. In the **Cluster-Aware Updating Wizard** window, click on **Next**.

14. In **Advanced Options**, specify any advanced options and click on **Next**.

15. In **Additional Options**, select **Give me recommended updates the same way that I receive important updates**, to also have recommended updates installed beside important ones, and click on **Next**.

16. In the **Confirmation** window, click on **Update** to start the update process; click on **Close** after completion.

17. Follow the update process using the default window for Cluster-Aware Updating, where you can check details such as the node name, update status, and progress. For advanced information, click on the **Log of Updates in Progress** tab, as shown in the following screenshot:

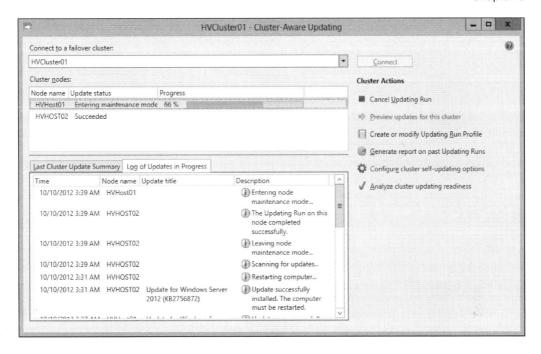

18. Wait until CAU updates all nodes, and close the window when finished.

How it works...

Cluster-Aware Updating is another feature that will change the way we update our clusters today, by creating automatic tasks that manage the entire update process for all cluster nodes with almost no downtime for virtual machines running on it.

There are two options for configuring CAU. The first one, demonstrated in the recipe, is **self updating**, where CAU creates a task to update the cluster periodically. The wizard to configure self updating allows you to select a daily, weekly, or monthly update frequency. During the wizard you can also add advanced options to set the way the task will behave. The default options are sufficient with all necessary configurations, but you can change the values, based on your needs. By using self updating, you can have a fully automated updating process that requires no user intervention whatsoever.

The second option is **remote updating**, where a remote computer running Windows Server 2012 or Windows 8, which have Failover Clustering Tools installed, can initiate an on-demand update process, using a default or custom update profile. This option can be used to start the orchestrated update process manually for critical updates or updates outside the schedule for self updating.

Another interesting option is **previewing updates**. This shows a list of available updates to be installed per host and can be used to review existing updates before installing them.

After configuring CAU, you can make sure all updates are being applied automatically to all cluster nodes.

There's more...

Using PowerShell to manage Cluster-Aware Updating

CAU offers full support for being managed using PowerShell. There are 17 commandlets available for CAU. To list all of them, type the following command:

```
Get-Command -Module ClusterAwareUpdating
```

For more information about a specific commandlet, type the following command:

```
Get-Help <cmdlet name>
```

Generating reports on past updating runs

If you want to check past updating runs made by CAU, you can use the **Generate report on past updating runs** option in the **Cluster-Aware Updating** window by specifying the start and end dates and clicking on **Generate Report**, as shown in the following screenshot:

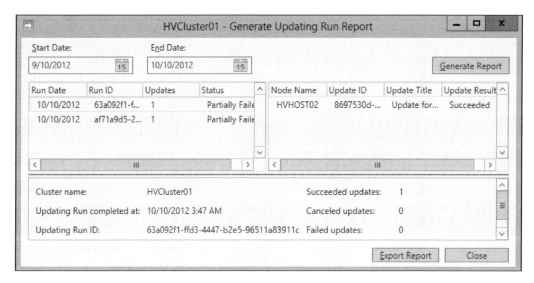

You can also export the report to a `.htm` file by clicking on **Export Report**.

See also

▸ The *Configuring Windows Update for Hyper-V* recipe in this chapter

Delegating control in Hyper-V

In some companies, it is common practice to have different access levels for systems, such as administrator, service desk, and auditor. When implementing virtual servers using Hyper-V, it is also important to reflect these access levels.

The new version of Hyper-V makes this task easier when you need to specify particular users or groups to be **Hyper-V Administrators**, but you also might face scenarios where different levels are required.

This recipe will show you how to use the new feature **Simple Authorization** and how to create advanced access levels for Hyper-V users.

Getting ready

During the task, to add advanced permissions to a user, you will need to use groups. You can create and use local groups or Active Directory groups. Make sure you have created them before you start.

How to do it...

The following steps show how to delegate control for a user by using the local Hyper-V Administrators group and by using Authorization Manager for advanced delegations:

1. To add users or groups as members of the local Hyper-V Administrators, open the Start menu and type `computer`. From **Search Results**, click on **Computer Management**.

2. In the **Computer Management** console, expand **System Tools | Local Users and Groups** and click on **Groups**.

3. In the group list, double-click on the **Hyper-V Administrators** group, as shown in the following screenshot:

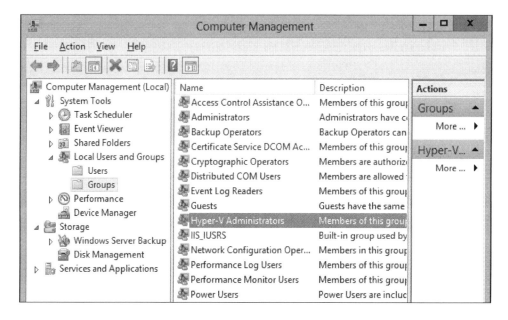

4. In the **Hyper-V Administrators Properties** window, click on **Add**, type the groups or users you want to add into the group, and click on **OK** twice.

5. To add advanced permissions for a group in Hyper-V, open the Start menu and type `azman.msc` to open the **Authorization Manager** console.

6. In the **Authorization Manager** console, right-click on **Authorization Manager** and select **Open Authorization Store**.

7. In the **Open Authorization Store** option, under **Store Name**, type the path `C:\ProgramData\Microsoft\Windows\Hyper-V\InitialStore.xml` and click on **OK**.

8. Under the **Authorization Manager** console, expand **Hyper-V services | Definitions**, right-click on **Role Definitions**, and select **New Role Definition**.

9. In the **New Role Definition** window, specify the name of the role you want to use.

10. Then, under **Description**, specify the role description and click on **OK**. Role Definitions will be listed as shown in the following screenshot:

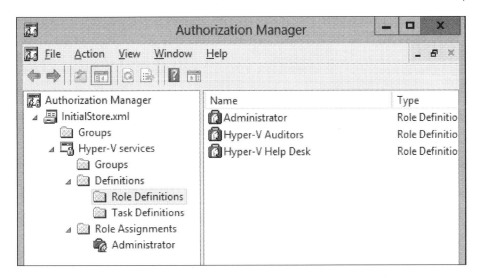

11. In the **Authorization Manager** console, right-click on **Task Definitions** and select **New Task Definition**.

12. In the **New Task Definition** window, under **Name**, specify the task name.

13. Then, under **Description**, add a description for your task and click on **OK**. The tasks will be listed in the right-hand pane, as shown in the following screenshot:

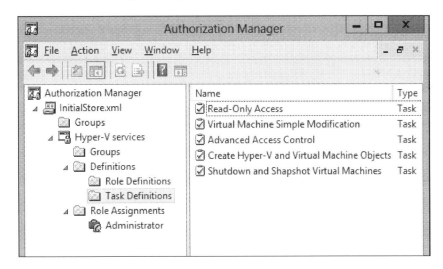

14. To add a definition into a task, click on **Task Definition** and double-click on a task.

15. Click on the **Definition** tab and select **Add**.

16. In the **Add Definition** window, select the **Operations** tab.

17. Select the operations you want from the list, as shown in the following screenshot, and click on **OK**:

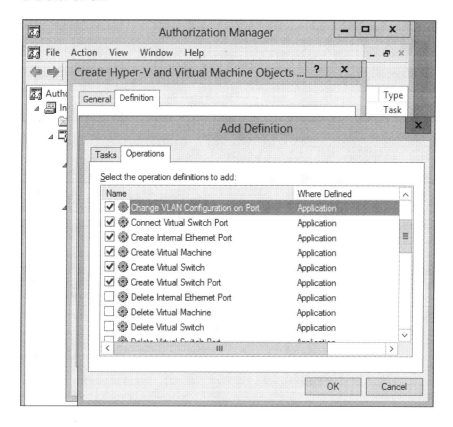

18. To add a Task Definition into a Role Definition, click on **Role Definitions** and select the role you want to change.

19. In the **Role Definition** properties, click on the **Definition** tab.

20. Under the **Definition** tab, click on **Add**.

21. In the **Add Definition** window, select the **Tasks** tab, select the tasks you want to link to the Role Definition, and click on **OK**.

 It is possible to add operations directly to a role group rather than a Task Definition, however it will be easier to change a task that is linked to other groups. When a task is changed, every group that has a link to it will have the changes applied by default.

22. To assign a role, right-click on **Role Assignments** and select **New Role Assignment**.

23. In the **Add Role** window, select the Role Definition you want to add, and click on **OK**.

24. To assign a user or a group to a role, right-click on the group you want, select **Assign Users and Groups**, and click on **From Windows and Active Directory...**, as shown in the following screenshot:

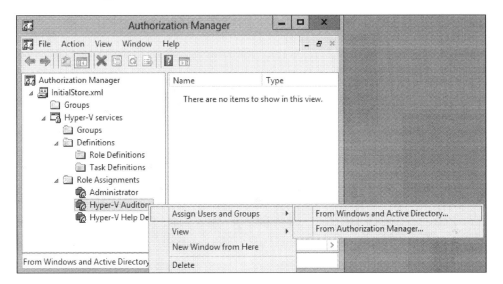

25. In the **Select Users or Groups** window, enter the object names and click on **OK**. After that, you can log in to Hyper-V as a user who is member of a group that was assigned to a role, to check the permissions that have been added.

How it works...

In Windows Server 2008 and 2008 R2, there is no local group to administer Hyper-V. Normally, to be able to manage Hyper-V, users are added into the local administrator group. That allows users to do whatever they want on that server.

In Windows Server 2012, during Hyper-V installation, a new group is created, named **Hyper-V Administrators**. When a user is added to this group, they can do anything on Hyper-V, but they don't have any other rights on the local computer.

Even with the local Hyper-V group, sometimes different access levels are required. For those scenarios, you have to use **Authorization Manager** (**Azman**). Azman is a framework that is used to manage the authorization policy that allows applications to perform access control. Hyper-V uses Azman to grant access based on roles and tasks. Hyper-V authorization policies are stored in a file named `InitialStore.xml`, located by the path `C:\ProgramData\Microsoft\Windows\Hyper-V\`. Once loaded through Azman, you can create and delete the access policies or apply them to groups and users.

The first things to be created on Azman are **Role Definitions**. These are for roles that are used to receive access policies named **Operations**. Hyper-V has 34 operations used to grant permissions, such as to create virtual machines, allow virtual machine snapshots, and stop virtual machines. Applying these policies to many groups can be a tough job, that's why Azman uses **Task Definitions**. Tasks Definitions can group operations in common, so that you can apply them to more than one Role Definition, making the modifications easier to make. The example in the recipe demonstrated the creation of a Task Definition named **Read-Only Access**, containing all operations necessary to allow a group to open and view the Hyper-V settings. Then, the task was assigned to a Role Definition named **Hyper-V Auditors**.

Once the operations or the tasks are assigned to a Role Definition, you have to assign the role to a local or an Active Directory group, so that it can get the policies that are in the Role Definition.

Using the operations and tasks, you can grant only the necessary access for users to access Hyper-V with more security and control.

Configuring Port ACLs

Using network limitations to limit access between computers and networks, even in virtual environments, is common practice. For instance, let's say you need to deny network access by a particular IP address or virtual machine to another virtual machine or to an entire network. In previous versions of Hyper-V, you would have needed additional software or a network device to define these rules, making it more complicated and expensive.

Hyper-V introduces a feature called **Port ACLs**, which enforces policies to block or allow network traffic on a virtual machine, on an IP address, or on a network range. These policies are created via PowerShell, and administrators can use them to control network traffic sent and received through the Hyper-V virtual switch.

Port ACLs will act as a network firewall and can be used to define the direction, address, and action for network rules.

This recipe will demonstrate how to create and analyze Port ACLs by using Hyper-V.

Getting ready

Before starting to create the Port ACLs rules, make sure your network infrastructure (such as subnets, routers, and IP address) is configured and is working properly.

How to do it...

You will see, through the following steps, how to use the Port ACLs cmdlets to add, visualize, and remove rules for virtual machines:

1. Launch the Start menu and type `powershell`, to open Windows PowerShell.

2. To block outbound access by a virtual machine to an IP range, use the `Add-VMNetworkAdapterAcl` command, specifying the virtual machine after `VMName` and the network range after `RemoteIPaddress`. The following example denies the virtual machine named `WinSRV2012` outbound connections to any IP in the `192.168.0.0/24` network.

   ```
   Add-VMNetworkAdapterAcl -VMName WinSRV2012 -RemoteIPAddress
   192.168.0.0/24 -Direction Outbound -Action Deny
   ```

3. To deny inbound access to a virtual machine by *any* IP address, type the following command. In the example, we used a virtual machine named `WinSRV2012` and had the inbound connections denied from `ANY` remote IP address.

   ```
   Add-VMNetworkAdapterAcl -VMName WinSRV2012 -RemoteIPAddress ANY -
   Direction Inbound -Action Deny
   ```

4. To allow a particular IP address outbound and inbound connection to a virtual machine, use the following command. In this example, the network adapter named `Network Adapter` in the virtual machine `WinSRV2012` had all connections allowed if the IP address was `10.10.0.10`.

   ```
   Add-VMNetworkAdapterAcl -VMName WinSRV2012 -RemoteIPAddress
   10.10.0.10 -Direction both -Action Allow -VMNetworkName "Network
   Adapter"
   ```

5. For bulk configuration for more than one virtual machine at the same time, create a filter using the `Get-VM` commandlet and add the actions you want. The following example gets every virtual machine starting with `SRVDMZ` and creates a rule to deny any connection from and to the IP address `131.107.1.1`.

   ```
   Get-VM -Name SRVDMZ* | Add-VMNetworkAdapterAcl -RemoteIPAddress
   131.107.1.1 -Direction both Action Deny
   ```

6. To view all Port ACLs rules per virtual machine, type the command `Get-VMNetworkAdapterACL`. The following screenshot shows a list with rules for every virtual machine:

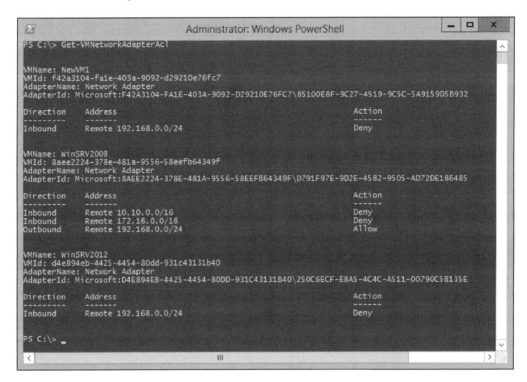

7. To remove an existing rule, use the commandlet `Remove-VMNetworkAdaterAcl`. In this example, the rule that allows connections from both directions has been removed.

    Remove-VMNetworkAdapterAcl –VMName WinSRV2012 –RemoteIPAddress 10.10.0.10 –Direction both –Action Allow –VMNetworkName "Network Adapter"

How it works...

Port ACLs is one of the features that can only be managed by using PowerShell. The three available commands to administer Port ACLs are:

►   `Add-VMNetworkAdapterAcl`

►   `Get-VMNetworkAdapterAcl`

►   `Remove-VMNetworkAdapterAcl`

The first command, `Add-VMNetworkAdapterAcl`, is used to create new rules. To create them, the command needs inputs such as the VM name, action, direction, and remote IP address.

The `Action` syntax can have one of these three values: `Allow`, `Deny`, and `meter`. It will define what the rule actually does when the policy attributes match.

The `Direction` input allows you to choose in which direction the rule will be applied. The available options are `inbound`, `outbound`, and `both`.

The `RemoteIPAddress` or `RemoteMacAddress` syntax specifies the destination for which you want to apply the rule. `RemoteIPAddress` accepts single IP addresses or IP addresses with the subnet mask, and `RemoteMacAddress` can be used to specify a particular MAC address.

After creating the rules, you can use the command `Get-VMNetworkAdapterAcl` to view all existing rules. You can see all policies by simply typing `Get-VMNetworkAdapterAcl` or by using syntaxes to create filters to show them by VM name, VM network adapter, computer name, management OS, and snapshot.

The command used to remove Port ACLs rules is `Remove-VMNetworkAdapterAcl`. The syntaxes used are the same as for `Add-VMNetworkAdapterAcl`. You can type the same command used to add a rule; just swap the `Add` with `Remove` to remove the existing rule.

Port ACLs will be very handy when you need to limit the communication for a particular IP address (or range) between virtual machines. This is already common in server scenarios, but now you don't need to rely on physical devices such as switches or routers to do so.

Using these three commandlets, you will be able to manage and automate all Port ACLs rules.

See also

> ▶ The *Learning and utilizing basic commands in PowerShell* recipe in *Chapter 4, Saving Time and Cost with Hyper-V Automation*

Installing and configuring BitLocker for data protection

Disk protection is becoming a security concern in datacenters. Data that is stored here is very important, and any leakage can lead to serious problems for company business.

BitLocker Drive Encryption is a Windows feature that enables data protection by using strong encryption to protect your data in case of theft. It is a perfect solution for branch offices or datacenters where there is no local security. BitLocker is a solution that protects the disk in case of lost, stolen, or inappropriately decommissioned hard drives. This protection is by way of a password or a smart card, and it also supports a recovery key in case of lost passwords.

In virtual environments, when using virtual hard disks, there's no encryption, by default. If one of your servers or storage is stolen, someone can open the virtual hard disk files with a double-click and get all the information they want.

When used in conjunction with a system that supports **Trusted Platform Module** (**TPM**), BitLocker also provides additional and advanced security features. TPM is a chipset present on servers that BitLocker can use to store the encryption key so that the system can identify, say whether the hard disk has been moved from one server to another. During the boot process, BitLocker and TPM verify the hardware and boot file integrity, allowing verification for any modification, say attaching a disk to another computer in an unauthorized manner.

This recipe shows how to enable BitLocker, to encrypt and protect your hard drives.

Getting ready

To enable the additional security features provided by TPM, you need to make sure your server has a TPM chipset and a **Trusted Computing Group BIOS**. You can check whether you have TPM by using Device Manager or the **TPM Management console** (type `tpm.msc` in the Start menu). The console will allow you to verify, enable, and configure TPM, if it is present.

It is a best practice to use a USB flash drive to store the startup key for a scenario without a TPM chipset. Add a flash drive before you start the BitLocker wizard.

If you don't have a TPM chipset, this recipe will also demonstrate how to enable BitLocker without the need to have TPM.

How to do it...

The following steps show how to enable and configure BitLocker for your partitions:

1. To install the BitLocker Drive Encryption feature, open the Server Manager console from the Taskbar.
2. In the **Server Manager** console, click on **Manage** at the top-right corner and select **Add Roles and Features**.
3. In the **Before you begin** section, click on **Next**.
4. In the **Select installation type** section, click on **Next**.
5. In the **Select destination server** section, click on **Next** twice.

6. In the **Select features** section, select the **BitLocker Drive Encryption** checkbox, as shown in the following screenshot:

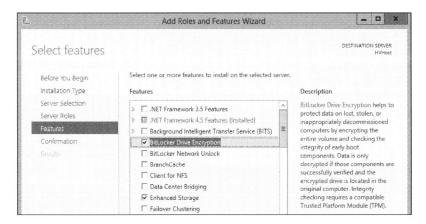

7. In the **Add Roles and Features Wizard** window, click on **Add Features**.

8. Click on **Next**, and on the **Confirm installation selections** screen, click on **Install**. Wait for the installation to be finished, and restart your server.

9. After the installation, to enable BitLocker in a hard disk drive, open the Control Panel.

10. In the Control Panel, click on **System and Security | BitLocker Drive Encryption**.

11. In the **BitLocker Drive Encryption** window, select the drive for which you want to enable BitLocker and click on **Turn on BitLocker**.

12. You can also access the same option by right-clicking on the volume or via Windows Explorer. To do this via Windows Explorer, open a new Windows Explorer window, click on **Computer** in the left-hand pane, select the drive you want to enable, select the **Drive** tab, click **BitLocker**, and click on **Turn on BitLocker**, as shown in the following screenshot:

13. If you receive an error message saying that BitLocker cannot be enabled because there is no TPM device, continue with the immediate next steps, otherwise continue from step 20.

14. To use BitLocker without a compatible TPM, launch the Start menu and type `gpedit.msc`. Click on the **gpedit** icon to open Local Group Policy Editor.

15. In the **Local Group Policy Editor** window, navigate to **Computer Configuration | Administrative Templates | Windows Components | BitLocker Drive Encryption**, and click on **Operating System Drives**.

16. Double-click on the policy **Require additional authentication at startup**, and click on **Enabled**.

17. Under **Options**, check the **Allow BitLocker without a compatible TPM (requires a password or a startup key on a USB flash drive)** checkbox and click on **OK**.

> For domain-joined servers, you can apply a Group Policy Object (GPO), rather than a local policy, for automation and central management.

18. Type the command `gpupdate /force` to make sure the local policy or GPO has been applied.

19. Open Windows Explorer or Control Panel to turn BitLocker on, as explained in steps 10 and 12.

20. In the **BitLocker Drive Encryption** wizard, specify a password that will be used every time your computer starts, and click on **Next**. If you are not encrypting a system partition, you can also elect to use a smart card to unlock the drive, by checking the **Use my smart card to unlock the drive** checkbox.

21. In the next window, a recovery key will be created. You need to specify where to save the key. Pick between **Save to a USB flash drive**, **Save to a file**, and **Print the recovery key**, as shown in the following screenshot:

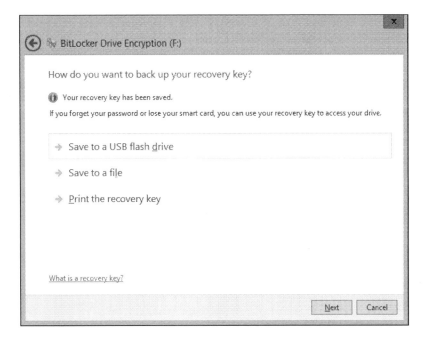

22. In the **Choose how much of your drive to encrypt** window, select the option **Encrypt used disk space only (faster and best for new PCs and Drives)** or **Encrypt entire drive (slower but best for PCs and drives already in use)** and click on **Next**.

23. If you are encrypting a system partition, the Wizard will show the **Are you ready to encrypt this drive** window to run the BitLocker system check. Click on **Continue** to start the test.

24. Restart your computer, add the password created during the BitLocker activation, and wait for drive encryption to be finished. The process to encrypt the drive can take some minutes, based on the data volume that is being encrypted.

25. To manage BitLocker configuration, such as recovery keys and passwords, and also to disable it, open the Control Panel and click on **System and Security | Manage BitLocker**.

How it works...

BitLocker has come very far since its release in Windows Vista.

It is a very common feature enabled on portable computers to allow disk protection in case they are stolen. The good news is that you can also use it on servers and storage to enable high protection.

The following are some new features that make the adoption of BitLocker easier in a server environment:

- It protects data on Failover Cluster Volumes and SANs
- If offers Cluster Shared Volumes (CSV) support
- Data volumes and OS volumes stored on SAN are accessed via iSCSI or Virtual Fibre Channel
- It offers support for Encrypted Hard Drives (EHDs)
- It allows standard users the ability to change the BitLocker password
- It offers the option to encrypt used disk space only
- It has network unlock

On Windows Server 2012, BitLocker is a feature and has to be installed in order to enable BitLocker on a disk drive. By default, you must also have a TPM chipset to use BitLocker. In case the server doesn't have TPM, you can disable the TPM requirement using group policies.

After installing, it is quite easy to get BitLocker enabled. There are several ways to do it, such as through Windows Explorer, by right-clicking on the disk drive, through the Control Panel, and through the command-line interface.

During the process of turning it on, you must specify a password; every time you initialize the disk, the password must be entered. The wizard also creates a recovery key that needs to be saved on another hard drive or even printed, in case you lose the password.

With these new features, you can apply and manage BitLocker in a vast list of scenarios and storage, including CSVs, and boot via SANs, which is very useful for branch offices with lower physical security, such as disaster recovery multisite cluster.

There's more...

BitLocker can also be enabled using two commands. The first one is `Manage-BDE`. Using the next example, you can enable BitLocker on `C:` and save the recovery key on `E:`. After typing the command, the system will prompt for the password and the encryption process will begin.

```
Manage-bde -on C: -Password -RecoveryKey H:\
```

If you prefer PowerShell, you can use the commandlet `Enable-BitLocker`. For more information, type `Help Enable-BitLocker`.

Configuring Hyper-V auditing

You have seen in the previous recipes how to protect your physical and virtual servers with Windows Updates, an antivirus, access control, and so on. However, a key factor needs to be considered to address security concerns when they happen, to track unsolicited access or unauthorized actions on your system, or to simply monitor when and how the Hyper-V administrators are managing it.

The best way to get these results is by setting an audit. By default, all Hyper-V events are logged in Event Viewer and can be used to diagnose a problem or track what has been done by the other Hyper-V admins.

You can also see all Hyper-V roles and authorization rights changes with Audit File System, which is not enabled by default.

This recipe will explain and show how to use the existing event logs as well as showing you how to enable Audit File System.

How to do it...

The following steps will demonstrate how to use the default data in Event Viewer to audit Hyper-V changes and how to use Object Access Auditing to check changes in the Hyper-V permissions.

1. To see specific Hyper-V event logs, launch the Start menu and type `event viewer`. From the search results, open **Event Viewer**.

2. In the **Event Viewer** console, expand **Application and Service Logs | Microsoft | Windows**.

3. Scroll down until you find the Hyper-V log folders, as shown in the following screenshot:

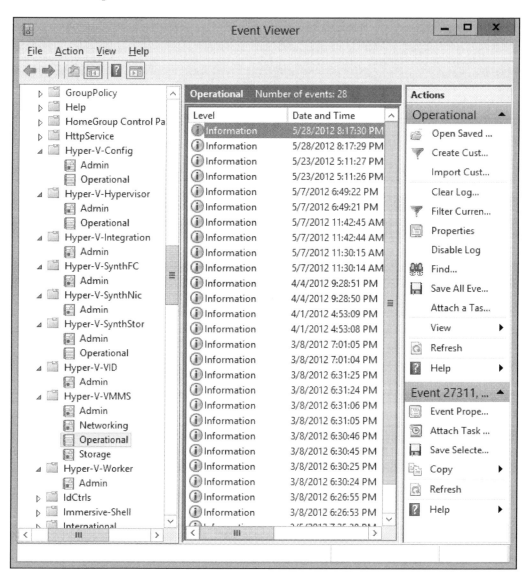

4. To use the default Event Viewer filter that shows all Hyper-V logs in a single view, click on **Custom Views**, expand **Server Roles**, and click on **Hyper-V**, in the **Event Viewer** console, as shown in the following screenshot:

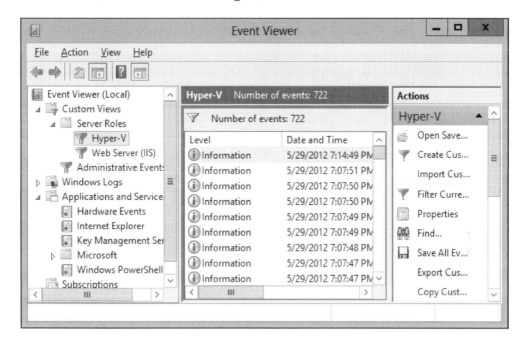

5. To enable auditing for Hyper-V roles and authorization rights, launch the Start menu and type `gpedit.msc`. Select **gpedit** from the search results, to open Local Group Policy Editor.

6. In the **Local Group Policy Editor** console, under **Computer Configuration**, expand **Windows Settings | Security Settings | Advanced Audit Policy Configuration | System Audit Policies**, and select **Object Access**.

7. In the right-hand pane, double-click on **Audit File System**.

8. In the **Audit File System Properties** window, check the **Configure the following audit events** checkbox.

9. Check the checkboxes for **Success** and **Failure** under **Configure the following audit events**, as shown in the following screenshot:

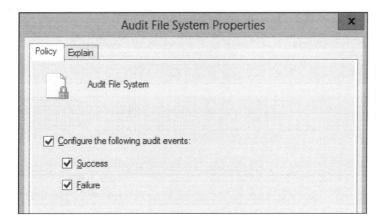

10. Click on **OK** and close the **Local Group Policy Editor** console.

11. Open Windows Explorer from the taskbar.

12. In the address bar, type the path `C:\ProgramData\Microsoft\Windows\Hyper-V` and press *Enter*.

13. In the results pane, right-click on the file named `InitialStore` and click on **Properties**.

14. In the **InitialStore Properties** window, select the **Security** tab and click on the **Advanced** button.

15. In the **Advanced Security Settings for InitialStore** window, select the **Auditing** tab and click on **Add**.

16. In the **Auditing Entry for InitialStore** window, click on the hyperlink **Select a principal**.

17. Type `Everyone` in the entry box and click on **OK**.

18. In the drop box next to **Type**, select **All**.

19. Under **Permissions**, select the **Full control** checkbox. The **Auditing Entry for InitialStore** window will look similar to the following screenshot:

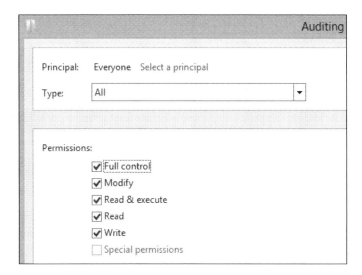

20. To verify the audit log entries, open Event Viewer again, expand **Windows Logs**, and click on the **Security** log.

21. The events will be listed with **File System** as the **Task Category** and with **Microsoft Windows security** as the **Source**. You also need to check under **Object Name** whether the file is `InitialStore.xml`.

22. In the following screenshot, an event shows that someone has successfully accessed the `Initialstore.xml` file:

How it works...

All Hyper-V actions, such as creating a new virtual hard drive, changing a virtual switch, and adding a fiber channel adapter, can be audited. All these logs can be viewed in Event Viewer.

The following are the Hyper-V logs in Event Viewer:

▶ **Hyper-V-Config**: This contains all the information related to the virtual machine configuration files

▶ **Hyper-V-Hypervisor**: This is used to log information about hypervisor activities

▶ **Hyper-V-Integration**: This shows events related to integration services

▶ **Hyper-V-SynthFC**: This concerns Virtual Fibre Channel details

▶ **Hyper-V-SynthNic**: This displays information about virtual switches

▶ **Hyper-V-SynthStor**: This has details about virtual hard disks

▶ **Hyper-V-VMMS**: This is dedicated to logs containing information about virtual machine management services

▶ **Hyper-V-Worker**: This shows logs about the worker process created by every running virtual machine

Using the descriptions for these log entries, you can find errors in or information about Hyper-V quicker; however, if you prefer to see all events at the same time, there is a custom view (created when the Hyper-V role is installed) that contains all Hyper-V log entries. It facilitates seeing all logs in the same window view.

The changes in the Hyper-V authorization rights are not logged by default in Event Viewer. To do so, the local Audit File System needs to be enabled via group policies. The `InitialStore.xml` file must also be configured to have file auditing. When both are configured, you can see the log entries for successful and failed access in the security log in Event Viewer.

With the Hyper-V event entries and file auditing for the Hyper-V authorization file, you will be able to track all changes and modifications in your host server that are related to virtual machines, hypervisor, virtual switches, and all other Hyper-V components.

7
Configuring High Availability in Hyper-V

In this chapter we will cover:

- ▶ Installing and configuring an iSCSI Target server in Windows Server 2012
- ▶ Installing and configuring the Windows Failover Clustering feature
- ▶ Enabling Cluster Shared Volumes 2.0
- ▶ Using Live Migration in a cluster environment
- ▶ Configuring VM Priority for Clustered Virtual Machines

Introduction

The adoption of and migration to the virtual environment has been implemented by almost all companies nowadays. Virtual servers provide benefits such as lower energy consumption, datacenter space, and costs. On the other hand, it can be very dangerous, since lots of virtual machines running on just one server creates a single point of failure. In this example, if a server with heaps of virtual machines is down, not only is one system affected, but also all VMs running on that server.

The good news is that Windows Server 2012 and Hyper-V come with the right tools and high availability solutions for almost all scenarios. In fact, Hyper-V and Failover Clustering are so deeply integrated, that in previous Windows Server versions, some of the features in Failover Clustering were only meant for Hyper-V use. This has also been improved in Windows Server 2012, so that you can take advantage of new features such as Hyper-V over SMB, built upon CSV2.0.

Small offices or huge datacenters in different locations; it doesn't matter which environment, you will find the correct configuration to make sure your servers are protected from any disaster that may occur, including natural disasters that can rip your datacenter off the map. The interesting thing is that all these magical tools and configurations are offered in the box, without the need to install third-party applications or expensive software.

In this chapter, you will see how to create an **iSCSI Target server** for low-cost storage, how to prepare and configure a **failover cluster** for Hyper-V, **Cluster Shared Volumes** (**CSV**), and other interesting things, to provide a high availability Hyper-V environment.

Installing and configuring an iSCSI Target server in Windows Server 2012

The disk performance and storage systems are normally one of the most expensive and important components in a server farm.

With different storage technologies such as **NAS** and **SAN**, and different methods to connect to them, such as **Fibre Channel** and **SCSI**, it becomes difficult to manage, integrate, and unify all these appliances. Windows Server 2012 makes this task much easier with the **iSCSI Target server**, which is now included in the operating system, giving you an easy and cheap solution for block storage.

iSCSI is a standard protocol that allows storage systems to communicate over **Ethernet**. It basically encapsulates all storage communication in TCP packets, allowing them to be sent over network connections. Using iSCSI Target in Windows Server 2012, you can create a unified server to add all your storage and allow other servers, either physical or virtual, to connect using a single protocol.

The benefits of using an iSCSI Target server on Windows Server 2012 include:

- ▸ A unified way to manage and access storage systems
- ▸ The ability to use local disks or low performance storage for development or test scenarios
- ▸ Diskless servers booting and running from an iSCSI Target server
- ▸ The ability to create virtual storage with storage pools and storage spaces
- ▸ Support for data deduplication to save disk space

In this recipe, you will see how to install and configure the iSCSI Target server, create iSCSI virtual disks, and connect hosts to the server using the iSCSI Initiator.

Getting ready

In production environments, storages such as NAS and SAN are the most common choices, but for test and development scenarios, you can also use the local disk on the server to create your iSCSI virtual disks, facilitating low-cost lab and test environments.

If you are using external storage, connect and configure the server that will be used as the iSCSI Target server, to have access to the storages before you begin.

Make sure network communication between the iSCSI Target server, the storages, and the servers that will connect to the iSCSI Target server is working properly too.

How to do it...

Carry out the following steps in order to install and configure an iSCSI Target server, create and attach virtual hard drives, and connect other servers to the Target Server:

1. To install the iSCSI Target server, open Server Manager from the taskbar.

2. In Server Manager, click on **Manage** and select **Add Roles and Features**.

3. Once in the **Before you begin** section, click on **Next** three times.

4. In the **Select server roles** section, expand **File And Storage Services | File and iSCSI Services** and select **iSCSI Target Server**, as shown in the following screenshot:

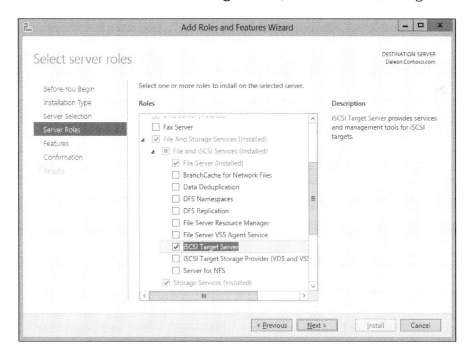

5. Click on **Next** twice, and click on **Install**. Wait for the installation to be completed.

6. After the installation, back on the **Server Manager** dashboard, click on **File and Storage Services** in the left-hand pane, and select **iSCSI**.

7. To create a new iSCSI virtual disk, click on **Tasks** and select **New iSCSI Virtual Disk**, on the **iSCSI** page.

8. In the **New iSCSI Virtual Disk Wizard** window, under **Select iSCSI virtual disk location**, select the storage location to create the virtual disk file and click on **Next**, as shown in the following screenshot:

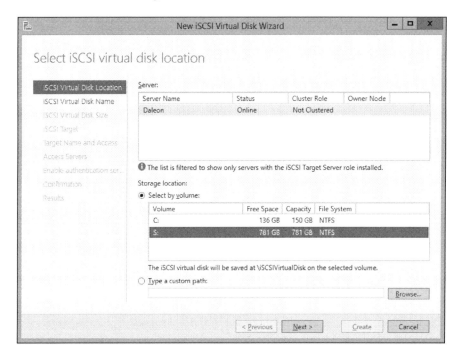

9. In the **Specify iSCSI virtual disk name section**, type the disk name and description and click on **Next**.

10. In the **Specify iSCSI virtual disk size** window, type the disk size and click on **Next**.

11. As no iSCSI Target server is configured yet, select **New iSCSI target** in the **Assign iSCSI target** window. This will allow the same wizard to create a new virtual disk and configure the iSCSI Target server.

12. In the **Specify target name** window, type a display name and the description for the iSCSI Target server and click on **Next**.

13. In **Specify access servers**, click on **Add** to configure the servers that will have access to the iSCSI virtual disk.

14. In the **Add initiator ID** window, specify the method to identify the initiator either by computer name (Windows Server 2012 only), initiator cache, or by the **iSCSI Qualified Name (IQN)**. The following screenshot shows an example of the method that uses the computer name to identify the initiator. Click on **OK** to add the server.

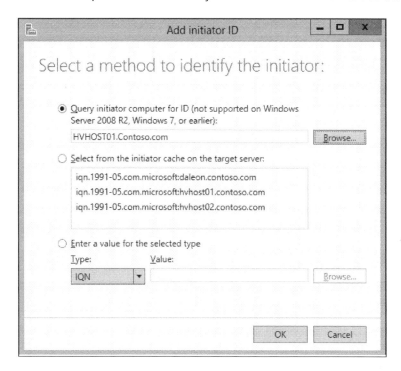

15. After adding all servers that will connect to the virtual disk, click on **Next**.

16. If you want to authenticate the initiator connections, in the **Enable Authentication** window, select either **Enable CHAP** or **Enable reverse CHAP**, provide the username and password, and click on **Next**.

17. Under **Confirm selections**, double-check the chosen options and then click on **Create and Close**.

18. When created, if you want to change, extend, disable, remove, or assign the iSCSI virtual disk, open the **iSCSI** page in Server Manager and right-click on the virtual disk. A list of options will appear, as shown in the following screenshot:

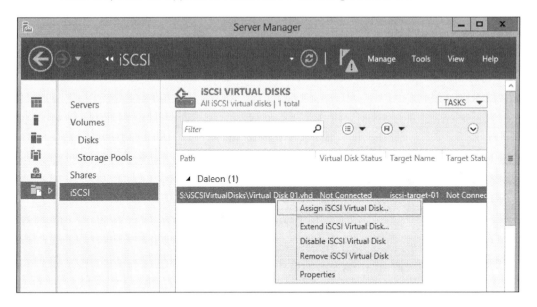

19. To connect the servers to the iSCSI Target server, launch the Start menu and type `initiator`. From the results list, click on **iSCSI Initiator**.

20. In the **Microsoft iSCSI** window, select **Yes** to enable the iSCSI service.

21. On the **iSCSI Initiator Properties** screen, type the iSCSI Target server name in the textbox named **Target** and click on **Quick Connect**.

22. In the **Quick Connect** window, confirm that the status is shown as **Connected** and select **Done**. The following screenshot shows an example of the connected server:

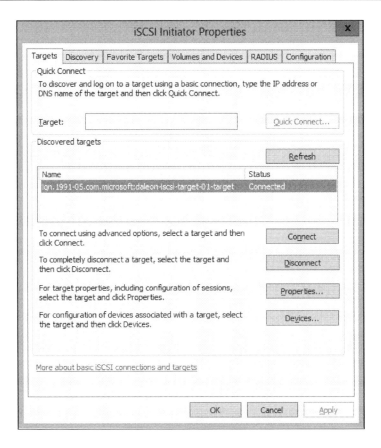

23. In the **iSCSI Initiator Properties** window, click on the **Volumes and Devices** tab, and click on **Auto Configure**, to add the available iSCSI virtual disks to the server. Click on **OK** to close the window.

24. After connecting to the iSCSI virtual disk, launch the Start menu and type `diskmgmt.msc` to open the **Disk Management** tool.

25. The iSCSI virtual disks will be listed in the **Disk Management** window. Right-click on the new disk and click on **Online**, as shown in the following screenshot:

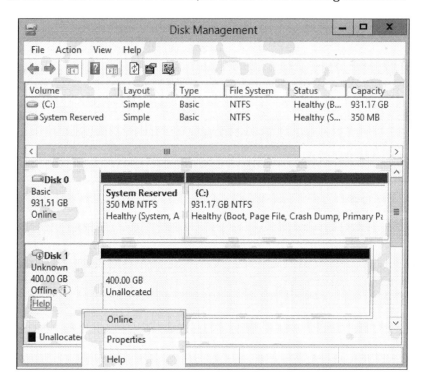

26. Initialize the disk and create new partitions to start using your new disk from the iSCSI Target server.

How it works...

The iSCSI Target server was introduced as a standalone tool in Windows Server 2008 R2, and it now comes as a role in Windows Server 2012.

The server is responsible for receiving and managing all computers that need access to storages. This client connection is known as **iSCSI Initiator**.

The first step is to install the iSCSI Target server through Server Manager. After its installation, you will need to create an **iSCSI Virtual Disk**. These virtual disks use the VHD file format to create **iSCSI Logical Unit Numbers** (**LUNs**) in your physical storage or local disks. A wizard will walk you through the virtual disk creation details and will also configure the iSCSI Target server when you create and assign a disk for the first time. During the server configuration, you have to specify which servers using iSCSI Initiator will be able to connect to the iSCSI Target server.

After configuration and disk assignment, the server will be ready to receive connections from other servers. Then, you need to use the iSCSI Initiator application from the servers you want to connect to the iSCSI Target server and then connect to the disks. Windows Server 2012 allows the server name to be used to identify the server rather than the **IQN.**

When connected, you will be able to open the **Disk Management** tool to bring the disk online, create the partitions, and manage the disks using the iSCSI protocol.

There's more...

All the iSCSI components in Windows Server 2012 can be managed by PowerShell.

To get all iSCSI Target commandlets, type the following on the command line:

```
Get-Command -Module iSCSITarget
```

To get a list of all iSCSI Initiator commandlets, type the following on the command line:

```
Get-Command -Module iSCSI
```

To get all existing commandlets that manage disks, volume partitions, and storage pools, type the following on the command line:

```
Get-Command -Module Storage
```

See also

▶ The *Installing and configuring the Windows Failover Clustering feature* recipe in this chapter

Installing and configuring the Windows Failover Clustering feature

In order to create high availability scenarios, Windows Server 2012 provides the **Failover Clustering** feature, which allows you to put roles or virtual machines into a high availability solution.

When installed and configured, Failover Clustering uses Failover Cluster Management Tools to bring all necessary cluster components, such as storage, network, roles, and nodes, together into a single console.

Failover Clustering is a Windows feature that creates a group of servers called **nodes** that are put together in a virtual space. A cluster is formed by nodes, storages, network devices, and the failover cluster itself (which acts as the management software) to bring all these components under just one console. All users and services that use the cluster connect to the virtual name created by Failover Clustering; however, this virtual entity can contain many nodes (up to 64) in the same cluster. In case one of the active nodes fails, the cluster services, such as virtual machines, will be started on another node, allowing you to deliver a high availability scenario.

Failover Clustering is not a new feature in Windows. It has been present since the first Windows Server version, however the new version of Windows Server 2012 brings heaps of features, such as:

- New limit of 64 nodes per cluster and up to 4,000 virtual machines running on the same cluster
- Cluster-Aware Updating (CAU), which includes a feature that automates the cluster updating process
- Simultaneous Live Migration
- Hyper-V Replica Broker to support Hyper-V Replica in a clustered environment
- Virtual machine application monitoring
- Cluster validation tests
- Multisite Support
- Dynamic Clusters
- iSCSI Software Target integration
- Cluster upgrade and migration
- Cluster Shared Volumes 2.0
- Virtual Fibre Channel support for clusters within a virtual machine
- VM Failover Prioritization
- Improved placement after failover
- Read Only Domain Controllers (RODCs) support
- Smart placement of Cluster Name Object (CNO), creating the account in the same OU as the nodes in the cluster
- Affinity Groups

These improvements make deployment, troubleshooting, and management much easier, helping you todeliver a reliable high availability environment.

In this recipe, you will see how to install the Failover Clustering feature and how to create a cluster to support Hyper-V virtual machines.

Getting ready

Failover Clustering needs an **Active Directory** (**AD**) environment requiring all nodes to be members of an AD domain. Make sure all nodes are members of the same Active Directory domain.

Before you begin, you also need to configure all storages and access within the nodes that will be used in the cluster. Check whether the disks are available on all nodes that will be members of the cluster.

If you want to use the cluster for virtual machines, make sure you have installed the Hyper-V role on all nodes that will participate in the cluster.

How to do it...

The following steps will show how to install the Failover Clustering components and how to create a new cluster:

1. To install the Failover Clustering feature, open Server Manager from the taskbar.

2. On the **Server Manager** dashboard, click on **Manage** and select **Add Roles and Features**.

3. On the **Before you begin** page, click on **Next** four times.

4. On the **Select features** screen, check the **Failover Clustering** checkbox, as shown in the following screenshot:

5. In the **Add Roles and Features Wizard** window, click on **Add Features** to add the required features to manage Failover Clustering.

6. Click on **Next** in the **Select features** window, and then click on **Install**.

7. To open the Failover Cluster Manager console in Server Manager, click on **All Servers** in the left-hand pane, right-click on the server you want to open, and select **Failover Cluster Manager**.

8. By default, there is no cluster created. To create a new cluster, select one of the three **Create Cluster** options in Failover Cluster Manager, as shown in the following screenshot:

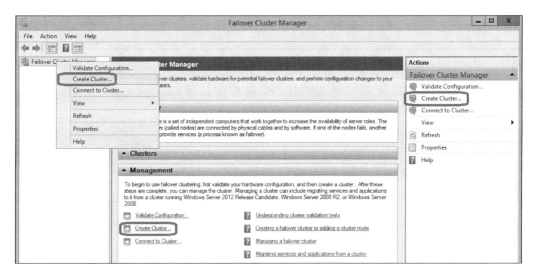

9. Click on **Next** in the **Before You Begin** section in the **Create Cluster Wizard** window.

10. In the **Select Servers** section, type the servers you want to add into your cluster, click on **Add**, and then click on **Next**. All added servers must have the Failover Clustering feature installed already.

11. In **Validation Warning**, select **Yes, When I click Next, run configuration validation tests, and then return to the process of creating the cluster**, and click on **Next**. A **Validate a Configuration Wizard** screen will be launched.

12. In the **Before You Begin** page, click on **Next**.

13. In **Testing Options**, select **Run all tests** or the new option **Run only tests I select** to run only a single test in case of running for the second time to fix an issue. For the first test, it is recommended that you select **Run all tests**, as shown in the following screenshot:

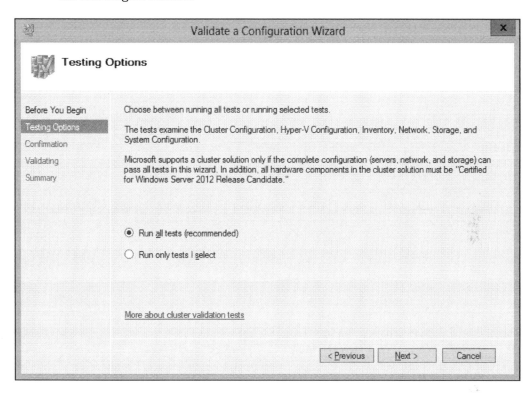

14. In the **Confirm information selections** section, click on **Next** to start the tests.

15. The validation tests will start to run and check all potential problems. When finished, click on **View Report** to see all results with success, warning, and error messages.

16. Use the report to identify any error or warning, and click on **Finish**.

17. Correct the errors and warnings mentioned in the report and run it again to make sure they are solved.

18. Back on the **Create Cluster Wizard** screen, in the **Access Point for Administering the Cluster** section, specify the name you want to use for your cluster, in **Cluster Name**. A Cluster Name Object will be created in AD in the same organizational unit that the nodes sit in.

19. On the same page, select the network and IP address for the cluster name and click on **Next**, as shown in the following screenshot:

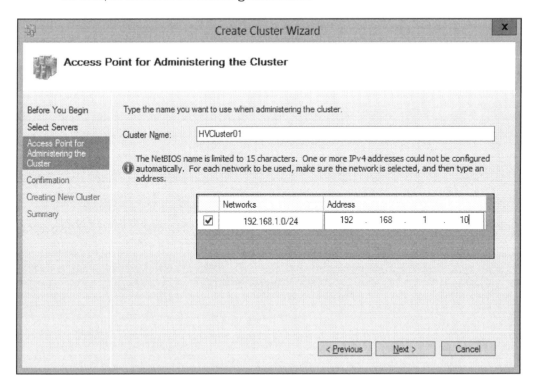

20. On the **Confirmation** page, check the **Add all eligible storage to the cluster** checkbox, if you want to automatically add all available storage in the nodes, and click on **Next**. The process to create a new cluster will start.

21. When the new cluster creation finishes, click on **View Report** to see detailed information about the creation, and click on **Finish**.

22. To add a virtual machine to your cluster, right-click on **Roles**, select **Virtual Machines**, and click on **New Virtual Machine**.

23. Select the node you want to create the new virtual machine in, follow the wizard, and click on **Finish**.

24. The new cluster will be listed in **Failover Cluster Manager**. To add, remove, or configure advanced settings for nodes, click on **Nodes** in the left-hand pane.

25. To manage, add, or change the disks or pools, click on **Storage**, in the left-hand pane.

26. To manage the network and network connections, click on **Networks**. The following screenshot shows some running virtual machines, the left-hand pane and all cluster resources such as **Nodes**, **Roles**, **Storage**, and **Networks**:

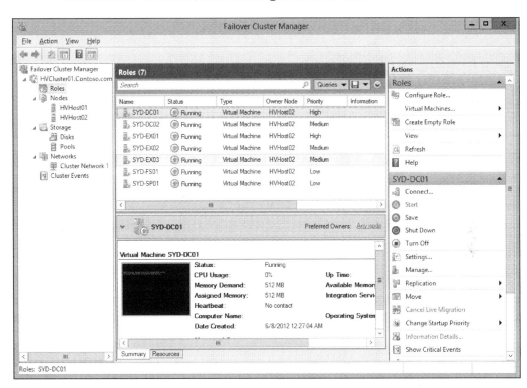

How it works...

After going through the easy Failover Clustering installation, the system installs all core features, tools, and PowerShell modules, to enable its administration.

One of these tools is **Failover Cluster Management Tools**. It allows you to manage not only the cluster, but its components, such as roles, nodes, storage, and networks. From a single view, you can carry out tasks such as adding a new disk, changing network settings, managing cluster roles, and much more. For virtual machines in a clustered environment, once the Hyper-V servers are members of a cluster, many of the actions you are used to performing in Hyper-V Manager (such as securing updates and correct configuration among the cluster nodes) should be carried out through Failover Cluster Manager.

The wizard to create a new cluster is very straightforward. You basically need to select which server will act as a node in your cluster and specify the cluster name and the IP address, and it's done. To make it even simpler, helping you to identify any error or misconfiguration that can compromise the cluster, **Validate a Configuration Wizard** is launched when your first cluster is created. It allows you to check tons of components and settings on every node, storage, network, and system configuration, and in Hyper-V. You won't be able to continue if the report shows any failed tests. You will need to correct the issue before you can create a failover cluster that is supported. You can rerun the validation tasks whenever you want, including for existing clusters, in case some update is made. All cluster reports are saved in `C:\Windows\Cluster\Reports` on each node. These reports are important and have to be kept in case you need them for errors or problems you might have in the future.

To add a virtual machine in the cluster, you need to create it from Failover Cluster Manager by right-clicking on **Roles**. It's recommended that you manage all virtual machines running in failover clusters by using Failover Cluster Manager rather Hyper-V Manager.

After creating your virtual machines, they will be in a high availability system managed by Failover Clustering.

There's more...

Like any other feature of Windows Server 2012, Failover Clustering can also be managed by using PowerShell. The PowerShell module for Failover Clustering is installed automatically with feature installation.

To list all available Failover Clustering commandlets, type the following command:

```
Get-Command -Module FailoverClusters
```

To see how easy is to manage Failover Clustering using PowerShell, look at the next example, which shows how to create a cluster with the same details as the one demonstrated in this recipe. The `New-Cluster` commandlet creates a new cluster called HVCluster01 with the static IP address `192.168.1.10` and also adds two nodes with the names HVHost01 and HVHost02.

```
New-Cluster -Name HVCluster01 -StaticAddress 192.168.1.10 -Node
HVHost01,HVHost02
```

To check all cluster details, type the following command:

```
Get-Cluster | Format-List -Property *
```

See also

> ▶ The *Enabling the Hyper-V role* recipe in *Chapter 1, Installing and Managing Hyper-V in Full or Server Core Mode*

- The *Learning and utilizing basic commands in PowerShell* recipe in *Chapter 4, Saving Time and Cost with Hyper-V Automation*

- The *Enabling Cluster Shared Volumes 2.0* recipe in this chapter

- The *Configuring Cluster-Aware Updating for cluster nodes* recipe in *Chapter 6, Security and Delegation of Control*

Enabling Cluster Shared Volumes 2.0

Windows Server 2012 includes a new version of one of the most interesting features when working with Failover Clustering. When enabled, **Cluster Shared Volume** (**CSV**) 2.0 allows multiple nodes to simultaneously access the same **NTFS** file system, providing your cluster environment with flexibility and reliability. CSV also brings all disks in the cluster to a single location, improving access and management, and it also improves operational efficiency by increasing availability.

The new version brings CSV to other roles such as file servers, not only for Hyper-V as with the previous version.

This is the list with the most important improvements and features of CSV 2.0:

- Support for Bitlocker

- Direct I/O for file data access

- CSV proxy file system

- Online check disk (`chkdsk`)

- Multisubnet support

- Support for SMB 3.0

- Integration with Storage Spaces

- No authentication dependencies

- Improvements for file backup

CSV is strongly recommended when using Hyper-V with Failover Clustering. That said, you will also see how to enable CSV to your disks within Failover Clustering.

Getting ready

CSV is only available through Failover Clustering. Before you start, make sure you have a cluster with the storage already added. The *Installing and configuring the Windows Failover Clustering feature* recipe in this chapter is a good start if you have not created your cluster yet.

How to do it...

The following steps will demonstrate how to add your cluster disks into a Cluster Shared Volume:

1. To enable CSV to your disks, launch the Start menu and type `Cluadmin.msc` to open Failover Cluster Manager.

2. In the **Failover Cluster Manager** window, in the left-hand pane, expand **Storage** and click on **Disks**.

3. A list with the added disks will be displayed. Select the disk or disks on which you want to enable CSV, and click on **Add to Cluster Shared Volumes** using either one of the options shown in the following screenshot:

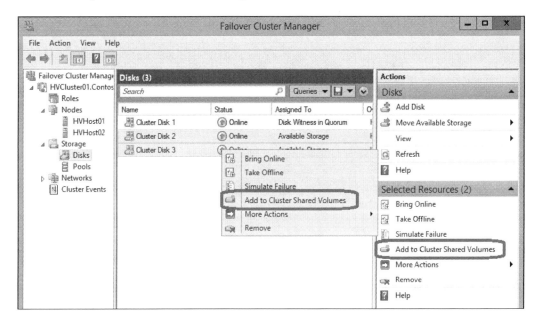

4. Every disk will now be listed and accessed in the path `C:\ClusterStorage`. To see the available disks within the CSV, open Windows Explorer and navigate to the folder `C:\ClusterStorage`.

5. To use the CSV disk, when creating your virtual machines, select one of the volumes within the `ClusterStorage` folder.

How it works...

CSV is a Failover Clustering feature to be used by Hyper-V. It is simply an NTFS volume that accepts read and write operations by all nodes in the cluster. By default, CSV is not enabled, but it is a best practice to enable it when using in conjunction with Hyper-V virtual machines. The process of enabling CSV has been improved in Windows Server 2012. To do so, you must open Failover Cluster Manager, select the disk you want, and click on **Add to Cluster Shared Volume**; as simple as that! When enabled, CSV puts all disks as folders in `C:\ClusterStorage`. It makes management and access easier once all disks are shown in a single path.

CSV drastically reduces the number of LUNs required for your virtual machines. Rather than using one LUN per virtual machine, you can place more virtual machines within a CSV volume.

Disks with CSV enabled now appear as **CSV Proxy File system** (**CSVFS**). Although it is still using NTFS as the filesystem, CSVFS is used as a label in the disks, enabling applications to know they are running under CSV disks.

There's more...

You can also add available disks in a CSV volume by using the command `Add-ClusterSharedVolume`. The following command gets all disks and adds them in the CSV:

```
Get-ClusterResource *disk* | Add-ClusterSharedVolume
```

Configuring CSV Cache for Hyper-V Environments

One of the abilities of CSV in Windows Server 2012 is to enable the CSV cache. When the cache is configured, all read-only unbuffered I/O is cached, which is ideal for **Virtual Desktop Infrastucture** (**VDI**) scenarios. CSV Cache uses RAM to write the cache information, delivering a high performance for your applications. Thus, some applications running on a virtual machine that require high read requests improve in performance.

As CSV Cache depends on the workload and application requirements, it's disabled by default. To enable CSV Cache, you first need to specify the cache in MB. Only 20 percent of the available RAM can be used for CSV Cache.

The following command can be used to set the cache size. The cache used in this example (512 MB) is a default value that is recommended in most scenarios.

```
(Get-Cluster).SharedVolumeBlockCacheSizeinMB = 512
```

After setting the cache value, you must enable it on the disks you want to use CSV Cache for. The following command shows how to enable it for a disk called `Cluster Disk 1`:

```
Get-ClusterSharedVolume "Cluster Disk 1" | Set-ClusterParameter
CsvEnableBlockCache 1
```

When the second command is typed, a warning message is displayed saying that the disks must be taken offline to apply the changes.

Make sure the disk is not being used by any role or services, open Failover Cluster Manager, expand **Storages**, and click on **Disks**. Select the disk you want to bring offline, right-click on it, and select **Take Offline**, as shown in the following screenshot:

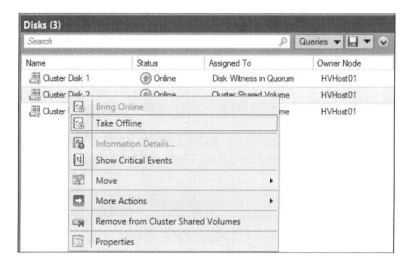

In the **Offline Cluster Shared Volume** message, click on **Yes** to confirm and take the disk offline. To bring the disk online again, right-click on the disk and select **Bring Online**.

See also

▶ The *Installing and configuring the Windows Failover Clustering feature* recipe in this chapter

Using Live Migration in a cluster environment

One of the core concepts of a private cloud is elasticity and mobility. In a cluster environment, you can distribute running virtual machines across different servers, based on components and metrics such as workload, physical host resources, and VM availability. Using **Live Migration**, you can move virtual machines from one physical server to another without any downtime or disruption of the services provided by the VMs, making their reallocation to other servers possible with two or three clicks. A good example is when you need to bring a host offline for maintenance or when you need to add more hardware resources to a VM. With Live Migration, you can quickly move the VMs to another host, providing the necessary agility, productivity, and load balance for your virtual servers.

Windows Server 2012 brings many new features and improvements to Live Migration. One of the most exciting features is the ability to use Live Migration without a cluster environment, called **Shared Nothing Live Migration**. It allows you to move a virtual machine from one host to another with a single network adapter, with no requirement of Failover Clustering or shared storage.

New core improvements make Live Migration 70 percent faster than the previous version in Windows Server 2008 R2. You can also use Live Migration on more than one virtual machine at the same time and create priorities and other interesting features that will be covered later in this chapter.

In this recipe, you will learn how to configure and use Live Migration in a cluster environment.

Getting ready

This recipe will guide you on how to use Live Migration for virtual machines in a clustered environment. Make sure you have a cluster up and running with a couple of virtual machines on it.

How to do it...

The following steps will show how to enable, configure, and move VM between nodes in a cluster, using the Live Migration feature:

1. Before moving virtual machines with Live Migration, you must configure the Hyper-V Live Migration settings. To do so, open Hyper-V Manager, click on **Hyper-V Settings** in the right-hand pane, and click on **Live Migrations** in the left-hand pane.

2. In the **Live Migrations** settings, check **Enable incoming and outgoing live migrations**.

3. Under **Authentication protocol**, select **Use Credential Security Support Provider (CredSSP)** or **Use Kerberos**.

4. Under **Simultaneous live migrations**, specify the number of simultaneous live migrations.

5. Under **Incoming live migrations**, choose between the options **Use any available network for live migration** and **Use these IP addresses for live migration**.

6. When finished with all configurations shown in the following screenshot, click on **OK** to close the **Hyper-V Settings** window:

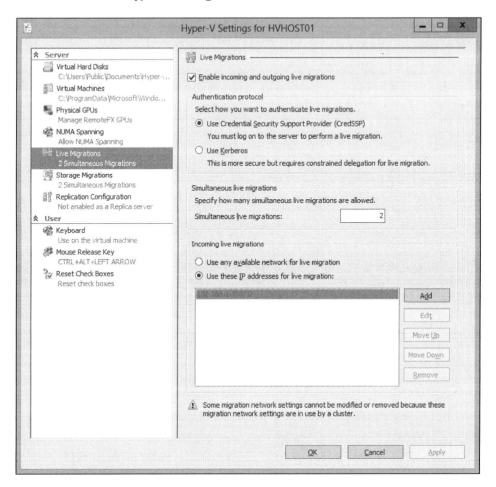

7. To configure the network adapter that will be used by Failover Clustering to move VMs, launch the Start menu, type `Cluadmin.msc`, and click on **Failover Cluster Manager**.

8. In the **Failover Cluster Manager** window, right-click on **Networks** and click on **Live Migration Settings**.

9. In the **Live Migration Settings** window, select the network that will be used for live migration, as shown in the following screenshot, and click on **OK**.

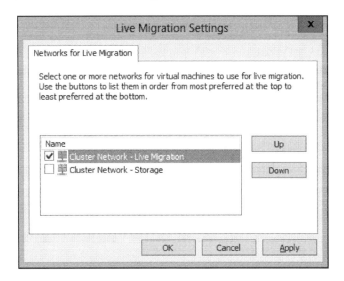

10. To live migrate a VM, click on **Roles** in the left-hand pane, in **Failover Cluster Manager**.

11. In the list containing all running virtual machines, select the virtual machines you want to live migrate and right-click on them.

12. In the virtual machine menu, select **Move | Live Migration**, and choose between **Best Possible Node** to migrate to the best available node and **Select Node...** to select a specific node, as shown in the following screenshot:

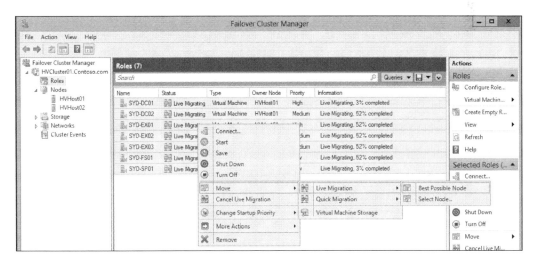

13. Specify the node you want to move your VMs to and click on **OK**. Hyper-V will start to live migrate the virtual machines to the selected node.

14. During the migration, you can follow the status by checking the **Information** column, as shown in the following screenshot:

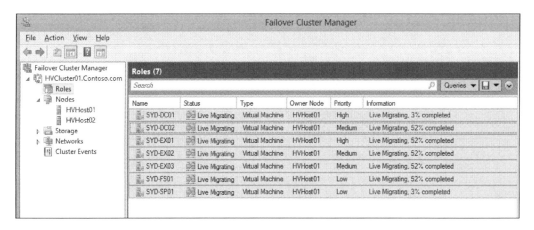

15. To confirm the migration, check the column named **Owner Node** to see if the server listed is the selected server, when finished.

How it works...

After enabling the Hyper-V hosts to support Live Migration, you can configure some options through Hyper-V and Failover Clustering.

The first thing to do is to configure Live Migration settings in Hyper-V. Using Hyper-V Manager, you can disable live migrations, change the authentication protocol used to authenticate live migrations, change the number of simultaneous live migrations, and set the incoming live migration configuration. The first authentication protocol, CredSSP, allows you to migrate your VMs with no preconfiguration, but you can only move them when logged on the source server where you want to migrate the VM from. Kerberos gives you the option to migrate your VMs from remove servers, but it requires preconfiguration on Active Directory prior to the migrations. To see how to use Kerberos, refer to the *Migrating the virtual machines using Shared Nothing Live Migration* recipe in *Chapter 2, Migrating and Upgrading Physical and Virtual Servers*.

The second step is to use Failover Cluster Manager to specify which network will be used to live migrate your VMs. Using the Live Migration settings in **Networks**, you can select the networks for live migration. It's best practice to have a dedicated network adapter purely for live migration.

After these two steps, you can start to move your virtual machines, using Failover Clustering. You can move a single VM or a bunch of VMs by selecting them and clicking on **Move | Live Migration**. Rather than simply moving the VM, now you can select either the best possible node or specify a node. When the **Best Possible Node** option is used, each VM is placed based on the node with best available resources.

The migration will start simultaneously, based on the limit specified in the Hyper-V settings. In case you migrate more VMs than the limit, a queue will be created to live migrate the VMs. Another factor used during the migration is the virtual machine priority, which can be configured per VM. The VMs with high priority will be migrated first, followed by those with medium and low priorities.

When live migration starts, the source host server connects to the destination server, transfers the VM configuration data, and allocates the necessary memory to the VM that will be transferred. Then, the idle memory is synchronized between the source and the destination host. After that, the active pages are synchronized. When the minimum number of written memory pages exists, the storage handle is given to the destination host, which takes control of the running virtual machine, bringing it online. During the whole migration, the virtual machine is still running and no downtime happens.

Now you can live migrate your VMs to other servers, helping to distribute, reallocate, and plan host maintenances.

There's more...

Here, we have another example showing how PowerShell can simplify our lives. Using the command `Move-VM`, you can move VMs to remote servers with very little work. In this next example, a VM called `WinSRV2012` is being moved to a remote server called `HVHost02`:

```
Move-VM "WinSRV2012" HVHost02
```

For more information about the `Move-VM` command, use the following commandlet:

```
Get-Help Move-VM
```

See also

- ▶ The *Migrating the virtual machines using Shared Nothing Live Migration* recipe in *Chapter 2, Migrating and Upgrading Physical and Virtual Servers*
- ▶ The *Installing and configuring the Windows Failover Clustering feature* recipe in this chapter
- ▶ The *Configuring VM Priority for Clustered Virtual Machines* recipe in this chapter

Configuring VM Priority for Clustered Virtual Machines

When using Failover Clustering with heaps of virtual machines distributed across hosts, you might face a scenario where many VMs need to be live migrated to other hosts or when they are started at the same time. In both examples, all VMs will be moved to another host with no priority. That can cause services failures when, for example, a service starts before the necessary requirement services. To make it simpler, let's say you have VMs with Exchange, SQL, and SharePoint Server, and all of them start before the Active Directory VMs during a failover. All these services require Active Directory to be online first so that the authentication and authorization can happen. In this example, all services will fail and you will need to restart them to guarantee they will start after the Active Directory VM. With VM Priority, you can specify a priority for every VM, allowing them to be moved or started in order, based on their priority.

This recipe will guide you through the steps to configure **VM priorities** in your virtual machines within a cluster.

Getting ready

VM Priority is a feature available only for virtual machines within a cluster. Make sure you have a cluster with a few virtual machines on it before you start.

How to do it...

The following steps will show how to configure different priorities for your virtual machines in a clustered environment:

1. To set priorities for your VM, launch the Start menu, type `Cluadmin.msc`, and click on **Failover Cluster Manager**.

2. Expand your cluster in the left-hand pane, and click on **Roles** to see the list with virtual machines.

3. Right-click on the virtual machine for which you want to configure priority, select **Change Startup Priority** and select between **High**, **Medium**, **Low**, and **No Auto Start**, as shown in the following screenshot:

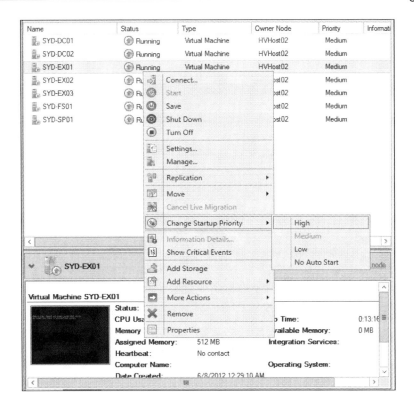

Name	Status	Type	Owner Node	Priority	Informati
SYD-DC01	Running	Virtual Machine	HVHost02	Medium	
SYD-DC02	Running	Virtual Machine	HVHost02	Medium	
SYD-EX01	Running	Virtual Machine	HVHost02	Medium	
SYD-EX02	Ru		st02	Medium	
SYD-EX03	Ru		st02	Medium	
SYD-FS01	Ru		st02	Medium	
SYD-SP01	Ru		st02	Medium	

Connect...
Start
Save
Shut Down
Turn Off
Settings...
Manage...
Replication ▶
Move ▶
Cancel Live Migration
Change Startup Priority ▶ | High
Information Details... | Medium
Show Critical Events | Low
Add Storage | No Auto Start
Add Resource ▶
More Actions ▶
Remove
Properties

SYD-EX01

Virtual Machine SYD-EX01

Status:
CPU Usa: Time: 0:13:16
Memory   vailable Memory: 0 MB
Assigned Memory: 512 MB   Integration Services:
Heartbeat: No contact
Computer Name: Operating System:
Date Created: 6/8/2012 12:29:10 AM

4. When you move VMs, start more than one VM at the same time, or fail VMs over to another server, they will be processed based on the set priority. Use the **Priority** column in **Failover Cluster Manager** to check the priority configuration. The following screenshot shows an example of VMs being started as the hosts where they sit go offline:

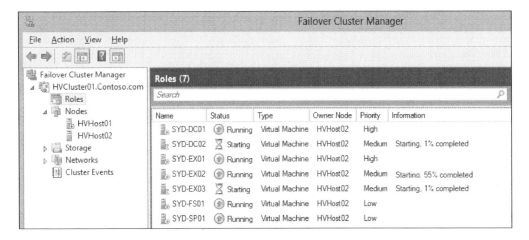

Failover Cluster Manager

File   Action   View   Help

Failover Cluster Manager
   HVCluster01.Contoso.com
     Roles
     Nodes
       HVHost01
       HVHost02
     Storage
     Networks
     Cluster Events

Roles (7)

Search

Name	Status	Type	Owner Node	Priority	Information
SYD-DC01	Running	Virtual Machine	HVHost02	High	
SYD-DC02	Starting	Virtual Machine	HVHost02	Medium	Starting, 1% completed
SYD-EX01	Running	Virtual Machine	HVHost02	High	
SYD-EX02	Running	Virtual Machine	HVHost02	Medium	Starting, 55% completed
SYD-EX03	Starting	Virtual Machine	HVHost02	Medium	Starting, 1% completed
SYD-FS01	Running	Virtual Machine	HVHost02	Low	
SYD-SP01	Running	Virtual Machine	HVHost02	Low	

How it works...

VM priorities can be configured in all clustered resources, enabling administrators to set an order for the start or placement of virtual machines and other roles. When the host where the VMs sit goes offline, when you live migrate them to other hosts, or when you start more than one VM at the same time, the priority will determine which VM will be processed first, allowing you to control the way that the cluster handles the VMs.

These are the four priority options available in Failover Clustering:

- High
- Medium
- Low
- No Auto Start

The default option is **Medium**. Every resource will have the same priority when created. When live migrated or started, the VMs with high priority will be processed first, followed by those with medium and low. The option **No Auto Start** causes the virtual machine or the role to not start automatically.

 It's important to know that both high and medium priorities move the VMs on the fly, using **Live Migration**, without downtime, but the low priority uses **Quick Migration** by pausing and moving the VM to save network performance and bandwidth.

There's more...

To set VM Priority using PowerShell, type the following command:

```
Get-ClusterResourceType "Virtual Machine" | set-ClusterParameter
MoveTypeThreshold 3000
```

8

Disaster Recovery for Hyper-V

In this chapter we will cover the following topics:

- ► Backing up Hyper-V and virtual machines using Windows Server Backup
- ► Restoring Hyper-V and virtual machines using Windows Server Backup
- ► Configuring Hyper-V Replica between two Hyper-V hosts using HTTP authentication
- ► Configuring Hyper-V Replica broker for a Failover Cluster
- ► Configuring Hyper-V Replica to use certificate-based authentication using an Enterprise CA
- ► Using snapshots in virtual machines

Introduction

Hyper-V and Windows Server 2012 come with tools and solutions to make sure that your virtual machines will be up, running, and highly available. Components such as Failover Cluster can ensure that your servers are accessible, even in case of failures. However, disasters can occur and bring all the servers and services offline. Natural disasters, viruses, data corruption, human errors, and many other factors can make your entire system unavailable.

People think that **High Available (HA)** is a solution for **Disaster Recovery (DR)** and that they can use it to replace DR. Actually HA is a component of a DR plan, which consists of process, policies, procedures, backup and recovery plan, documentation, tests, **Service Level Agreements (SLA)**, best practices, and so on. The objective of a DR is simply to have business continuity in case of any disaster.

In a Hyper-V environment, we have options to utilize the core components, such as Hyper-V Replica, for a DR plan, which replicates your virtual machines to another host or cluster and makes them available if the first host is offline, or even backs up and restores to bring VMs back, in case you lose everything.

This module will walk you through the most important processes for setting up disaster recovery for your virtual machines running on Hyper-V.

Backing up Hyper-V and virtual machines using Windows Server Backup

Previous versions of Hyper-V had complications and incompatibilities with the built-in backup tool, forcing the administrators to acquire other solutions for backing up and restoring.

Windows Server 2012 comes with a tool known as **Windows Server Backup** (**WSB**), which has full Hyper-V integration, allowing you to back up and restore your server, applications, Hyper-V, and virtual machines. WSB is easy and provides for a low cost scenario for small and medium companies.

This recipe will guide you through the steps to back up your virtual machines using the Windows Server Backup tool.

Getting ready

Windows Server Backup does not support tapes. Make sure that you have a disk, external storage, network share, and free space to back up your virtual machines before you start.

How to do it...

The following steps will show you how to install the Windows Server Backup feature and how to schedule a task to back up your Hyper-V settings and virtual machines:

1. To install the **Windows Server Backup** feature, open **Server Manager** from the **taskbar**.

2. In the **Server Manager Dashboard**, click on **Manage** and select **Add Roles and Features**.

3. On the **Before you begin** page, click on **Next** four times.

4. Under the **Add Roles and Features Wizard**, select **Windows Server Backup** from the **Features** section, as shown in the following screenshot:

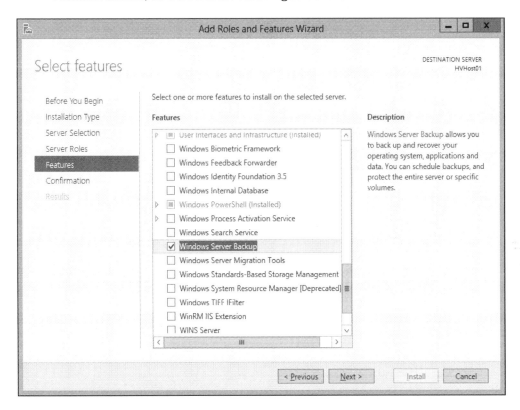

5. Click on **Next** and then click on **Install**. Wait for the installation to be completed.

6. After the installation, open the **Start** menu and type `wbadmin.msc` to open the **Windows Server Backup** tool.

7. To change the backup performance options, click on **Configure Performance** from the pane on the right-hand side in the **Windows Server Backup** console.

8. In the **Optimize Backup Performance** window, we have three options to select from—**Normal backup performance**, **Faster backup performance**, and **Custom**, as shown in the following screenshot:

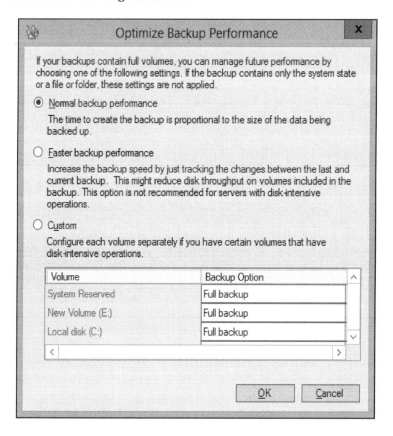

9. In the **Windows Server Backup** console, in the pane on the right-hand side, select the backup that you want to perform. The two available options are **Backup Schedule** to schedule an automatic backup and **Backup Once** for a single backup. The next steps will show how to schedule an automatic backup.

10. In the **Backup Schedule Wizard**, in the **Getting Started** page, click on **Next**.

11. In the **Select Backup Configuration** page, select **Full Server** to back up all the server data or click on **Custom** to select specific items to back up. If you want to backup only Hyper-V and virtual machines, click on **Custom** and then **Next**.

12. In **Select Items for Backup**, click on **Add Items**.

13. In the **Select Items** window, select **Hyper-V** to back up all the virtual machines and the host component, as shown in the following screenshot. You can also expand **Hyper-V** and select the virtual machines that you want to back up. When finished, click on **OK**.

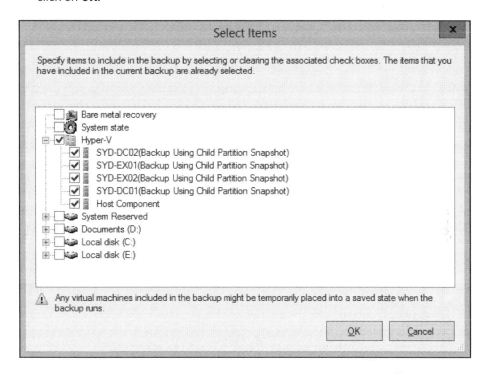

14. Back to the **Select Items for Backup**, click on **Advanced Settings** to change **Exclusions** and **VSS Settings**.

15. In the **Advanced Settings** window, in the **Exclusions** tab, click on **Add Exclusion** to add any necessary exclusions.

16. Click on the **VSS Settings** tab to select either **VSS full Backup** or **VSS copy Backup** as shown in the following screenshot. Click on **OK**.

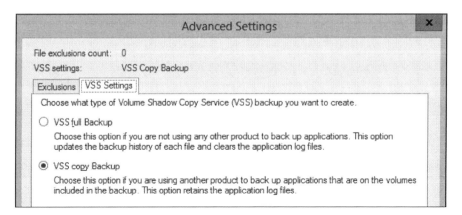

17. In the **Select Items for Backup** window, confirm the items that will be backed up and click on **Next**.

18. In the **Specify Backup Time** page, select **Once a day** and the time for a daily backup or select **More than once a day** and the time and click on **Next**.

19. In the **Specify Destination Type** page, select the option **Back up to a hard disk that is dedicated for backups (recommended)**, **back up to a volume**, or **back up to a shared network folder**, as shown in the following screenshot and click on **Next**.

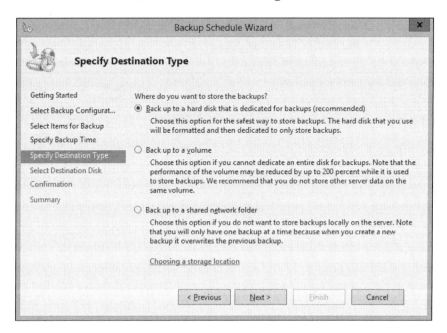

20. In **Select Destination Disk**, click on **Show All Available Disks** to list the disks, select the one you want to use to store your backup, and click on **OK**. Click on **Next** twice.

21. If you have selected the **Back up to a hard disk that is dedicated for backups (recommended)** option, you will see a warning message saying that the disk will be formatted. Click on **Yes** to confirm.

22. In the **Confirmation** window, double-check the options you selected and click on **Finish**, as shown in the following screenshot:

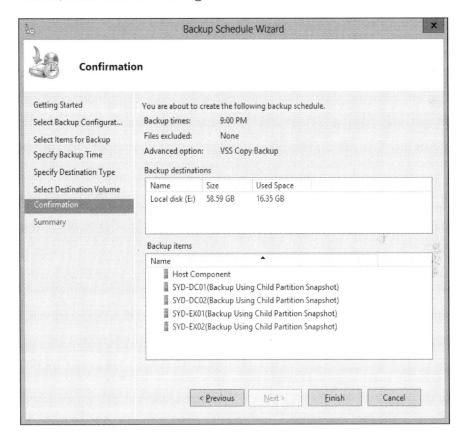

23. After that, the schedule will be created. Wait until the scheduled time to begin and check whether the backup has been finished successfully.

How it works...

Many Windows administrators used to miss the **NTBackup** tool from the old Windows Server 2003 times because of its capabilities and features. The **Windows Server Backup** tool, introduced in Windows Server 2008, has many limitations such as no tape support, no advanced schedule options, fewer backup options, and so on. When we talk about Hyper-V in this regards, the problem is even worse. Windows Server 2008 has minimal support and features for it.

In Windows Server 2012, the same tool is available with some limitations; however, it provides at least the core components to back up, schedule, and restore Hyper-V and your virtual machines.

By default, WSB is not installed. The feature installation is made by Server Manager. After its installation, the tool can be accessed via console or command lines.

Before you start the backup of your servers, it is good to configure the backup performance options you want to use. By default, all the backups are created as normal. It creates a full backup of all the selected data. This is an interesting option when low amounts of data are backed up. You can also select the **Faster backup performance** option. This backs up the changes between the last and the current backup, increasing the backup time and decreasing the stored data. This is a good option to save storage space and backup time for large amounts of data.

A backup schedule can be created to automate your backup operations. In the **Backup Schedule Wizard**, you can back up your entire server or a custom selection of volumes, applications, or files. For backing up Hyper-V and its virtual machines, the best option is the customized backup, so that you don't have to back up the whole physical server. When Hyper-V is present on the host, the system shows Hyper-V, and you will be able to select all the virtual machines and the host component configuration to be backed up. During the wizard, you can also change the advanced options such as exclusions and **Volume Shadow Copy Services** (**VSS**) settings. WSB has two VSS backup options—**VSS full backup** and **VSS copy backup**. When you opt for VSS full backup, everything is backed up and after that, the application may truncate log files. If you are using other backup solutions that integrate with WSB, these logs are essential to be used in future backups such as incremental ones. To preserve the log files you can use VSS copy backup so that other applications will not have problems with the incremental backups.

After selecting the items for backup, you have to select the backup time. This is another limitation from the previous version—only two schedule options, namely **Once a day** or **More than once a day**. If you prefer to create different backup schedule such as weekly backups, you can use the WSB commandlets in PowerShell.

Moving forward, in the backup destination type, you can select between a dedicated hard disk, a volume, or a network folder to save your backups in.

When confirming all the items, the backup schedule will be ready to back up your system.

You can also use the option **Backup once** to create a single backup of your system.

There's more...

To check whether previous backups were successful or not, you can use the details option in the WSB console. These details can be used as logs to get more information about the last (previous), next, and all the backups.

To access these logs, open **Windows Server Backup**, under **Status** select **View details**. The following screenshot shows an example of the **Last backup**.

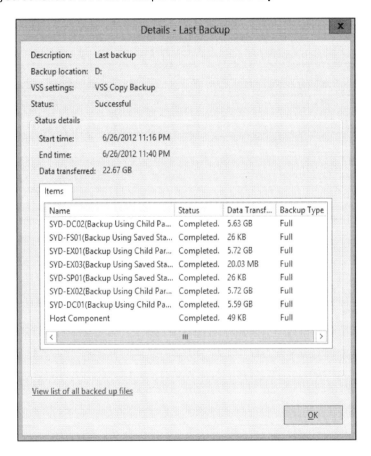

To see which files where backed up, click on the **View list of all backed up files** link.

Checking the Windows Server Backup commandlets

Some options such as advanced schedule, policies, jobs, and other configurations can only be created through commandlets on PowerShell.

To see all the available Windows Server Backup commandlets, type the following command:

```
Get-Command -Module WindowsServerBackup
```

See also

> ▶ The *Learning and utilizing basic commands in PowerShell* recipe in *Chapter 4, Saving Time and Cost with Hyper-V Automation*

> ▶ The *Restoring Hyper-V and virtual machines using Windows Server Backup* recipe in this chapter

Restoring Hyper-V and Virtual Machines using Windows Server Backup

Cluster, Hyper-V Replica, Storage Migration, and other features makes for a higher availability for Hyper-V virtual machines, but it is impossible to provide 100 percent assurance in any system. When we lose a host computer, for example, not only is a single system offline, but also all the virtual machines that are running in there. It does not matter if it is only an application, a virtual machine, or the entire Hyper-V host that needs to be restored. In simple words, you have to be prepared to bring your systems online as soon as possible in case of a failure.

One of the benefits of Windows Server Backup is that it is easy to use and it is present in the OS already. With a couple of clicks, your hosts and its VMs are up and running.

This recipe will guide you through the steps to restore your virtual machines using Windows Server Backup.

Getting ready

Windows Server Backup only supports restores of backups that were made by it. Make sure that you have the access to these backups before you begin.

How to do it...

In the following steps, you will see steps how to restore a backup containing virtual machines and the host components using Windows Server Backup:

1. If the computer on which you restore the data does not have **Windows Server Backup** installed, proceed with the following steps. In case it is already installed, go to *step 7*.

2. To install the **Windows Server Backup** feature, open **Server Manager** from the taskbar.

3. In the **Server Manager Dashboard**, click on **Manage** and select **Add Roles and Features**.

4. In the **Before you begin** page, click on **Next** four times.

5. In **Select features**, select **Windows Server Backup**, as shown in the following screenshot:

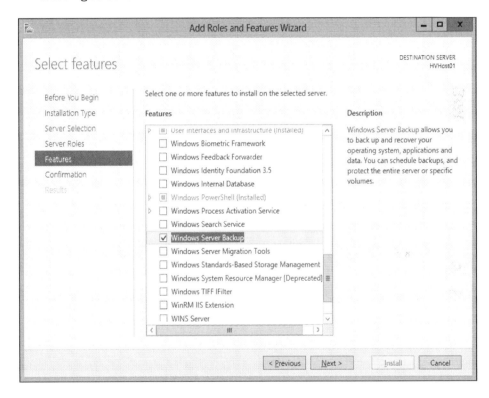

6. Click on **Next** and then click on **Install**. Wait for the installation to be completed.

7. To open WSB, in the start menu, type wbadmin.msc.

8. In the **Windows Server Backup** console, in the pane on the right-hand side, click on **Restore**.

9. In the **Recovery Wizard** window, under **Getting Started**, select **This server** if the backup is stored locally, or select **A backup stored on another location** if the backup is in a storage or network folder, as shown in the following screenshot. Then click on **Next**.

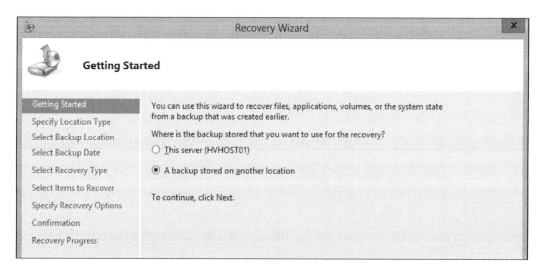

10. In the **Specify Location Type** window, you can select from the options **Local drives** or **Remote shared folder**. Select the option where your backup files are situated and click on **Next**.

11. In the **Select Backup Location** window, click on the drop-down list to select the backup location where the files are placed, and then click on **Next**.

12. In the **Select Server** window, select the server which you want to restore and click on **Next**.

13. In **Select Backup Date**, select the month, day, and time for restoring, as shown in the following screenshot. If you want to check the content of the backup, click on the hyperlink in front of **Recoverable items**. Click on **Next** when done.

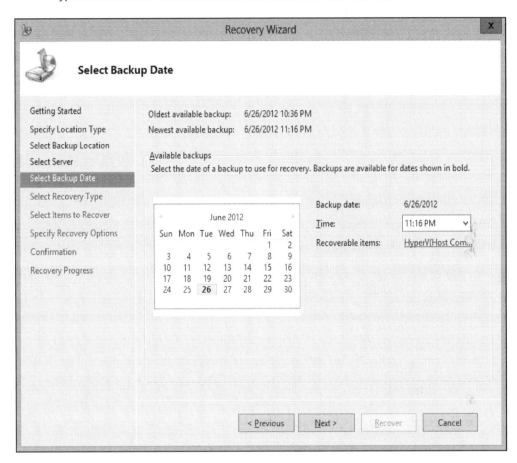

14. In the **Select Recovery Type** page, select what you want to recover. You can choose from the following options—**Files and folders**, **Hyper-V**, **Volumes**, **Applications**, and **System State**. To recover virtual machine and the host components, select **Hyper-V**, as shown in the following screenshot, and click on **Next**:

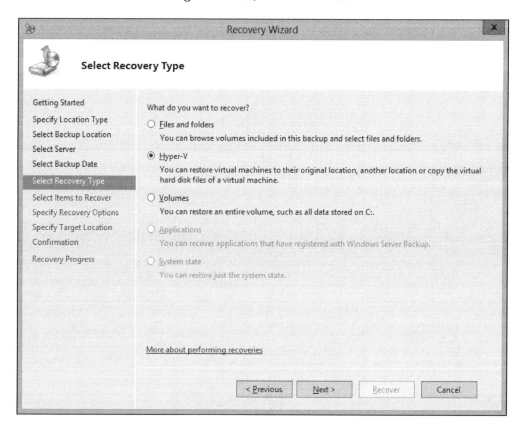

15. On the **Select Items to Recover** page, select the virtual machine that you want to restore, as shown in the following screenshot. If you need to recover the Hyper-V settings, check the **Host Component** option and click on **Next**.

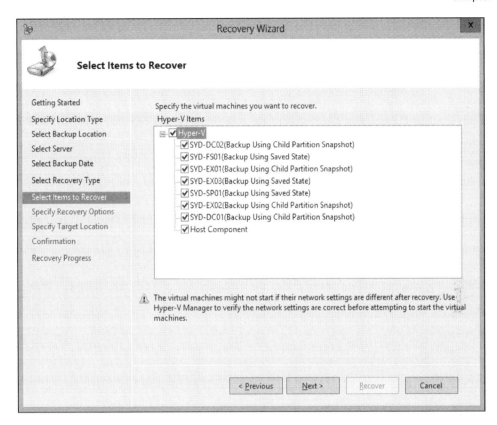

16. In the **Specify Recovery Options**, you can select from the following options—**Recover to original location**, **Recover to alternate location**, and **copy to folder**. Select the options that suits your environment and click on **Next**. In the **Confirmation** window, verify the recovery items that will be restored and click on **Recover**. Wait until the restore is complete and click on **Close** to close the **Recovery Wizard**.

17. To check the recovered items, in the **Windows Server Backup** console, under **Messages**, double click on the recovery event. The **Application recovery** window will open, as shown in the following screenshot:

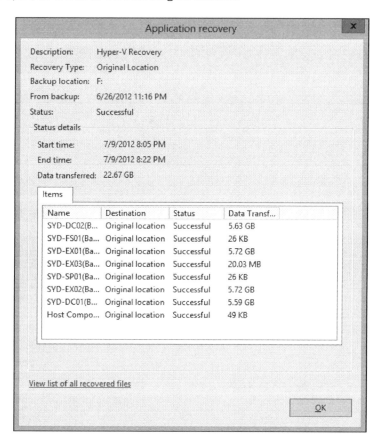

18. To check the recovered files, click on **View list of all recovered files** in the **Application recovery** window.

19. To check whether the restoration was successful, open the **Hyper-V Manager** and check whether the restored virtual machines are listed.

How it works...

After a host failure, file corruption, or any other kind of data loss, you might face a very stressful environment with users calling every minute, managers freaking out, and many other bad consequences of an offline system.

The good news is that Windows Server Backup makes these consequences a little less painful. If you have backed up your virtual machines (and I am sure you did), it can restore them with a very intuitive wizard.

It can be used to restore files, folders, volumes, applications, the entire system state, and the new option introduced in Windows Server 2012, to recover Hyper-V.

In a scenario where you need to restore a virtual machine, the first thing to do is to make sure that WSB is already installed and the backup files are accessible from the computer where you want to restore the data.

In the Recovery Wizard, you can restore the server by specifying the backup location. The location can be a local drive such as attached disks and storages, or it can be a remote shared folder. Then the wizard shows a schedule from which you can select the last backup file. After selecting the backup date and time, the recovery type Hyper-V option must be selected to recover virtual machines. A list with the available virtual machines will be displayed, from which you can select the ones to be restored to the original or alternate location. The next step is just to wait for the restore process to finish and make sure that everything is online again.

See also

▶ The *Enabling the Hyper-V role* recipe in *Chapter 1, Installing and Managing Hyper-V in Full or Server Core Mode*

▶ The *Learning and utilizing basic commands in PowerShell* recipe in *Chapter 4, Saving Time and Cost with Hyper-V Automation*

▶ The *Backing up Hyper-V and virtual machines using Windows Server Backup* recipe in this chapter

Configuring Hyper-V Replica between two hyper-V hosts using HTTP authentication

Disaster Recovery (DR) is a very important component for every IT system. Good DR infrastructure normally involves datacenters, servers, storage, network bandwidth, and other expensive solutions. All these factors can make a DR plan more complicated for small- and medium-sized companies. The high cost and complexity would make it very difficult to accomplish.

Hyper- V on Windows Server 2012 comes with a new feature, called **Hyper-V Replica** to solve this problem. It is a feature that allows the virtual machines to be replicated to another server, such as a remote disaster recovery site server, using a single network connection.

The Hyper-V Replica components consist of a **primary server** that hosts all the virtual machines running in production, and a **replica server** that hosts replicas of each virtual machines on the primary server. It allows the administrators to automatically replicate the virtual machines that are to be used in case of a planned failover, such as moving VMs to the replication site, or even a failover in unplanned events where the primary server is offline.

The Hyper-V Replica replication engine has a module called **change tracking** that captures every "write" within the virtual hard disk file of all the running virtual machines and creates a log file. The replication happens in the **Virtual Hard Disk** (**VHD**) level, making it even easier to allow any virtual machine to be replicated. The replication using these logs occurs periodically and asynchronously through an HTTP or HTTPS connection. All the data that must be replicated to the replica server uses the **network module**, which optimizes the workload to work in slow network connections such as WANs. All you need are two physical servers running Hyper-V and a network connection between then. That's it. It does not need any third-party hardware or software applications. Also, it has the option to create **recovery points** so that you can restore virtual machines to any point in time. You don't have to worry about database corruption or virus replication when using the recovery points.

Hyper-V Replica is designed to give small- and medium-sized companies a full disaster recovery infrastructure solution for their virtualized environments with few requirements in terms of cost and components.

While allowing you to have replicas on the same network, the idea of Hyper-V Replica is to have a replica on a different network where you can run your VMs in case of a disaster, making it fully compliant with almost all the disaster recovery policies in place today.

In this recipe, you will see how to create a single Hyper-V Replica infrastructure with a primary and recovery server using HTTP based replication. That's not everything about Hyper-V Replica. The next recipes will show advanced configurations such as certificate-based replication and the integration between Hyper-V Replica and Failover Cluster.

Getting ready

Hyper-V Replica requires only two servers with the Hyper-V role installed and a network connection. It's as simple as that!

How to do it...

In the following tasks, you will see how to prepare and configure two servers to work with Hyper-V Replica and how to enable replication of a virtual machine. The tasks will illustrate setting up the primary server (**HVHost01**) and the replica server (**HVHost02**). At the end of the tasks, you will see how to fail the virtual machine over to in the replica server in case of disaster.

1. Open the **Hyper-V Manager** on the server that will be used as replica server.

2. In the **Hyper-V Manager**, click on **Hyper-V Settings** in the pane on the right-hand side.

3. In the **Hyper-V Settings** window, select **Replication Configuration**.

4. Click on **Enable this computer as a Replica server**.

5. Under **Authentication and ports**, select **Use Kerberos (HTTP)** and specify the port to be used.

6. Under **Authorization and storage**, select **Allow replication from any authenticated server** and specify the default location to store the replica files; or, you can select **Allow replication from the specified servers**. If you select the second option, specify the **Primary Server**, **Storage Location**, and **Trust Group**.

7. In the following screenshot, the port **80** has been used to replicate with HTTP. The primary server ***.contoso.com** has been added to allow replication from any server from the **contoso.com** domain, and a trust group called **HVServer**s has also been created. Click on **OK** when finished.

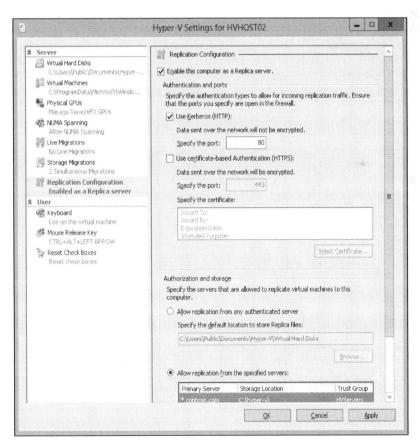

8. Repeat steps 1 through 7 for the **primary server** as well.

 Though it is not necessary, you can enable the primary server as a replica server for occasions where you need to fail back the VMs using a planned failover.

9. To enable a **Windows Firewall** exception for Hyper-V Replica, open **PowerShell** from the **Taskbar** and type the following command in both servers:

```
Enable-Netfirewallrule -displayname "Hyper-V Replica HTTP Listener
(TCP-In)"
```

10. Now, with the replica server up and running, right-click on the virtual machine that you want to replicate in the primary server, in the Hyper-V Manager, and select **Enable Replication**.

11. In the **Enable Replication Wizard**, click on **Next**.

12. In the **Specify Replica Server**, type the Hyper-V Replica server name in **Replica Server** and click on **Next**.

13. In **Specify Connections Parameters**, verify that **Use Kerberos authentication (HTTP)** is selected. In case of slow network connections, verify that the **Compress the data that is transmitted over the network** option is checked, as shown in the following screenshot, and click on **Next**.

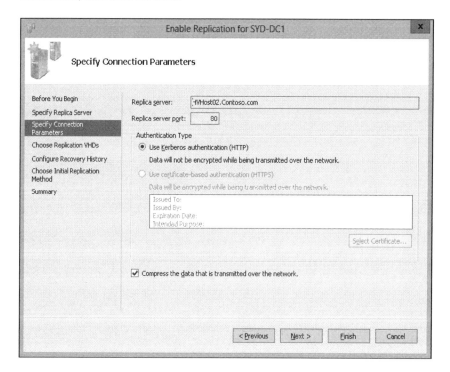

14. Under **Choose Replication VHDs**, deselect the virtual hard disks file that you don't want to replicate and click on **Next**.

15. In **Configure Recovery History**, select **Only the latest recovery point** to have only the last recovery point in the replica server, as shown in the next screenshot. You can select **Additional recovery points** if you want to allow the replica server to receive additional recovery points. If you select this option, specify the number of recovery points in **Number of additional recovery points to be stored**; to replicate incremental snapshots using the **Volume Shadow Copy** (**VSS**), select the checkbox **Replicate Incremental VSS copy every:** and use the slider to specify the frequency at which the snapshots are taken.

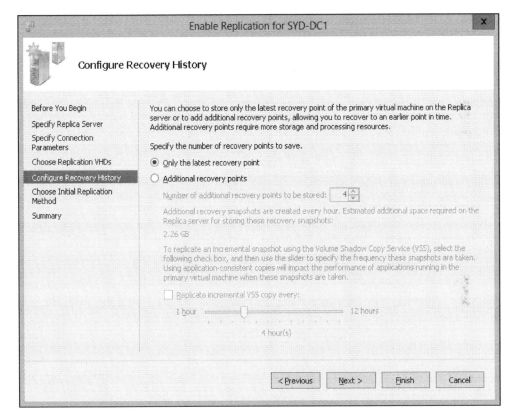

 The slider to specify the time is only applied to the frequency the of snapshots being taken. It can be confused with the time to replicate the virtual machine data to the replica server. The default value is 5 minutes and cannot be changed.

16. In the **Choose Initial Replication Method** window, under **Initial Replication Method**, select **Send initial copy over the network**, as shown in the next screenshot, to use the network connection to copy the VM files. Select **Send initial copy using external media** to export the VM data and locally import it in the replica server. You may select the **Use an existing virtual machine on the Replica server as the initial copy** option if you have a restored copy of the virtual machine on the replica server.

17. Under **Schedule Initial Replication**, select **Start replication immediately**, as shown in the following screenshot, to send the virtual machine data straight away after the wizard is completed. You may alternatively select **Start replication on** and set the time and date for scheduled replication to schedule the initial replication. Once done, click on **Next**.

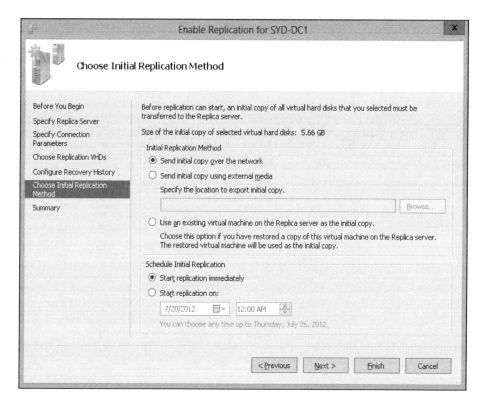

18. In the **Completing the Enable Replication** wizard, check the settings and click on **Finish**. The virtual machine data will be transferred to the replica server on the scheduled time and date.

19. In case of a disaster and the primary server is offline, right-click on the virtual machine in the replica server, select **Replica**, and click on **Failover**.

20. In the **Failover** window, select the recovery point to use in the drop-down list and click on **Fail Over**, as shown in the following screenshot:

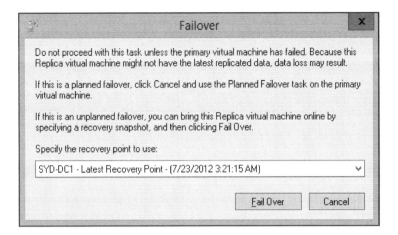

How it works...

Hyper-V Replica needs two servers to replicate the virtual machine data. The principal server that runs the virtual machines is known as **primary server**. The secondary server, called **replica server** is used in case of a failover. The first thing is to enable the replica server in the **Hyper-V Settings**. The settings are divided in two classes—**authentication** and **authorization**. In authentication, there are two options to transfer the virtual machine files over the network—HTTP, which does not encrypt the data and doesn't require any additional configuration and HTTPS, which encrypts the content using digital certificates for authentication. You must request and install an authentication certificate in order to use HTTPS. This option will be covered in the next recipe.

The replica server also needs to be configured to receive data from other servers. That's the role of the authorization part of the window. You can select the option to **Allow replication from any authenticated server** or specify a list of servers and the path to store the virtual machine files. In the server list you can also use wildcards like ***.contoso.com** to allow any server from the `contoso.com` domain to replicate data to the server. You can use **Trusted Groups** to separate different areas or customers, creating a sort of tagging. This is an interesting option in case you have different customers and want to make sure their data will be in different locations.

Although the primary server does not need these replica server options, it would be a best practice to enable it in the primary servers so that you can use the Planned Failover feature and transfer the VM back to the primary server after an outage.

After this, a firewall exception must be configured to allow Windows Firewall to receive the HTTP (or HTTPS, if you are using the certificates) requests from the primary server. If you configured the primary server as a replica server, you also must run the PowerShell command.

That's basically all you need to set up the host computers with Hyper-V Replica. The next step is to enable the replication on the virtual machines that you want. This is done by selecting the option **Enable Replication** on the VM.

The first step of the wizard is to select the replica server. After that, you can select the protocol to send the VM files. You can use either HTTP or HTTPS. On the same screen, you can uncheck the option to compress the data over the network. As the primary and replica servers are intended to run on different sites, this option is checked by default. The next option is to select the VHD that needs to be replicated. In case the VM has more than one VHD, you can select the one VHD that will be present in the replica server. For better performance and to reduce the amount of data that's being replicated, it's recommended to use a different VHD for the page file within the VM and exclude it from being replicated.

In the **Recovery History** window, you can choose to have only the last recovery point of a VM or more points. You can select the number of recovery points and the interval to create the additional recovery points. The last step is to select the initial replication method and schedule. The default method is to send the initial copy over the network. In case of large virtual machines over slow networks, you can export the VM data to an external media and import in the replica server. In case the VM that you want to replicate already exists in the replica server, you can use it for the initial copy. Then, you can start the replication immediately or schedule the initial replication. It is important to say that the schedule is only applicable during the initial replication. The log replication occurs every 5 minutes and cannot be changed.

When a virtual machine is enabled to replicate, the Hyper-V Replica modules start to monitor the changes in the VHD and create a log to be replicated. This is done by the change tracking module in the **Hyper-V Virtual Storage Stack**. The replication starts using an asynchronous method, replaying the log files in reverse order.

Then, the unexpected happens: a disaster occurs. No need to panic (at least with your VMs). The failover process is manual. To do so, you must select the virtual machine and fail it over. You can also select the recovery point to restore the VM. It comes in very handy if you have a virus infection in one of your virtual machine, for example.

As a last tip, it is recommended to monitor the health of your replica using the default views and tools, to make sure that you will be able to restore a recent version of your virtual machines in case of failure.

There's more...

You might be wondering what happens when a virtual machine with a static IP address fails over onto another datacenter with a different subnet and network configuration. For example, on datacenter A, where the primary server sits, you have a VM with IP address, default gateway, DNS settings, and so on. On datacenter B, where the replica server is, there are different network configurations, causing problems on all the VMs that failover to access the network.

When the VM starts on the replica server, it will lose the network settings. Even if you keep the same network configuration, it will not work because the VM is running on a different network.

That's why Hyper-V allows you to add failover network configuration settings, which can be used when you failover it to the replica server. It is also important to note that this requires a **synthetic virtual network adapter** on the VM and doesn't work with legacy virtual network adapters.

To configure these settings, open the virtual machine settings, expand the attached network adapter, and click on **Failover TCP/IP**, as shown in next screenshot:

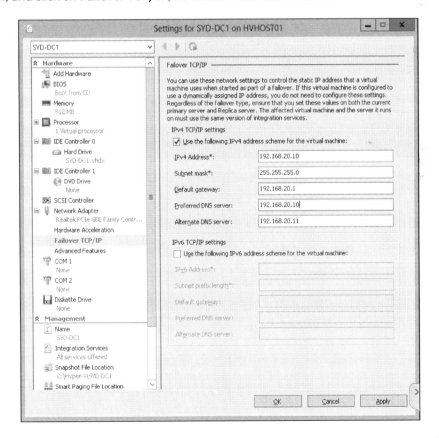

Check the **Use the following IPv4 address scheme for the virtual machine** option and add the network configuration that you want your VM to use when it fails over the other network.

Using PowerShell to configure and enable Hyper-V Replica

PowerShell is also present as a secondary configuration option for Hyper-V Replica and sometimes it makes things very handy and easy, as shown in the next examples.

You can use the command `Set-VMReplicationServer` to configure your server as a replica server. The next example shows a server being enabled using **Kerberos** as authentication type, with the default storage location point to `C:\Hyper-V` and with the option to receive replication from any server enabled.

```
Set-VMReplicationServer -ReplicationEnabled $true
-AllowedAuthenticationType Kerberos -DefaultStorageLocation C:\Hyper-V
-ReplicationAllowedFromAnyServer $true
```

To enable replication to a VM you can use the command `Enable-VMReplication`. The next example shows how to enable replication to all the virtual machines at the same time using port `80` on server `HVHost02`.

```
Enable-VMReplication -VMName * -ReplicaServerName HVHost02
-ReplicaServerPort 80 -AuthenticationType Kerberos
```

The `Start-VMInitialReplication` command starts the initial replication for your virtual machines. The next example shows how to start it on every virtual machine:

```
Start-VMInitialReplication -VMName *
```

To list all the Hyper-V Replica commandlets on PowerShell, type the following command:

```
Get-Command -Module Hyper-V *Replica*
```

See also

- The Configuring *Hyper-V Replica Broker for a Failover Cluster* recipe in this chapter
- The *Configuring Hyper-V Replica to use certificate-based authentication using an Enterprise CA* recipe in this chapter
- The *Tuning your Hyper-V server* recipe in *Chapter 9, Monitoring, Tuning, and Troubleshooting Hyper-V*

Configuring Hyper-V Replica Broker for a Failover Cluster

If you have either the primary or the replica server as a member of a **Failover Cluster** environment, you will need to configure the **Hyper-V Replica Broker** role. This role is necessary to enable a cluster to be part of a Hyper-V Replica so that it can support seamless replication. In this scenario, you can have a standalone server and a cluster working as primary or replica server, or a cluster for each.

When configuring a Hyper-V Replica for a virtual machine, a different virtual name called **Client Access Point** (**CAP**) must be used. The CAP is created during the Hyper-V Replica Broker configuration.

In this recipe, you will see how to configure Hyper-V Replica Broker to use your cluster servers in the Hyper-V Replica scenario.

Getting ready

You will need a Failover Cluster environment already configured with a cluster created as well. For more information on how to install and configure it, have a look at the *Installing and configuring the Windows Failover Cluster* recipe in *Chapter 7, Configuring High Availability in Hyper-V*.

How to do it...

These steps will guide you through the Hyper-V Replica Broker configuration, enabling a failover cluster to participate in a Hyper-V Replica infrastructure.

1. To configure Hyper-V Replica Broker, open the Start menu and type `Cluadmin.msc` to open the **Failover Cluster Manager**.
2. Select the existing cluster and click on **Configure Role**.
3. In the **High Availability Wizard** window, click on **Next**.

4. In **Select Role**, select **Hyper-V Replica Broker**, as shown in the following screenshot, and click on **Next**.

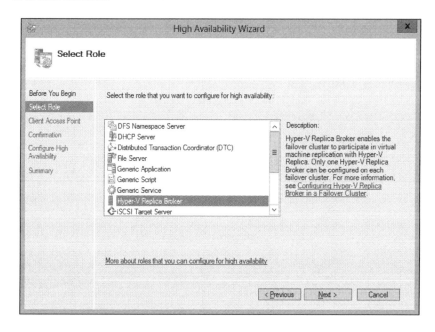

5. In the **Client Access Point** window, specify the name and the IP address for your CAP and click on **Next**, as shown in the following screenshot:

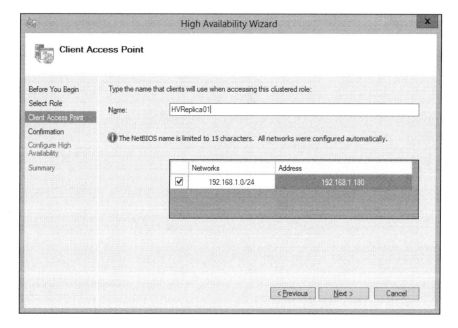

6. In the **Confirmation** window, click on **Next** and then **Finish**.

7. After the configuration, open the **Failover Cluster Manager** again, expand your cluster, click on **Roles**, right-click on the **Hyper-V Replica Broker** object, and click on **Replication Settings**.

8. In the **Hyper-V Replica Broker Configuration** window, select **Enable this cluster as a Replica server**.

9. Under **Authentication and ports**, select either **Use Kerberos (HTTP)** or **Use certificate-based Authentication (HTTPS)**. For the last option, you must have a digital certificate installed first.

10. Under **Authorization and storage**, select **Allow replication from any authenticated server** or **Allow replication from the specified servers** and specify the location to store the replica files. When finished, click on **OK**, as shown in the next screenshot:

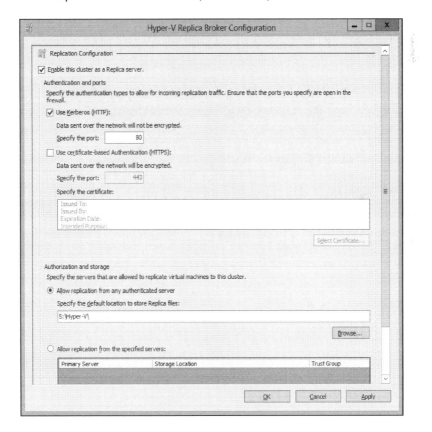

11. After configuring the Hyper-V Replica Broker, when enabling a virtual machine for replication, for the **Client Access Point** field type `Replica Server`.

How it works...

Hyper-V Replica does support cluster, but it cannot use the cluster name while you are enabling replication in the virtual machine. That's why you need to configure the Hyper-V Replica Broker. It creates a virtual name and IP address that can be used in the wizard to create a virtual machine replica.

Hyper-V Replica Broker is a role that is enabled in the **Failover Cluster Manager**. During its creation, you just need to add the Client Access Point name and the IP address. Then you must enable and configure Hyper-V Replica in the role, as done in a normal host that will be used as a replica server. After adding the authentication and authorization options, your cluster will be ready to start working as part of a Hyper-V Replica infrastructure.

See also

 ▸ The *Configuring Hyper-V Replica between two Hyper-V hosts* recipe in this chapter
 ▸ The *Configuring Hyper-V Replica to use certificate-based authentication using an Enterprise CA* recipe in this chapter

Configuring Hyper-V Replica to use certificate-based authentication using an Enterprise CA

Hyper-V Replica brings you all that you need to build your **Infrastructure as a Service (IaaS)** and also provides you with a Disaster Recovery environment for your virtualized workloads.

With its simple configuration and a couple of clicks, you can start replicating your virtual machine to a different site with low cost and high reliability. However, the out-of-box experience using HTTP to replicate data does not provide encryption during the transfer to the other site.

This recipe will show you how to use an **Enterprise Certification Authority (CA)** to obtain a certificate to replicate the virtual machine data using HTTPS.

Getting ready

In order to request a digital certificate, you will need to have an Enterprise CA already installed and configured. Use the Server Manager to install **Active Directory Certificate Services** and then to configure an Enterprise CA in case you don't have one.

How to do it...

The following steps will show how to create a certificate template in the Enterprise CA, how to request and install a certificate to be used on Hyper-V Replica and how to enable Hyper-V Replica to use certificate-based authentication for replication.

1. To create a certificate template to be used to issue certificates for Hyper-V, type `certsrv.msc` from your CA server, to open the **Certification Authority** console.

2. Expand your local CA (make a note of the CA name, you will need it during step 16), right-click on **Certificate Templates**, and select **Manage**.

3. In the **Certificate Templates Console**, right-click on the **Workstation Authentication** template and select **Duplicate Template**, as shown in the following screenshot:

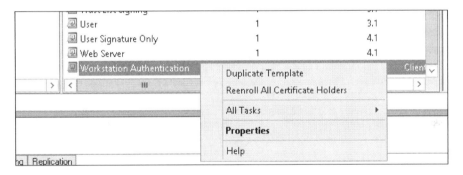

4. In the **Properties of New Template** pane, go to the **General** tab and fill in the **Template display name** and the **Template name** fields. In the following screenshot, `Hyper-V Replica Template` was added as the **Template name**.

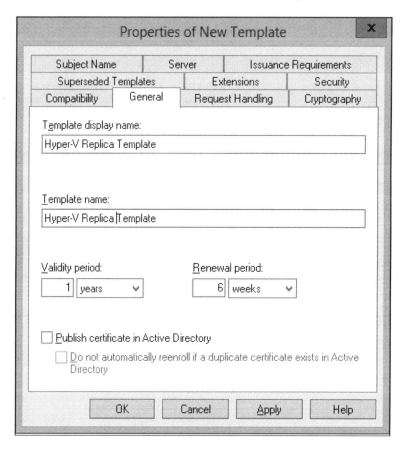

5. Go to the **Issuance Requirements** tab and check the **CA certificate manager approval** option to manually approve the certificates using the new template. Although it is optional, you can provide more security and control for new certificates.

6. Click on the **Security** tab, select the **Authenticated Users** group and allow the **Enroll** permission, as shown in the following screenshot:

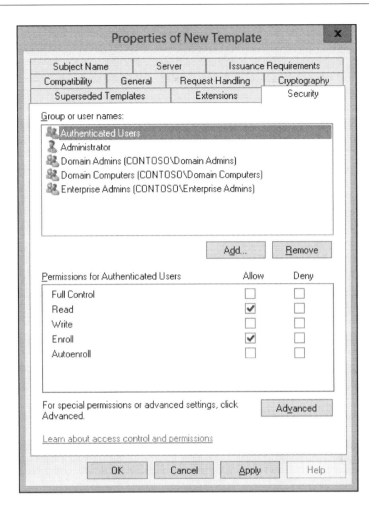

7. Click on the **Subject Name** tab and select **Supply** in the request to enable the subject name to be added during the request.

8. Click on the **Extensions** tab, make sure that **Application Policies** is selected, and click on **Edit**.

9. In the **Edit Application Policies Extensions** window, click on **Add**.

10. In the **Add Application Policy** screen, select **Server Authentication** from the list and click on **OK** twice. Under **Description of Application Policies**, you will see both **Client** and **Server Authentication** as shown in the following screenshot. Click on **OK** to confirm the new certificate template creation and close the **Certificate Templates Console** window.

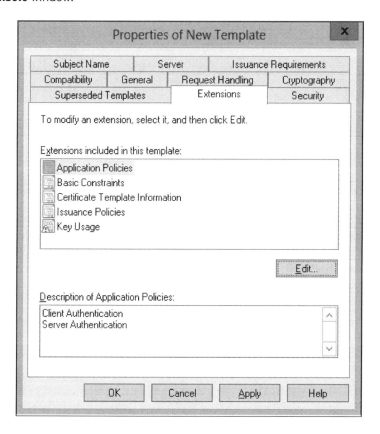

11. Back in the **Certification Authority** console, right-click on **Certificate Templates**, navigate to **New**, and click on **Certificate Template to Issue**.

12. In the **Enable Certificate Templates** window, select the new certificate template, and click on **OK**.

13. From the server that will be used as member of the Hyper-V Replica, open Notepad and use the following text as an example code to create a `.inf` file to request your certificate. Replace the **Subject** line value "`CN=HVHost01.contoso.com`" with your server's **Fully Qualified Domain Name** (**FQDN**). Replace the **CertificateTemplate** value "`Hyper-V Replica Template`" with the name used in the *step 4*:

```
[Version]
Signature="$Windows NT$"


[NewRequest]
Subject = "CN=HVHost01.contoso.com"
Exportable = TRUE
KeyLength = 2048
KeySpec = 1
KeyUsage = 0xA0
MachineKeySet = True
ProviderName = "Microsoft RSA SChannel Cryptographic Provider"
ProviderType = 12
RequestType = CMC


[RequestAttributes]
CertificateTemplate = "Hyper-V Replica Template"
```

14. Save the file as a `.inf` file and close Notepad. In the next example, the file that will be used is `C:\HVhost01.inf`.

15. Open the command prompt as administrator and type the following command to create a new request file:

```
Certreq -new C:\HVHost01.inf C:\HVHost01.req
```

16. Type the next command to submit the request using the `.req` file that was created in the previous task. Replace the name "`Daleon\Contoso-CA`" with your CA server name and the CA name, as shown in *step 2*.

```
Certreq -submit -config "Daleon\Contoso-CA" C:\HVHost01.req C:\
HVHost01.cer
```

17. In the command results, make a note of the **request ID**.

18. In case you need to approve the pending request, as configured in step 5, open the **Certificate Authority** console back in the CA server, click on **Pending Requests**, right-click on the request, select **All Tasks**, and click on **Issue**, as shown in the following screenshot:

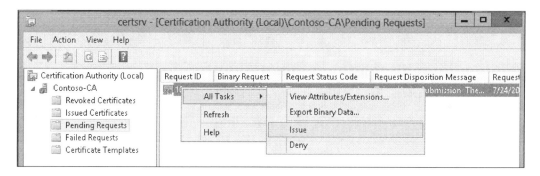

19. Open the command prompt back in the Hyper-V host again and type the next command to retrieve the approved certificate. Replace the request ID 10 with the one from step 17.

    ```
    Certreq -retrieve 10 HVHost01.cer
    ```

20. Right-click on the `.cer` file created in the previous step and click on **Install Certificate**.

21. In the **Certificate Import Wizard**, select **Local Machine** under **Store Location** and click on **Next**.

22. In **Certificate Store**, select **Place all certificates in the following store**, click **Browse**, select **Personal**, click on **OK**, **Next**, and then on **Finish** to import the certificate.

23. To enable Hyper-V Replica in the local **Windows Firewall**, open PowerShell from the taskbar and type the following command in both the servers:

    ```
    Enable-Netfirewallrule -displayname "Hyper-V Replica HTTPS
    Listener (TCP-In)"
    ```

24. Now with the certificate installed locally, open the **Hyper-V Manager**, click on **Hyper-V Settings** on the pane on the right-hand side, and check the **Enable this computer as a Replica server** option.

25. Check the **Use certificate-based Authentication (HTTPS)** option and click on **Select Certificate**.

26. In the **Windows Security** window, confirm the imported certificate and click on **OK**, as shown in the next screenshot:

27. Verify the certificate settings, as shown in the following screenshot, and click on **OK**.

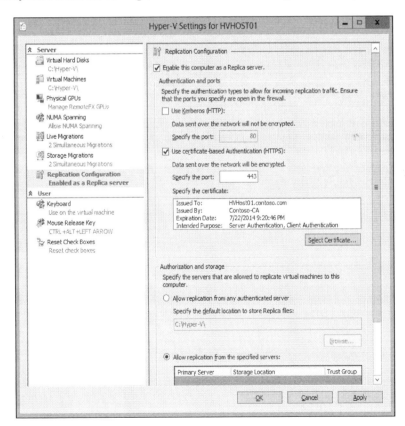

28. Repeat steps 13 to 27 to request and install a certificate to the other Hyper-V Server.

29. When enabling the replica for a virtual machine, under **Specify Connection Parameters**, select **Use certificate-based authentication (HTTPS)**, as shown in the next screenshot, click on **Select Certificate** and click on **OK**.

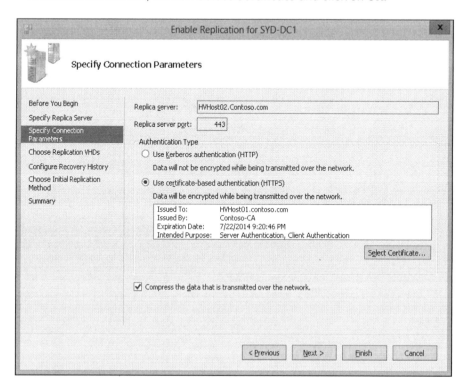

How it works...

A **digital certificate** is one of the most common and safest methods used today by applications, websites, and many other solutions to provide communication authenticity and encryption.

Hyper-V Replica can use this technology to encrypt and protect replication data. In this recipe, an Enterprise CA was used as an example for internal certificate requests. Although Enterprise CAs are more common internally, you can also use standalone or even external CAs to create requests for your certificates.

By using an Enterprise CA, you have some benefits such as Active Directory integration, auto enrolment of certificates, and certificate templates.

In the recipe, a template was created with the necessary advanced options required for Hyper-V Replica configuration.

After template creation, a `.inf` file containing the certificate details must be used to create a request file so that you can issue it from the CA server.

When the certificate is issued and installed on both servers that will be used to configure Hyper-V Replica, you can enable it by using certificate-based authentication and replicate the virtual machines between them.

See also

▶ The *Configuring Hyper-V Replica between two Hyper-V hosts* recipe in this chapter

▶ The *Configuring Hyper-V Replica Broker for a Failover Cluster* recipe in this chapter

Using snapshots in virtual machines

In the IT field, it is easy to have problems, errors, mistakes, and other issue that might need a deep troubleshooting process or even worse, such as a system restore. With virtual machines, the administrators have a very interesting option that is not available in physical servers. What if you could rollback a VM before the error occurred? What if you could prepare the VM for some change that can cause an issue. That's what **snapshots** are made for. You can take a VM snapshot on the fly, do whatever you need to do, and roll it back in case of errors.

This comes very handy and can save our lives, making the problem prevention two clicks away.

To illustrate some scenarios to use snapshots, consider the following examples:

▶ System upgrades or migration

▶ Software updates

▶ Software installation and configuration

▶ Registry changes

▶ Troubleshooting problems

This list can go on and on, but the idea of snapshots is to give you the opportunity to recover the virtual machine in a fast and an easy way. With them, you can revert the virtual machine to a previous state before the error. That's why snapshots are very common in developing, staging, and testing the environments.

This recipe will show the different ways to create and manage snapshots, as well as its tricks and best practices.

Getting ready

Snapshots can be created on any existing virtual machine. The only prerequisite in this recipe is to have Hyper-V with at least one virtual machine.

How to do it...

The following steps will show how to create and manage virtual machine snapshots.

1. To take a snapshot of a virtual machine, open **Hyper-V Manager**, right-click on the virtual machine and click on **Snapshot** or click on **Snapshot** in the pane on the right-hand side, as shown in the following screenshot:

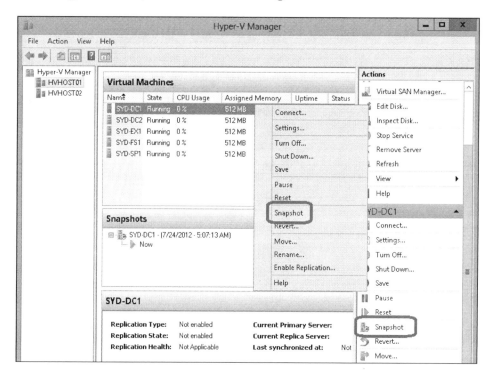

2. To take a snapshot and add a name during its creation, double-click on a virtual machine to open the **Virtual Machine Connection** window, click on **Action** in the menu, and then click on **Snapshot**.

3. On the **Snapshot Name** window, type the snapshot name, as shown in the next screenshot, and click on **Yes**.

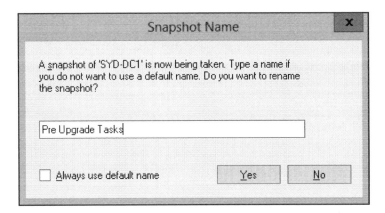

4. To apply, rename, delete, and see the snapshot settings, select any virtual machine, select the snapshot to be managed, and right-click on it, as shown in the following screenshot:

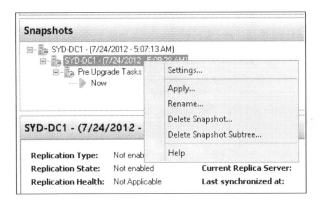

How it works...

As shown in the simple tasks in the recipe, Hyper-V offers several ways to create snapshots. When a new one is created, it captures the virtual machine state, configuration, and all its content, and stores them into an **Automatic Virtual Hard Disk** (**AVHD**) file within the virtual machine folder.

When a virtual machine has a snapshot taken, an AVHD file is created and a link between the new file and the current VHD is created. All the "writes" start getting stored in the AVHD file, while the "reads" happen in both files. When you delete the snapshot, Hyper-V merges the AVHD file with the VHD file. The AVHD file is then deleted as along with the link with the VHD file. Because of different disks to read and write and the possibility to create snapshot trees, you can have poor disk performance in the virtual machine. That's why snapshots are intended to be used temporarily.

In previous versions of Hyper-V, snapshot merges happened only with the virtual machine offline. The AVHD file was deleted only when the VM was turned off. One of the principal improvements on Windows Server 2012 is the ability to have a real-time merge between AVHD and VHD files.

In some situations, people might think that snapshots can replace a VM backup at times. They can also create lots of snapshots for a single VM. As a Hyper-V administrator, you must know that snapshots are temporary actions that can never replace any backup of your virtual machines.

There's more...

Using snapshots via PowerShell can be tricky. In PowerShell, snapshots are know by a different name **checkpoint**. The command `Create-CheckPoint` is used to take a snapshot from a virtual machine. You can also use `Remove-VMSnapshot`, `Restore-VMSnapshot`, `Get-VMSnapshot`, and `Rename-VMSnapshot`.

Exporting a virtual machine out of a snapshot

There is a new and special commandlet in PowerShell that can export a virtual machine from an existing snapshot called `Export-VMSnapshot`.

The following code snippet gets a snapshot called **Pre Upgrade Task** from the VM `SYD-DC1` and export to the folder `C:\Hyper-V`. After that, you can import and create a new VM from the snapshot.

```
Export-VMSnapshot -Name "Pre Upgrade Tasks" -VMName SYD-DC1 -Path C:\
Hyper-V
```

See also

- ▶ The *Exporting and importing virtual machines* recipe in *Chapter 2, Migrating and Upgrading Physical and Virtual Servers*
- ▶ The *Backing up Hyper-V and virtual machines using Windows Server Backup* recipe in this chapter
- ▶ The *Restoring Hyper-V and virtual machines using Windows Server Backup* recipe in this chapter

9

Monitoring, Tuning, and Troubleshooting Hyper-V

In this chapter we will cover:

- ▶ Using real-time monitoring tools
- ▶ Using Perfmon for logged monitoring
- ▶ Using VM Monitoring
- ▶ Monitoring Hyper-V Replica
- ▶ Using Resource Metering
- ▶ Tuning your Hyper-V server
- ▶ Using Event Viewer for Hyper-V troubleshooting

Introduction

Virtual machines running on Hyper-V are responsible for all system and **Line of Business** (**LOB**) applications for your company. As a virtualization administrator, it is your responsibility to check the host and the virtual machine health with monitoring applications, extract reports to verify workload increases, and then make possible tunings to get incremental performance increases, if needed.

It is highly recommended that you monitor your physical and virtual servers, making sure they are working as expected. Some tools and utilities will also show when something is not behaving as normal, helping you to identify when tuning is necessary or whether a problem exists.

In some cases, errors will occur, and you will have to be prepared to react immediately. Monitoring solutions will allow you to be notified, so that you can start the troubleshooting process to solve problems as soon as possible.

In this chapter, we will see how to use the default tools in Windows Server 2012 to monitor our physical and virtual servers, how to troubleshoot, and how to tune our Hyper-V servers.

Using real-time monitoring tools

The process of monitoring their servers is an important task for a server administrator.

By monitoring the performance of physical and virtual servers, you obtain data that can be used to understand the workload and its effects, identify bottlenecks and resource trends, diagnose issues, and optimize the system.

There are two options to monitor your system: real-time monitoring and logged monitoring.

Real-time monitoring is normally used to check server performance for troubleshooting purposes, to quickly and easily identify the cause of poor performance, for example. Logged monitoring is used to measure and collect performance data, so that you can identify workload problems and trends.

In this recipe, we will walk through some default tools that can be used for real-time monitoring.

Getting ready

Before you begin, make sure your account is a member of the local administrators group. The **Performance Monitor Users** group also can be used (for monitoring purposes only).

How to do it...

In the following steps, you will see how to open and explore Task Manager:

1. To open Task Manager, launch the Start menu and type `task manager`. Select **Task Manager** from the result list.

2. In the **Task Manager** window, click on **More Details** to see the hidden tabs and advanced options shown in the following screenshot:

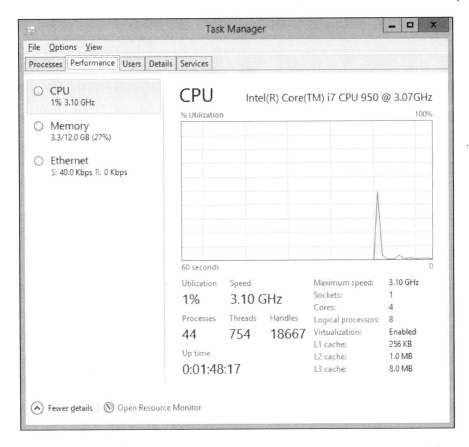

3. Navigate through the tabs **Process**, **Performance**, **Users**, **Details**, and **Services**, to check current information.

In the following steps, you will see how to open and explore Resource Monitor:

1. To open **Resource Monitor**, launch the Start menu and type `resource monitor`. Select **Resource Monitor** from the result list.

2. In the **Resource Monitor** window, use the tabs **Overview**, **CPU**, **Memory**, **Disk**, and **Network** to get resource details, as shown in the following screenshot:

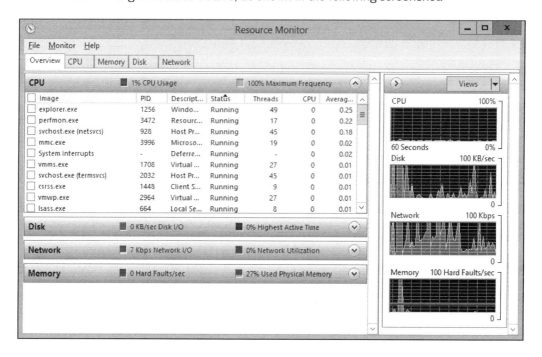

3. To manage a running process or application, right-click on the object from the list and select one of the existing options, such as **End Process**, **End Process Tree**, **Analyze Wait Chain**, **Suspend Process**, **Resume Process**, or **Search Online**.

In the following steps, you will see how to open and explore Performance Monitor:

1. To open Performance Monitor, type `perfmon.msc` at the Start menu and press *Enter*.

2. In the **Performance Monitor** window, under **Performance**, expand **Monitoring Tools** and click on **Performance Monitor**.

3. Right-click on the monitor area and click on **Add Counters**.

4. In the **Add Counters** window, select the counter you want to monitor.

5. Under **Instances of selected object**, select the instance you want to monitor, if available.

6. After selecting the counter and the instance, click on **Add**, as shown in the following screenshot:

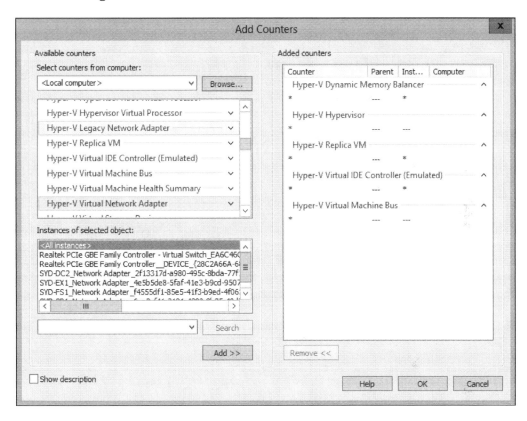

7. After adding the counters, click on **OK**. The results will be shown in the monitoring area.

8. During monitoring, select the counter from the counter list to check information such as **Last**, **Average**, **Minimum**, **Maximum**, and **Duration**, as shown in the following screenshot:

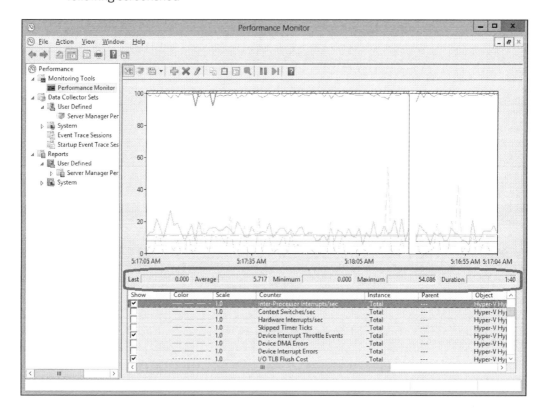

How it works...

Real-time tools are your best friends for quickly analyzing and checking any problem being caused by applications, services, roles, or even the hardware. In case your server is running too slow or something stops working, you can have a look in one of the real-time monitoring tools to see what is really happening.

There are three different levels of information that you can get. For each level, there is a particular tool. The first and the second ones, with less information, can show you quick system details, while the last one is more advanced and complicated but can show you almost every little detail of all local components of your server.

The first and most common one is **Task Manager**. With its new version, there are two different views, the light one, which is opened by default and shows only running applications, and the advanced one, with more detail and with five tabs that allow you to check the processes, performance, users, details, and services of your local server.

The second tool is **Resource Monitor**. It is a sort of advanced task manager showing tabs with information about the four most important subsystems of your server: **CPU**, **Memory**, **Disk**, and **Network**. This is the right tool to quickly check your hardware performance.

Performance Monitor, or just **Perfmon**, is the last default tool that can be used for advanced monitoring. Perfmon contains many counters, each one with lots of instances for all components in the system, such as services, hardware, application, roles, and features. Perfmon also supports remote monitoring, allowing you to monitor a bunch of servers in just one console. This is the right tool if you need high-level details about something, which the first two tools cannot provide.

Using these default and free real-time monitoring tools, you can find issues quickly, making troubleshooting even easier in times of performance problems.

There's more...

Using Tabs on Hyper-V Manager to Monitor Virtual Machines

Hyper-V Manager also comes with improvements to help administrators to more easily understand what is going on in virtual machines.

By just clicking on a virtual machine within Hyper-V Manager, you can see advanced information about the VM, memory, networking, and replication.

These details are shown by the four new tabs at the bottom of the console when a VM is selected. Using **Integration Components** on the VM, Hyper-V checks (for example) the VM summary, memory utilization, IP addresses, and replication health. This option is very simple and helpful, as you don't have to connect to the virtual machine or use advanced tools to check its details.

The following screenshot shows an example of the **Replication** tab with the most common replication data:

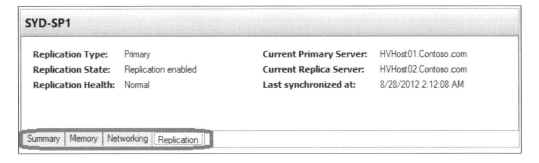

See also

► The *Using Perfmon for logged monitoring* recipe in this chapter
► The *Using VM Monitoring* recipe in this chapter

Using Perfmon for logged monitoring

After all preconfiguration, installation, and setting up of virtual machines, everything is up and running normally. However, what you really need to consider is *what is normal*. What is the regular performance and system utilization for your physical and virtual servers?

Logged monitoring will help you to answer that question, measuring realistic conditions and helping you to identify the needs of servers and hardware upgrades, optimization, and tunings, by using trend analysis. That's an example of what you can get using baselines. A baseline is the level of system performance that you decide is acceptable. Normally, they are decided before deployment, during the planning phases.

Using **data collector sets** from Perfmon, you can get realistic and advanced trend information and create baselines that can start and stop automatically, based on your schedule.

This recipe will show you how to use Perfmon to create baselines for your physical and virtual machines.

Getting ready

Baselines must track the server activities during a specific period of time. You can create daily, weekly, monthly, or any other schedule you need. Before you start, decide what you want to monitor, such as processor, memory, disk, and network, and for how long it will be monitored.

How to do it...

The following steps will show you the default system data collector sets and how to create user-defined collector sets:

1. To use the default data collector sets, launch the Start menu, type `perfmon.msc`, and press *Enter*.

2. In the **Performance Monitor** window, under **Performance**, expand **Data Collector Sets** and click on **System**, as shown in the following screenshot:

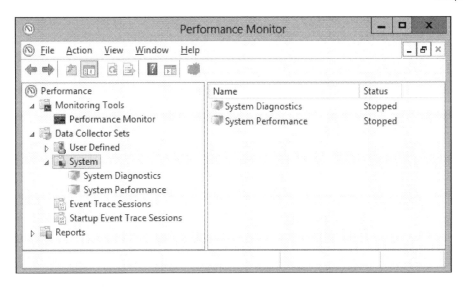

3. There are two default data collector sets named **System Diagnostics** and **System Performance**. To start either of them, right-click on it and select **Start**.

4. To see the results, expand **Reports | System** and select the report you want to open.

5. To create a new data collector set, right-click on **User Defined** under **Data Collector Sets**, select **Data Collector Set**, and click on **New**.

6. In the **Create new Data Collector Set.** window, type a name, select **Create manually (Advanced)**, and click on **Next**.

7. On the **What type of data do you want to include?** screen, select the data type you want to use and click on **Next**.

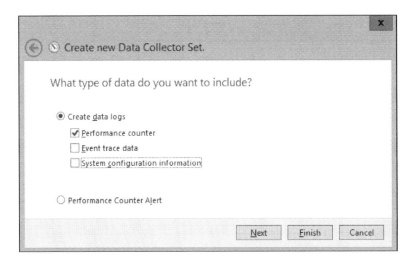

8. In the new window, select the computer from which you want to get the data for remote monitoring, select the counters and instances you want to add, and click on **Add**, as shown in the following screenshot. When finished, click on **OK**.

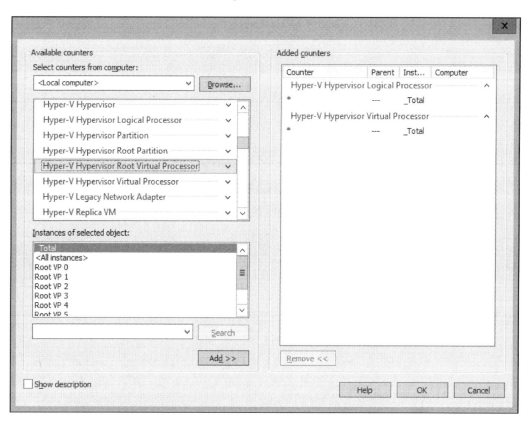

9. Under **Performance Counters**, under **Sample Interval and Units**, put the number and units you want to use to record the selected counters.

10. Check the selected counters and click on **Finish**.

11. After creating the new collector set, right-click on it under **User Defined** and click on **Properties** to change its options.

12. In the properties window, you can add a schedule to run the baseline automatically, create a stop condition (as shown with the example in the following screenshot), or change other options by using the tabs **General**, **Directory**, **Security**, **Schedule**, **Stop Condition**, and **Task**.

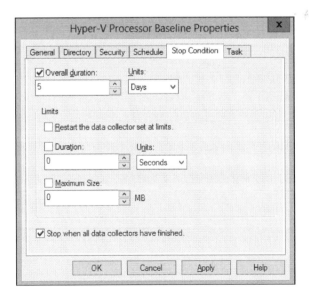

13. After running the data collector sets, to check the collected data, expand **Reports | User Defined** in the **Performance Monitor** window and open the folder for the collector set you created.

14. The report will be shown in the right-hand pane. Use the toolbar and the counter list to view and change the results windows, as shown in the following screenshot:

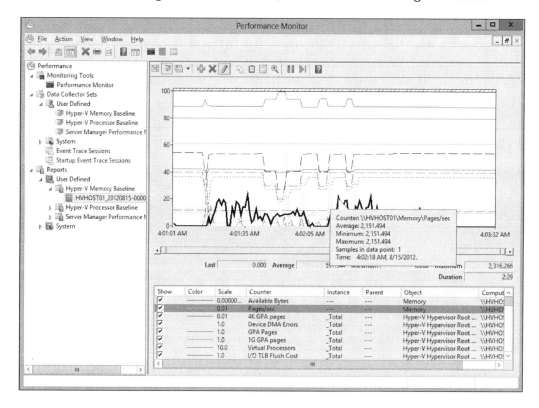

How it works...

On Windows Server, Perfmon is the only built-in tool that can be used for logged monitoring. It comes with two system collector sets that can be used to get advanced reports showing system diagnostics and system performance.

Under **User Defined**, you can create your own collector sets, based on the application or hardware you want to monitor.

For virtual environments, you can use only the host partition to analyze all the performance trends, but in some exceptions, a monitoring method within particular virtual machines is required.

Hyper-V has specific counters that let you know everything that is happening in the virtualization stack, virtual machines, and host resources. Some counters also have instances that can be triggered to monitor something more specific. For example, when using the **LogicalDisk** counter, you can select which disk (instance) you want to add.

Due to the high number of counters, the following list shows only a small selection of Hyper-V counters based on the subsystem that will be monitored. They can be used in conjunction to monitor parent and child partitions too.

Hyper-V general:

- ▶ \Hyper-V Hypervisor*
- ▶ \Hyper-V Virtual Machine Health Summary *
- ▶ Hyper-V VM Save, Snapshot, and Restore*

Physical and virtual processor:

- ▶ \Processor(_Total)*
- ▶ \Hyper-V Hypervisor Logical Processor(*)*
- ▶ \Hyper-V Hypervisor Root Virtual Processor (*) \ *
- ▶ \Hyper-V Hypervisor Virtual Processor (*) \ *
- ▶ \SynchronizationNuma(*)*
- ▶ \NUMA Node Memory(*)*
- ▶ \Hyper-V VM Vid Numa Node(*)*

Memory:

- ▶ \Hyper-V Hypervisor Partition(*)*
- ▶ \Hyper-V Hypervisor Root Partition(*)*
- ▶ \Hyper-V Dynamic Memory Balancer(*)*
- ▶ \Hyper-V Dynamic Memory Integration Services(*)*
- ▶ \Hyper-V Dynamic Memory VM(*)*
- ▶ \Hyper-V VM Vid Partition(*)*
- ▶ \Memory\Pages / Sec
- ▶ \Memory\Available Bytes

Disk:

- \Hyper-V Virtual IDE Controller (Emulated)(*)*
- \Hyper-V Virtual Machine Bus*
- \Hyper-V Virtual Storage Device(*)*
- \Physical Disk(*)\Current Disk Queue Length
- \Physical Disk(*)\Disk Bytes / sec
- \Physical Disk(*)\Disk Transfers/sec
- \Logical Disk(*)\Avg. Disk sec/Read
- \Logical Disk(*)\Avg. Disk sec/Write

Network:

- \Network Interface(*)*
- \Hyper-V Virtual Network Adapter(*)*
- \Hyper-V Virtual Switch(*)*
- \Hyper-V Virtual Switch Processor(*)*
- \Hyper-V Virtual Switch Port(*)*
- \IPv4*
- \Hyper-V Legacy Network Adapter(*)*
- \Per Processor Network Activity Cycles(*)*
- \Per Processor Network Interface Card Activity(*)*
- \TCPv4*

There is no standard for creating a baseline. Each environment is different from the other. You will need to identify which resources need to be monitored and then create your monitoring plan. The number of counters being monitored and the duration are also very important. If you have a data collector set with lots of counters that uses a small interval of time, you might have performance, storage, and network issues. Make sure the interval used is larger for longer monitoring windows. For instance, to monitor a server for just one day, you can use a 10-minute interval, and for one week of monitoring, a 1-hour interval.

 In case you don't have a plan and just want to run a baseline to track and analyze your system growth, you can create four baselines by using the counters from the previous lists: processor, memory, disk, and network.

Remember that these counters are just the normal ones for each subsystem, but you have many more options that can be used for advanced monitoring scenarios.

Now, with logged monitoring in place, you can analyze, investigate, and evaluate your existing environment, finding the normal baseline and using it to track any anomaly easily. The baseline results will also help you to identify when a tuning or an upgrade is necessary.

See also

▶ The *Using real-time monitoring tools* recipe in this chapter

Using VM Monitoring

System monitoring is the process of determining and finding problems in any of your servers, either physical or virtual.

VM Monitoring is a great assistant for virtual machine monitoring in clustered environments and helps to detect whether a virtual machine is running in a critical state. It will allow you to check the health of the VM service at the host level, identifying issues using events and status messages. VM Monitoring also enables the host to start a task to solve the problem in a proactive way, with no user interaction. In other words, it will check whether something is wrong, and if necessary, it will try to fix the problem automatically.

This recipe will show you how to prepare the virtual machine and the Management OS to use VM Monitoring.

Getting ready

There are some prerequisites that you need to note before you start. The first thing is that VM Monitoring is only available on virtual machines running on a cluster. All the host computer configurations are done through the **Failover Cluster Manager** console.

The virtual machine must be part of the same domain as the Management OS, and the user used to administer Failover Clustering must be a member of the local administrators group in the VM.

Last but not least, VM Monitoring is only available on virtual machines that run Windows Server 2012.

How to do it...

The following steps will demonstrate how to prepare the virtual machine to be monitored by VM Monitoring, how to enable it from the host so as to monitor a service, how to monitor Event Viewer entries within the VM, and how to check the VM Monitoring results:

1. To configure the VM to be monitored using VM Monitoring, open the **Failover Cluster Manager** console from one of the cluster nodes (or a machine that has Failover Cluster Manager installed) by typing `cluadmin.msc` on the Start menu.

2. In the **Failover Cluster Manager** window, expand your cluster, click on **Roles**, select the virtual machine that you want to prepare for use with VM Monitoring, and click on **Connect** in the right-hand pane.

3. Make sure the VM is started, and log in using a local administrator account.

4. To create a Windows Firewall exception, launch the Start menu and type `firewall`. In the right-hand pane, click on **Settings** and select **Windows Firewall**.

5. On the left-hand pane, click on **Allow an app or feature through Windows Firewall**.

6. In the **Windows Firewall** window, click on **Change settings**.

7. Under **Allowed apps and features**, select **Virtual Machine Monitoring** and select the networks you are connected with, as shown in the following screenshot:

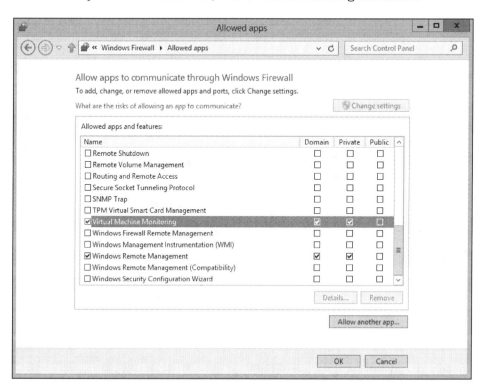

You can also configure the VM Monitoring firewall exception using the following command:

```
Set-NetFirewallRule -DisplayGroup "Virtual Machine
Monitoring" -Enabled True
```

8. To configure the recovery service action on the service that will be monitored, launch the Start menu and type `services.msc` to open the **Services** console.

9. In the **Services** console, in the service list, double-click on the service you want to monitor and click on the **Recovery** tab.

10. Select the actions for **First failure**, **Second failure**, and **Subsequent failures**, as shown in the following screenshot.

11. When finished, close all windows and virtual machine connections.

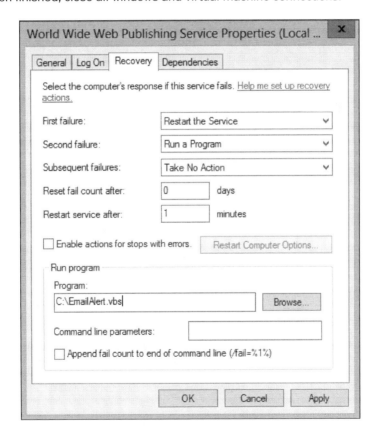

12. To configure VM Monitoring to monitor a service, from the Management OS, open the **Failover Cluster Manager** console again, right-click on the virtual machine you configured to enable VM Monitoring, select **More Actions**, and click on **Configure Monitoring**.

13. In the **Select Services** window, select the service you want to monitor and click on **OK**, as shown in the following screenshot:

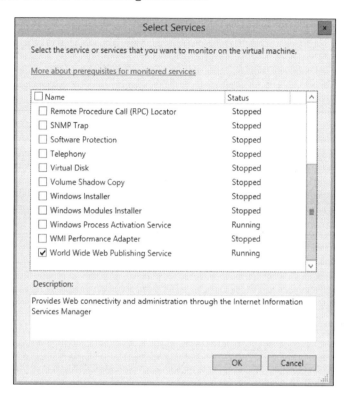

14. If you want to add a service that is not in the service list, type the following command from one of the failover cluster nodes, changing SYD-SP1 to the virtual machine name and MyApplication to the service name you want to add:

```
Add-ClusterVMMonitoredItem –VirtualMachine SYD-SP1 –Service
MyApplication
```

15. To configure VM Monitoring to monitor an event from Event Viewer, open the virtual machine connection again.

16. From the VM, open Server Manager.

17. In the **Server Manager** window, click on **Manage** in the right-hand pane and click on **Add Roles and Features**.

18. In the **Add Roles and Features Wizard** window, click on **Next** four times.

19. In the **Select features** section, expand **Remote Server Administration Tools | Feature Administration Tools | Failover Clustering Tools**, and select **Failover Cluster Modules for Windows PowerShell**, as shown in the following screenshot. Click on **Next** and then **Finish** to start the installation.

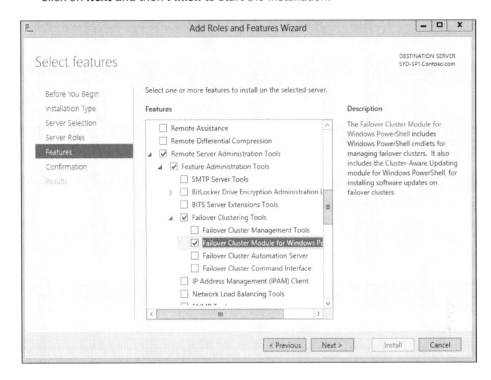

20. On the VM, open PowerShell and type the following command by replacing `Application` with the event log you want to monitor, `MyApplication` with the event source you will use, and `123` with the event ID VM Monitoring will monitor:

    ```
    Add-ClusterVMMonitoredItem -EventLog "Application" -EventSource
    "MyApplication" -EventID 123
    ```

21. To change the default action triggered on the host computer when one of these monitoring resources is alerted, open Failover Cluster Manager, select the virtual machine in **Roles**, and click on the **Resources** tab at the bottom.

22. In the **Resources** tab, right-click on the virtual machine and click on **Properties**.

23. In the properties window for the virtual machine, select the **Policies** tab and configure the response to resource failure options. The default configuration, which is shown in the following screenshot, will attempt to restart the virtual machine if one of the configured VM Monitoring is triggered. If the restart is unsuccessful, the VM will fail over to another node in the cluster.

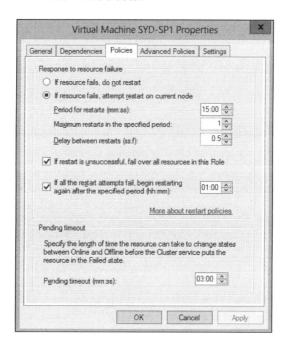

24. To check the virtual machine monitoring status, select the virtual machine in **Failover Cluster Manager** and check the **Status** details.

25. If the virtual machine has triggered one of the monitored options, a status showing **Running (Application in VM Critical)** will be displayed, as shown in the following screenshot:

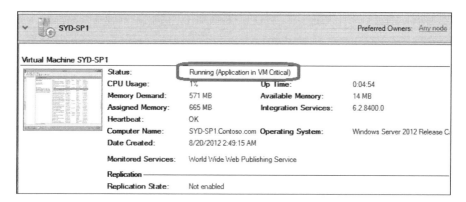

26. To check the status on all virtual machines using PowerShell, type the following command from one of the nodes that is a member of the cluster:

```
Get-ClusterResource | fl StatusInformation
```

27. To check the virtual machine status using Event Viewer, open Event Viewer in one of the failover cluster nodes.

28. In the **Event Viewer** window, expand **Windows Logs** and click on **System**. Click on **Event ID** to list events by ID, and double-click on the event with the ID **1250**; you will see the following screen:

How it works...

VM Monitoring can be enabled on every virtual machine with Windows Server 2012 running in a cluster, to monitor services and events from the host computer without the need to connect to the VM to check its status.

VM Monitoring requires that the virtual machine be in the same domain as the host computer. It also needs the failover cluster administrator that is used to set VM Monitoring to be a member of the local administrator group within the VM.

After these prerequisites, a firewall exception to allow VM Monitoring must be created to allow the **Management OS** to connect to the VM.

When monitoring a service, you can specify what will happen within the VM in case of service failure, by using the **Recovery** tab from the Services console. It allows three actions in a different order to be configured and can be used to automatically carry out an action, such as sending an e-mail or running a script to solve the problem.

Using Failover Cluster Manager, you can enable VM Monitoring by selecting which services you want to monitor. In case the service is not listed, the command `Add-ClusterVMMonitoredItem` can be used from the host computer, to add it to the list.

Although it is not available using the graphical interface, Event Viewer logs can also be monitored on your VMs, using PowerShell. The necessary commands used to enable Event Viewer monitoring are part of the Failover Clustering module and need to be installed within the VM.

From the node members of the cluster where the VMs sit, you can use the status information from Failover Cluster Manager or use Event Viewer, searching for the event ID 1250 on the system log, to check whether one of the monitored items was triggered.

When a problem is found by the cluster, the VM is restarted by default, and in case of failures, a failover process occurs. These failure actions can be changed through the virtual machine properties. Rather than carrying out an action, you can create an Event Viewer task to send an alert to the IT team with the status information, for example.

Although VM Monitoring is very handy, it is not enough. It is important to think about other monitoring tools that can give more details and alerts from your whole infrastructure, with reports and advanced features. A good example is **System Center Operations Manager**, a server where you can centralize all monitoring data, which can include servers, applications, network devices, desktops, and many other components from different brands and providers.

Monitoring Hyper-V Replica

Hyper-V Replica is one of the best features of Hyper-V so far. It is easy to set up, reliable, and comes with everything you need to have a great disaster recovery plan for your private cloud.

In case of a disaster, your servers or even the entire datacenter will be protected if Hyper-V Replica is in place. However, you need to ensure all your replica servers, virtual machines, logs, performance, and replication are working properly to certify that your servers will be up and running with the latest replication data in case of a failure.

This recipe will show you all the components on Window Server 2012 to provide the information, status, and reports you need to monitor Hyper-V Replica health.

Getting ready

These steps are based on an existing Hyper-V Replica environment. Perform the following steps on the primary Hyper-V server.

How to do it...

This recipe will show five options to monitor Hyper-V Replica: the Replication Health column, the Replication tab, the Replication Health window, Event Viewer, and Hyper-V Replica counters for Perfmon.

1. To enable the **Replication Health** column, open Hyper-V Manager, click on **View**, and select **Add/Remove Columns**.

2. In the **Add/Remove Columns** window, under **Available Columns**, select **Replication Health**, click on **Add**, and then click on **OK**. The column will be listed as shown in the following screenshot:

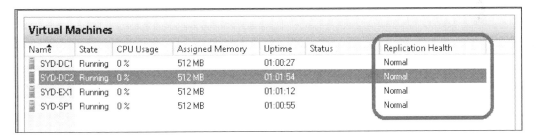

3. To visualize the **Replication** tab, select a virtual machine in Hyper-V Manager and click on **Replication** at the bottom, as shown in the following screenshot:

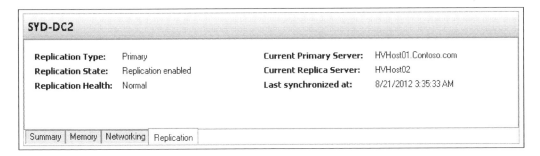

4. To view the replication health details, right-click on a virtual machine, select **Replication**, and click on **View Replication Health**. The VM's replication health will be shown as in the following screenshot:

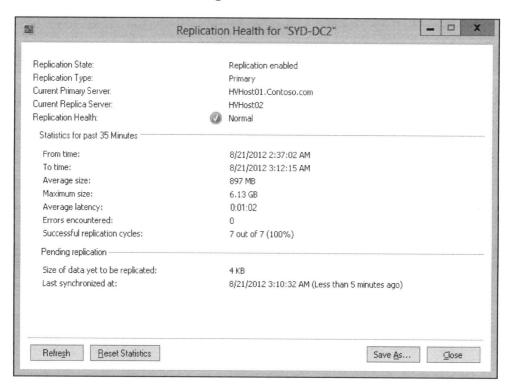

5. To verify the Event Viewer entries for Hyper-V Replica, open Event Viewer, expand **Application and Services Logs | Microsoft | Windows | Hyper-V-VMMS**, and click on **Admin**, as shown in the following screenshot:

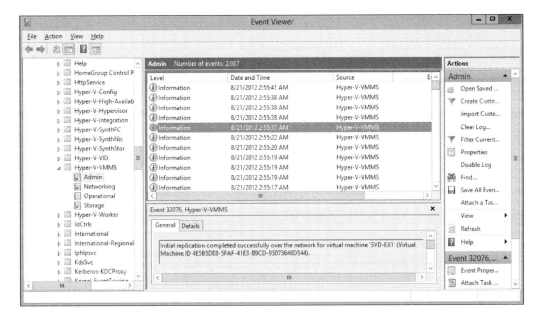

6. To monitor Hyper-V Replica counters, open Perfmon, expand **Monitoring Tools**, and click on **Performance Monitor**.

7. In the **Performance Monitor** view, press the *Ctrl + N* keys.

8. In the **Add Counters** window, scroll down and select **Hyper-V Replica VM**.

9. To monitor all virtual machines, click on **Add >>**, as shown in the following screenshot:

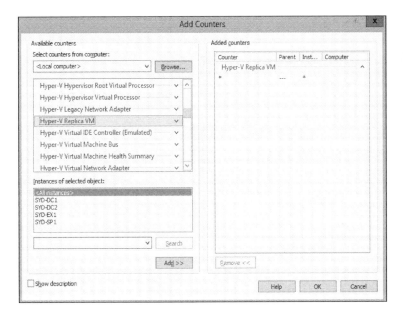

How it works...

Windows Server 2012 comes with different methods to monitor Hyper-V Replica, giving you all the necessary information you need to check its health.

The first and simplest one is the column **Replication Health** in Hyper-V Manager. This is the quickest and easiest view you can use to check if there is any problem with VM replication. Though it does not provide advanced details, it helps to quickly identify whether something is wrong.

Another easy way to check the replica status, but with more details, is the **Replication** tab, accessed from Hyper-V Manager as well. It shows the following information:

- ▶ **Replication Type**
- ▶ **Replication State**
- ▶ **Replication Health**
- ▶ **Current Primary Server**
- ▶ **Current Replica Server**
- ▶ **Last synchronized at**

To get a better replication health overview for Hyper-V, you can use the **Replication Health** window. It works like a small report that can be exported into a CSV file, showing replication details, statistics, and pending replication.

For advanced logs and data, an Event Viewer log named **Admin** under **Hyper-V-VMMS** shows all event entries for Hyper-V Replica. It is very helpful for advanced Hyper-V Replica troubleshooting.

The last one, for real-time and logged monitoring, is the group of counters in Perfmon to monitor everything about Hyper-V Replica and help you to identify performance errors, create baselines, and get advanced replication details when replication occurs.

From simple views to advanced logs and counters, Windows helps you to achieve all required info to make sure Hyper-V Replica is up and running.

There's more...

Using PowerShell to monitor Hyper-V Replica

You can also use simple commandlets from PowerShell to get replication details. The two available commands to check this data are `Get-VMReplication` and `Measure-VMReplication`. The following screenshot shows the output for both commands:

```
                      Administrator: Windows PowerShell

PS C:\Users\administrator.CONTOSO> Get-VMReplication

Name     State       Health Mode    PrimaryServer ReplicaServer ReplicaPort AuthType
----     -----       ------ ----    ------------- ------------- ----------- --------
SYD-DC1  Replicating Normal Primary HVHost01      HVHost02      80          Kerberos
SYD-DC2  Replicating Normal Primary HVHost01      HVHost02      80          Kerberos
SYD-EX1  Replicating Normal Primary HVHost01      HVHost02      80          Kerberos
SYD-SP1  Replicating Normal Primary HVHost01      HVHost02      80          Kerberos


PS C:\Users\administrator.CONTOSO> Measure-VMReplication

Name     State       Health LReplTime              PReplSize(M) AvgLatency AvgReplSize(M) SuccReplCount
----     -----       ------ ---------              ------------ ---------- -------------- -------------
SYD-DC1  Replicating Normal 8/21/2012 3:50:10 AM   0.0039       00:01:19   479.79         13 of 13
SYD-DC2  Replicating Normal 8/21/2012 3:50:33 AM   0.0039       00:00:29   418.97         15 of 15
SYD-EX1  Replicating Normal 8/21/2012 3:50:39 AM   0.0039       00:01:21   500.49         13 of 13
SYD-SP1  Replicating Normal 8/21/2012 3:50:21 AM   0.0039       00:01:19   482.52         13 of 13
```

See also

▸ The *Configuring Hyper-V Replica between two Hyper-V hosts using HTTP authentication* recipe in *Chapter 8, Disaster Recovery for Hyper-V*

Using Resource Metering

In private cloud environments, you might have different scenarios for each department, location, business unit, or even client, in the case of service providers. One of the benefits a cloud can offer is the ability to measure and bill your clients based on the current consumption of services. Tracking utilization for these resources can be difficult and complex, requiring proper applications and systems.

Hyper-V makes that simple with **Resource Metering**. This allows you to track and measure the current usage for virtual machines and resources pools, helping the IT department to bill clients based on the usage of cloud resources.

These are some examples of metrics that can be collected with Resource Metering:

▸ Average, minimum, and maximum VM memory usage

▸ Average VM processor usage

▸ Total VM disk allocation

▸ Network traffic reports (incoming and outgoing)

▸ Resource pool measurement for all types of resources within a pool

With Resource Metering, companies can implement advanced billing strategies, creating a cost-effective way to track resource utilization, based on virtual machines and resource pools.

You will see in this recipe how Resource Metering can be enabled for virtual machines and resource pools and how to extract its results.

Getting ready

Although it is not configured by default, Resource Metering can be enabled on every virtual machine in Windows Server 2012, using PowerShell. Make sure you have a PowerShell console opened as administrator before you begin.

How to do it...

The following steps will walk you through the Resource Metering PowerShell commandlets.

1. To enable Resource Metering for all virtual machines in a host, type the following command:

   ```
   Enable-VMResourceMetering –VMName *
   ```

2. If you want to enable it for a particular virtual machine, type the following command, replacing SYD-EX1 with the virtual machine name:

   ```
   Enable-VMResourceMetering –VMName SYD-EX1
   ```

3. To extract the measurement details for a virtual machine, use the command Measure-VM, as shown in the following screenshot:

```
PS C:\Users\administrator.CONTOSO> Measure-VM -VMName SYD-SP1

VMName   AvgCPU(MHz) AvgRAM(M) MaxRAM(M) MinRAM(M) TotalDisk(M) NetworkInbound(M) NetworkOutbound(M)
------   ----------- --------- --------- --------- ------------ ----------------- ------------------
SYD-SP1  165         814       968       512       130048       1698              14
```

4. To see more Resource Metering details for a virtual machine, use the command shown in the following screenshot:

```
PS C:\Users\administrator.CONTOSO> Measure-VM -VMName SYD-SP1 | Format-List

ComputerName              : HVHOST01
VMId                      : e9dbb93e-ea72-45b7-ac5d-a3574815f37e
VMName                    : SYD-SP1
MeteringDuration          : 00:12:35.1410000
AverageProcessorUsage     : 163
AverageMemoryUsage        : 818
MaximumMemoryUsage        : 968
MinimumMemoryUsage        : 512
TotalDiskAllocation       : 130048
NetworkMeteredTrafficReport : {Microsoft.HyperV.PowerShell.VMNetworkAdapterPortAclMeteringReport,
                            Microsoft.HyperV.PowerShell.VMNetworkAdapterPortAclMeteringReport,
                            Microsoft.HyperV.PowerShell.VMNetworkAdapterPortAclMeteringReport,
                            Microsoft.HyperV.PowerShell.VMNetworkAdapterPortAclMeteringReport}
AvgCPU                    : 163
AvgRAM                    : 818
MinRAM                    : 512
MaxRAM                    : 968
TotalDisk                 : 130048
```

5. To verify which virtual machine has Resource Metering enabled, type this command:

```
Get-VM * | Format-List Name,ResourceMeteringEnabled
```

6. For more details about inbound and outbound network utilization traffic, type the command shown in the following screenshot:

```
PS C:\Users\administrator.CONTOSO> (Measure-Vm -VMName SYD-SP1).NetworkMeteredTrafficReport

LocalAddress RemoteAddress Direction TotalTraffic(M)
------------ ------------- --------- ---------------
             0.0.0.0/0     Outbound  32
             0.0.0.0/0     Inbound   4202
             ::/0          Outbound  1
             ::/0          Inbound   1
```

7. To enable Resource Metering for a resource pool, type the following command to change the resource pool name to `Primordial` and the resource pool type to `Memory`:

```
Enable-VMResourceMetering –ResourcePoolName Primordial
–ResourcePoolType Memory
```

8. To measure the resource pool data, use the command `Measure-VMResourcePool`, as shown in the following screenshot.

```
PS C:\Users\administrator.CONTOSO> Measure-VMResourcePool -Name Primordial -ResourcePoolType Memory

Name       ResourcePoolType AvgCPU(MHz) AvgRAM(M) TotalDisk(M) NetworkInbound(M) NetworkOutbound(M)
----       ---------------- ----------- --------- ------------ ----------------- ------------------
Primordial {Memory}                     2405                   0                 0
```

9. Use the commandlet `Reset-VMResourceMetering` to reset the resource utilization data collected by Resource Metering. The following command shows how to reset the data for a virtual machine called `SYD-SP1`:

```
Reset-VMResourceMetering –VMName SYD-SP1
```

10. To disable Resource Metering, use the command `Disable-VMResourceMetering`. The following command shows how to disable Resource Metering for a virtual machine called `SYD-SP1`:

```
Disable-VMResourceMetering –VMName SYD-SP1
```

How it works...

Although there is no graphical interface to configure it, Resource Metering is quite easy to manage using PowerShell. The commands let you enable, measure, reset, and disable the counters for virtual machines and resource pools. It is also easy to create reports with measurement outputs, by using the output values to create advanced methods to charge your clients based on utilization of resources.

The four resources that can be monitored on a VM are processor (in megahertz) and memory, network, and disk (in megabytes).

The results can be collected and reset at any time, helping you to measure the virtual machine or resource pool usage based on your company's needs.

Now, with resource utilization details, you can create your billing system or simply track the resource information from your virtual machines and resource pools.

Tuning your Hyper-V server

To help refine Hyper-V servers, you can think of what can be changed to improve their performance, security, and administration. The problem is that most people do it only when something is wrong.

You can save resources and improve performance by fine-tuning changes and by configuration that can be done before implementation or even in running servers.

This recipe is a little bit different from the others. Rather than tasks, it will provide you with tips and best practices from previous recipes, listing the principal features and configuration options that can help with server tuning.

Getting ready

Most of the listed information was already described in other chapters and recipes.
Have a look at the *See also* section (at the end of this recipe) for links and references.

How to do it...

The following best practices help improve your Hyper-V server performance:

▶ **Use Server Core wherever possible**: The lower hardware consumption and number of updates and resources involved will enable higher performance and security for Hyper-V servers.

▶ **Use dedicated servers for Hyper-V**: In other words, don't combine different roles in just one server. Other roles can share and steal important resources from Hyper-V and vice versa.

▶ **Use only supported virtual machines**: Due to integration services, the virtual machine OS and version will have a huge impact when no supported VMs are running in production.

▶ **Use Dynamic Memory for virtual machines**: The process of lending memory from low workload VMs to other VMs in need is carried out automatically It can use the necessary memory, based on the VM necessity.

▶ **Use the new VHDX format instead of VHD**: The new format has a 64-TB limit, 32 times larger than the old one, but that is not the only new enhancement. Other improvements include native 4K disk alignment, for better performance, larger block sizes, and security enhancements. There is no reason to use VHD in a Windows Server 2012 environment anymore.

▶ **Enable SR-IOV and Network Teaming**: Do this for large virtual machine network workloads and get better performance, bypassing the virtual switch (SR-IOV) and segregating more than one network to create a teaming (Network Teaming).

▶ **Attach Virtual Fibre Channel adapters**: This allows virtual machines to access your LUNs directly, providing improved performance and enabling guest clustering scenarios even more easily.

▶ **Use data deduplication in VHDs libraries**: This saves disk space. The amount of disk space you can save can reach up to 85 percent.

▶ **Use SMB 3.0 to store VMs on shared folders**. The new protocol, used most commonly to access files on the network, can now host virtual machines on a shared folder. It is a perfect option for small business that can create a cluster using a shared folder as storage, running low workload on virtual machines in there.

▶ **Create and use Storage Pools**: They can add disks logically, creating high availability pools with a great performance for virtual machine disks, such as RAID 5 and RAID 1+0.

▶ **Use PowerShell**: Almost every recipe in this book has examples of commandlets that can save your time administering Hyper-V. With the new version, PowerShell is even easier to adopt.

▶ **Create a separate disk for page files**: When configuring Hyper-V Replica, create a separate disk for the page file within the VMs, and exclude it from being replicated. The page file causes lots of replication requests, and it can save a huge amount of performance and network utilization for replica servers.

How it works...

As you can see, simple configurations can be added or changed, and the results will surprise you. You can improve disk, memory, security, processor, administration, and much more on Hyper-V using the built-in tools and features, without the need for third-party products.

This is the list summary used in the recipe:

▶ Server Core

▶ Dedicated Hyper-V servers

▶ Supported virtual machines

▶ Dynamic Memory

▶ VHDX

- SR-IOV
- NIC Teaming
- Virtual Fibre Channel adapters
- Data deduplication
- SMB 3.0
- Storage Pools
- PowerShell

These features are used based on the workload and necessary performance needed on virtual machines and host computers. The use of all of them for every server is not recommended, so you need to analyze which one is the perfect match for your current environment. Some examples, such as Server Core and dedicated Hyper-V servers, are best practices and absolute musts for every host server with Hyper-V installed, due to the performance and security they can offer; some other options, such as data deduplication and Virtual Fibre Channel, should only be used in particular scenarios.

Dynamic Memory and VHDX can help with performance, and they can also be used without any limitation, on every virtual machine.

SR-IOV, NIC Teaming, and Virtual Fibre Channel are great (the best in the matter of performance) but can be expensive in some scenarios. For that reason, SR-IOV should be used only for virtual machines that require a large network I/O, whereas for network adapter high availability, use either Virtual Fibre Channel adapters or NIC Teaming.

Other simple things on Windows Server 2012 that can help are:

- Data deduplication, to save disk space
- SMB 3.0, for small and medium size companies, allowing them to have high availability virtual machines using two Hyper-V servers and a single shared folder
- Storage Pools, to aggregate disks logically to create pools

Last but not least is PowerShell. It is the most powerful management tool that administrators can use to save time and effort while managing virtual environments.

Combining all these features based on the scenarios you have will guarantee your servers have the best configuration and practices for Hyper-V tuning.

See also

- The *Enabling and disabling the graphical interface in Hyper-V* recipe in *Chapter 1, Installing and Managing Hyper-V in Full or Server Core Mode*
- The *Creating and adding virtual hard disks* recipe in *Chapter 3, Managing Disk and Network Settings*
- The *Using advanced settings for virtual networks* recipe in *Chapter 3, Managing Disk and Network Settings*

▶ The *Enabling and adding NIC Teaming to a virtual machine* recipe in *Chapter 3, Managing Disk and Network Settings*

▶ The *Configuring and adding Hyper-V Virtual Fibre Channel to virtual machines* recipe in *Chapter 3, Managing Disk and Network Settings*

▶ The *Learning and utilizing basic commands in PowerShell* recipe in *Chapter 4, Saving Time and Cost with Hyper-V Automation*

▶ The *Using small PowerShell commands for daily tasks* recipe in *Chapter 4, Saving Time and Cost with Hyper-V Automation*

▶ The *Setting up dynamic memory for virtual machines* recipe in *Chapter 5, Hyper-V Best Practices, Tips, and Tricks*

▶ Read about supported Hyper-V guest operating systems at `http://technet. microsoft.com/library/hh831531`

▶ Read about data deduplication at `http://technet.microsoft.com/en-us/ library/hh831602.aspx`

▶ Read about Storage Spaces at `http://technet.microsoft.com/en-us/ library/jj713504.aspx`

▶ For more information about SMB 3.0, see the article at `http://support. microsoft.com/kb/2709568`

Using Event Viewer for Hyper-V troubleshooting

The time may come when you face a Hyper-V issue that needs to be repaired. You will have to be prepared on how to troubleshoot any issue on Hyper-V when that happens, and the best way to start is using **Event Viewer** in Windows.

Almost all events on Hyper-V are logged in Event Viewer, however they are divided between different event logs. You need to be able to know how to obtain more details about an error and where to look in case of a Hyper-V problem.

This recipe will show how you can find the Hyper-V Event Viewer entries and what information each of them has.

Getting ready

Make sure you are using an administrative user account to view the Event Viewer details. You can use the dedicated local group named **Event Log Readers** to add users who need permissions only to see event logs.

How to do it...

The following steps will show how to locate the Hyper-V event logs, how to check all the events in just one view, and how to see the event cluster entries through Failover Cluster Manager:

1. To see the specific Hyper-V event logs, launch the Start menu and type `eventvwr`. From the search results, open **Event Viewer**.

2. In the **Event Viewer** console, expand **Application and Service Logs | Microsoft | Windows**.

3. Scroll down till you find the Hyper-V log folders, as shown in the following screenshot:

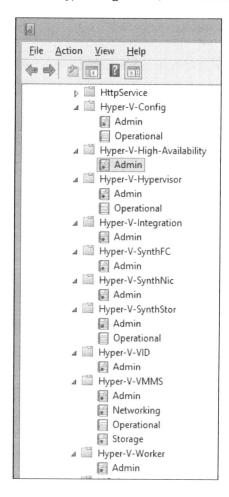

4. To use the default Event Viewer filter that shows all Hyper-V logs in a single view, in the **Event Viewer** console, click on **Custom Views**, expand **Server Roles** and click on **Hyper-V**, as show in the following screenshot:

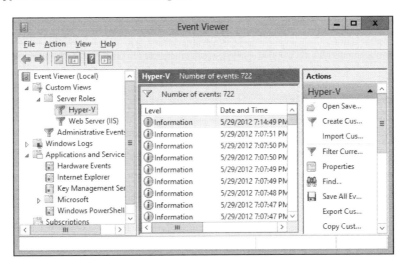

5. To check the cluster events, type `cluadmin.msc` in one of the nodes and open the **Failover Cluster Manager** console.

6. In the **Failover Cluster Manager** console, click on **Cluster Events**, as shown in the following screenshot:

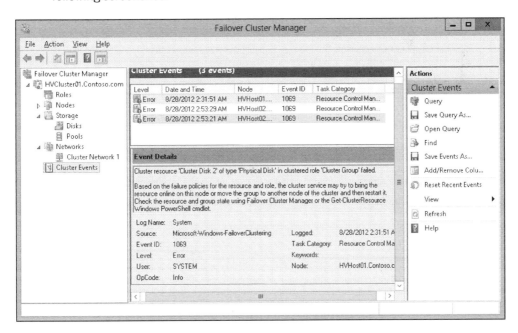

How it works...

When Hyper-V is installed on a host computer, event logs are created during the installation to show all the details about the different Hyper-V configurations. The **Hyper-V-High-Availability** log is also created when the Hyper-V host is member of a cluster.

The logs show admin, operational, networking, and storage details. The following list shows the description of the log entries:

- **Hyper-V-Config**: Contains all the information related to the virtual machine configuration files

- **Hyper-V-High-Availability**: Available in Hyper-V Cluster nodes and shows the Hyper-V entries regarding Failover Clustering

- **Hyper-V-Hypervisor**: Used to log information about hypervisor activities

- **Hyper-V-Integration**: Shows events about integration services

- **Hyper-V-SynthFC**: Related to Virtual Fibre Channel details

- **Hyper-V-SynthNic**: Information about virtual switches

- **Hyper-V-SynthStor**: Details about virtual hard disks

- **Hyper-V-VID**: Shows logs about the virtual interface driver

- **Hyper-V-VMMS**: Dedicated to logs containing information about the Virtual Machine Management service

There is a custom view that could be handy if you want to see all Hyper-V events in just one single view. It can be used to export and save all Event Viewer logs or as a filter to easily find a specific event.

The event entries have different levels, such as information, warnings, and errors. Every entry has details such as ID, time, source, user and computer, which can be used in filters or to get more online information.

Event Viewer should also be used as part of prevention or security health checks to analyze any problem that may occur with no apparent symptom. An administrator must monitor event viewer data constantly to make sure the server and Hyper-V are not expecting any issues.

See also

- The *Exporting and importing virtual machines* recipe in *Chapter 2, Migrating and Upgrading Physical and Virtual Servers*

- The *Backing up Hyper-V and virtual machines using Windows Server Backup* recipe in *Chapter 8, Disaster Recovery for Hyper-V*

- The *Restoring Hyper-V and virtual machines using Windows Server Backup* recipe in *Chapter 8, Disaster Recovery for Hyper-V*

Hyper-V Architecture and Components

Virtualization is not a new feature or technology that everyone decided to have in their environment overnight. Actually, it's quite old. There are a couple of computers in the mid 60s that were using virtualization already, such as the **IBM M44/44X**, where you could run multiple virtual machines using hardware and software abstraction. It is known as the first virtualization system and the creation of the term **virtual machine**.

Although Hyper-V is in its third version, Microsoft virtualization technology is very mature. Everything started in 1988 with a company named **Connectix**. It had innovative products such as **Connectix Virtual PC** and **Virtual Server**, an x86 software emulation for Mac, Windows, and OS/2.

In 2003, Microsoft acquired Connectix and a year later released **Microsoft Virtual PC** and **Microsoft Virtual Server 2005**. After lots of improvements in the architecture during the project Viridian, Microsoft released Hyper-V in 2008, the second version in 2009 (Windows Server 2008 R2) and the current version in 2012.

In the past years, Microsoft has proven that Hyper-V is a strong and competitive solution for server virtualization and provides scalability, flexible infrastructure, high availability, and resiliency. To better understand the different virtualization models, and how the virtual machines are created and managed by Hyper-V, it is very important to know its core, architecture, and components. By doing so, you will understand how it works, you can compare with other solutions, and troubleshoot problems easily.

This appendix includes well-explained topics with the most important Hyper-V architecture components compared with other versions.

Understanding Hypervisors

The **Virtual Machine Manager** (**VMM**), also known as **Hypervisor**, is the software application responsible for running multiple virtual machines in a single system. It is also responsible for creation, preservation, division, system access, and virtual machine management running on the Hypervisor layer.

These are the types of Hypervisors:

 ▸ VMM Type 2
 ▸ VMM Hybrid

VMM Type 1VMM Type 2

This type runs Hypervisor on top of an operating system, as shown in the following diagram. **Microsoft Virtual PC** is an example of software that uses **VMM Type 2**.

Virtual machines pass hardware requests to the Hypervisor, host OS, and finally reaching the hardware. That leads to performance and management limitation imposed by the host OS.

It is common for test environments—virtual machines with hardware restrictions—to run on software applications that are installed in the host operating system.

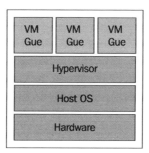

VMM Hybrid

When using the **VMM Hybrid** type, the Hypervisor runs on the same level as the operating system, as shown in the following diagram. As both Hypervisor and the OS are sharing the same access to the hardware with the same priority, it is not as fast and safe as it could be. This is the type used by the Hyper-V predecessor named **Microsoft Virtual Server 2005**.

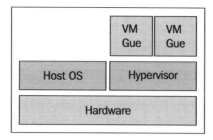

VMM Type 1

VMM Type 1 is a type that has the Hypervisor running in a tiny software layer between the hardware and the partitions, managing and orchestrating the hardware access. The host operating system, known as **Parent Partition**, runs on the same level as the **Child Partitions**, known as virtual machines, as shown in the next figure. Due to the privileged access that the Hypervisor has on the hardware, it provides more security, performance, and control over the partitions. This is the type used by Hyper-V since its first release.

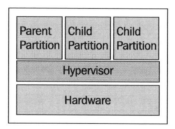

Hyper-V architecture

Knowing how Hyper-V works and how its architecture is constructed will make it easier to understand its concepts and operations. The following sections will explore the most important components in Hyper-V.

Windows before Hyper-V

Before we dive in the Hyper-V architecture details, it will be easy to understand what happens after Hyper-V is installed, by looking at Windows without Hyper-V, as shown in the following diagram:

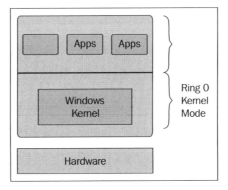

In a normal Windows installation, the instructions access is divided by four privileged levels in the processor called **Rings**. The most privileged level is **Ring 0**, with direct access to the hardware and where the Windows Kernel sits. **Ring 3** is responsible for hosting the user level, where most common applications run and with the least privileged access.

Windows after Hyper-V

When Hyper-V is installed, it needs a higher privilege than Ring 0. Also, it must have dedicated access to the hardware. This is possible due to the capabilities of the new processor created by Intel and AMD, called **Intel-VT** and **AMD-V** respectively, that allows the creation of a fifth ring called **Ring -1**. Hyper-V uses this ring to add its Hypervisor, having a higher privilege and running under Ring 0, controlling all the access to the physical components, as shown in the following diagram:

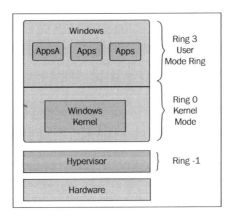

The OS architecture suffers several changes after Hyper-V installation. Right after the first boot, the **Operating System boot loader file** (`winload.exe`) checks the processor that is being used and loads the Hypervisor image on Ring -1 (using the files `Hvix64.exe` for Intel processors and `Hvax64.exe` for AMD processors). Then, Windows Server is initiated running on top of the Hypervisor and every virtual machine that runs beside it.

After Hyper-V installation, Windows Server has the same privilege level as a virtual machine and is responsible for managing VMs using several components.

Hyper-V architecture components

Hyper-V has many components that are responsible for providing an end-to-end management solution for virtual machines and the Management OS. The following diagram shows the most important components of Hyper-V, which will be explained in the later sections:

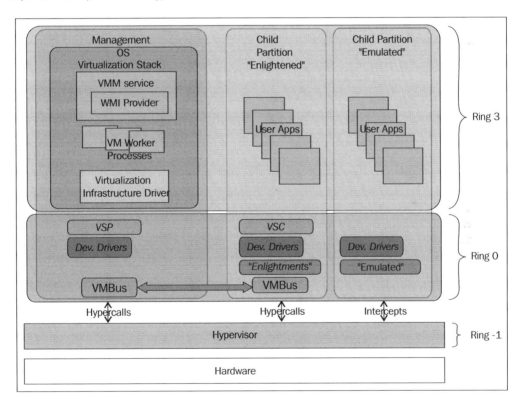

Hypervisor

The small Hyper-V Hypervisor (almost 20 MB) is responsible for managing, separating, and controlling all the partition access. Also, it is in charge of isolating all the partitions from each other with high security and reliability.

Partitions

When Hyper-V is present, the host operating system and the virtual machines run and share the same access and privilege to Hypervisor, and both are known as partitions. However, the host OS runs a series of components to manage the virtual machines and for that reason, the host partition is called **parent partition** or **management OS**, and virtual machines are called **child partitions** or **guests OS**.

Virtualization stack

The virtual machine creation and management is made by a series of virtual devices and software components called **virtualization stack**, which is executed in the parent partition. These series of components work in conjunction with the Hypervisor.

Virtualization Service Provider (**VSP**) is a software component that controls I/O requests on behalf of the virtual machines in the parent partition. **Virtual Machine Bus** (**VMBus**) is responsible for data transfer, service, and device delivery between Parent and Child partitions through a dedicated channel available between the **Virtualization Service Providers** (**VSPs**) and **Virtualization Service Clients** (**VSCs**). VSP uses VMBus to communicate with child partitions using VSCs to provide the synthetic drivers that run in the child partitions.

For every virtual machine that is started, a **Worker Process** is created in the parent partition. Worker process and **Virtual Machine Management Service** (**VMMS**) are user mode components that provide the ability for parent partition to create, start, stop, save, and delete virtual machines. All these tasks are coordinated by the **Virtual Infrastructure Driver** (**VID**), which manages the communication between parent and child partitions.

Enlightened versus emulated

The access between partitions and the Hypervisor is made by a special interface called **Hypercalls**. They guarantee that the virtual machines can have access to the hardware using components such as VID, VMBus, VSCs, and VSPs. These mechanisms are present during the **Integration Components** (**ICs**) installation. Some Windows and Linux operating systems have integration components packages already installed in their Kernel. Virtual machines that have these components are called **Enlightened VMs**. For old or non-supported operating systems, the parent partition intercepts the virtual machine communication, emulating the Hypercalls. The result is poor performance and limitations to access the hardware, since the management OS needs to work as a bridge to allow the VM to access the hardware. That's why it is very important to ensure that all the virtual machines are running with the latest IC version.

Differences between Hyper-V, Hyper-V Server, Hyper-V Client, and VMware

There are three different versions of Hyper-V—the role that is installed on Windows Server 2012, its free version called Hyper-V Server and the Hyper-V that comes in Windows 8 called Hyper-V Client. The following sections will explain the differences between all the versions and a comparison between Hyper-V and its competitor, VMware.

Hyper-V limitations improvements

Hyper-V has impressively improved since its first version. The new limits compared with the previous version sometimes are 16 times bigger. Quite impressive for a third release.

The following table shows the improvements based on Hyper-V of Windows Server 2008 R2:

Resource	Windows Server 2008 R2 Hyper-V	Windows Server 2012 Hyper-V
Logical Processors	64	320
Physical Memory	1TB	4TB
Virtual CPUs per Host	512	2048
Virtual CPU per VM	4	64
VM Memory	64GB	1TB
Active VMs per Host	384	1024
Maximum Nodes	16	64
Maximum VMs per Cluster	1000	8000

Windows Server 2012 Hyper-V

Hyper-V is one of the most fascinating and improved role on Windows Server 2012. Its third version goes beyond virtualization and helps us deliver the correct infrastructure to host your cloud environment.

Windows Server 2012 can be installed as a role in both Windows Server **Standard** and **Datacenter** editions. The only difference is that in the Standard edition, two free Windows Server OSes are licensed whereas there are unlimited licenses in the Datacenter edition.

Microsoft Hyper-V Server 2012

Hyper-V Server 2012, the free virtualization solution from Microsoft, has all the features included on Windows Server 2012 Hyper-V.

The only difference is that Microsoft Hyper-V Server does not include virtual machine licenses and a graphical interface. The management can be done remotely using Hyper-V Manager from another Windows Server 2012 or Windows 8.

All the other Hyper-V features and limits, including Failover Cluster, Shared Nothing Live Migration, and Hyper-V Replica are included in the Hyper-V free version.

Hyper-V Client

One of the new features of Windows 8 is **Hyper-V Client**. Users can have the same experience from Windows Server 2012 Hyper-V on their desktops or tablet, making their test and development virtualized scenarios much easier.

Hyper-V client is present only in the Windows 8 Pro or Enterprise version and requires a CPU feature called **Second Level Address Translation** (**SLAT**).

Although Hyper-V client is very similar to the server version, there are some components that are only present on Windows Server 2012 Hyper-V, as shown in the following list:

- Hyper-V replica
- Remote FX capability to virtualize GPUs
- Live Migration and Shared Nothing Live Migration
- SR-IOV Networks
- Virtual Fibre Channel
- Network Virtualization
- Failover Clustering
- VM Monitoring

Even with these limitations, Hyper-V Client has very interesting features such as Storage Migration, VHDX, VMs running on SMB 3.0 File Shares, PowerShell integration, Hyper-V Manager, Hyper-V Extensible Switch, Quality of Services, the same VM hardware limits as Windows Server 2012 Hyper-V, Dynamic Memory, DHCP Guard, Port Mirroring, and much more.

Windows Server 2012 Hyper-V X VMware vSphere 5.1

VMware is the existing competitor of Hyper-V and the current version 5.1 offers the **VMware vSphere** as a free and a standalone Hypervisor, vSphere Standard, Enterprise, and Enterprise Plus.

The following list compares all the features existing in the free version of Hyper-V with VMware Sphere and Enterprise Plus:

Feature	Windows Server 2012 Hyper-V	VMware vSphere 5.1	VMware vSphere 5.1 Enterprise Plus
Logical Processors	320	160	160
Physical Memory	4TB	32GB	2TB
Virtual CPU per VM	64	8	64
VM Memory	1TB	32GB	1TB
Active VMs per Host	1024	512	512
Maximum Nodes	64	N/A	32
Maximum VMs per Cluster	8000	N/A	3000
Native 4-KB Disk Support	Yes	No	No
Maximum Virtual Disk Size	64TB	2TB	2TB
Maximum Pass Through Disk Size	256TB+	64TB	64TB
Extensible Network Switch	Yes	No	Third part vendors
Network Virtualization	Yes	No	Requires vCloud networking and security
IPSec Task Offload	Yes	No	No
SR-IOV with Live Migration	Yes	No	No
Guest OS Application Monitoring	Yes	No	No
Guest Clustering with Live Migration	Yes	N/A	No
Guest Clustering with Dynamic Memory	Yes	N/A	No

The following table lists a comparison of features between Windows Server 2008 R2, Windows Server 2012, and vSphere 5.0 Enterprise Plus:

Category	Resource		Microsoft		VMware
			Windows Server 2008 R2	Windows Server 2012	vSphere 5.0 Enterprise Plus
Scalability, performance, density	Virtual machine	Active virtual machines per host	384	1,024	512
		Memory per virtual machine	64 GB	1 terabyte	1 terabyte
		Virtual processors per virtual machine	4	64	32
	Cluster	Maximum nodes	16	64	32
		Maximum virtual machines	1,000	4,000	3,000
	Network	High performance with SR-IOV	No	Yes	No
Storage		Native 4 KB disk support	No	Yes	No
		Maximum virtual disk size	2 terabytes	64 terabytes	2 terabytes
		Encrypted cluster storage	No	Yes	No
Secure multitenancy		Open extensible switch	No	Yes	No
Flexible infrastructure		1 GB simultaneous live migrations	1	Unlimited	4
		10 GB simultaneous live migrations	1	Unlimited	8
		Shared-nothing live migration	No	Yes	No
		Network virtualization	No	Yes	Partner
High availability		Virtual machine replication	No	Yes	No
		Guest OS application monitoring	Yes	Yes	Partner
		Guest clustering with live migration	No	Yes	No

Hyper-V comparing technologies

To understand the Hyper-V technologies better, the following table that is created by the Hyper-V Program Manager Ben Armstrong illustrates in which scenarios the conflicting Hyper-V features can be used:

	Zero Downtime	Protects against hardware failure	Protects against site failure	Protects against data corruption	Automatic response to failure	Workgroup compatible
Live Migration	Happy	Sad	Sad	Sad	Sad	Sad
Storage Migration	Happy	Sad	Sad	Sad	Sad	Happy
Import / Export	Sad	Sad	Sad	Sad	Sad	Happy
Clustering	Neutral	Happy	Neutral	Sad	Happy	Sad
Hyper-V Replica	Sad	Happy	Happy	Neutral	Sad	Happy
Backup	Sad	Happy	Neutral	Happy	Sad	Happy

References

- ▶ Working with Virtualized Domain Controllers: `http://technet.microsoft.com/en-us/library/jj574191.aspx`

- ▶ Hyper-V Network Virtualization Overview: `http://technet.microsoft.com/en-us/library/jj134230.aspx`

- ▶ Free online courses on Microsoft: `http://www.microsoftvirtualacademy.com/Home.aspx`

- ▶ My blog with news, articles and updates about Hyper-V, System Center, and Private Cloud: `http://leandroesc.wordpress.com`

Index

O

on past updating runs option 138
Operating System boot loader file (winload. exe) 269

P

parent partition 11, 250, 270
partitions 11, 270
pass-through disk
  adding, to virtual machines 61
Perfmon
  using, for logged monitoring 236-242
Performance Monitor. *See* Perfmon
Physical and virtual processor 241
physical computers
  converting, to virtual machines 53-55
  converting to virtual machines, command line used 55
Physical to Virtual (P2V) conversion 55
Port ACLs 144
Port mirroring 79
post installation settings
  configuration, steps 24-28
PowerShell
  about 87, 212
  basic commands 95-98
  remote connection, enabling 105-108
  scripts, enabling for execution on 104
  used, for configuring Hyper-V Replica 212
  used for creating HTML reports, with BPA results 113, 114
  used, for creating multiple VMs in single command line 98
  used, for enabling Hyper-V Replica 212
  used, for managing dynamic memory for virtual machines 119
  used, for setting VM Priority 186
  using, to manage CAU 138
PowerShell commands
  about 51
  using, for daily tasks 99-103
PowerShell ISE
  used, for advanced script editing 103
PowerShell Remoting feature 105
Pre Upgrade Task 228

previewing updates 138
Preview Updates window 136
Primary Server 204, 209
Primary Server (HVHost01) 204
Private Switch 100

Q

Quality of Services (QoS) policy 73
Quick Migration 186

R

Read Only Domain Controllers (RODCs) 168
real-time monitoring tools
  about 230
  tabs, using on Hyper-V Manager 235
  using 230-234
  working 234, 235
Recovery Points 204
remote connection
  enabling 105-108
  working with 105-108
RemoteIPAddress syntax 147
RemoteMacAddress syntax 147
remote management
  enabling, for Hyper-V in workgroup environments 119-124
remote updating 138
Remove-VMSnapshot command 228
Rename-VMSnapshot command 228
Replica Server 204, 209
Replica Server (HVHost02) 204
Replication Health window 254
Reset-VMResourceMetering command 257
Resource Metering
  about 255
  using 256
  using, steps 256, 257
  working 257, 258
Resource Monitor 235
resource pools
  creating, steps for 65-69
Restore-VMSnapshot command 228
Ring 0 268
Ring 3 268
Ring -1 11, 268, 269
Rings 268

Thank you for buying
Windows Server 2012 Hyper-V Cookbook

About Packt Publishing

Packt, pronounced 'packed', published its first book "*Mastering phpMyAdmin for Effective MySQL Management*" in April 2004 and subsequently continued to specialize in publishing highly focused books on specific technologies and solutions.

Our books and publications share the experiences of your fellow IT professionals in adapting and customizing today's systems, applications, and frameworks. Our solution-based books give you the knowledge and power to customize the software and technologies you're using to get the job done. Packt books are more specific and less general than the IT books you have seen in the past. Our unique business model allows us to bring you more focused information, giving you more of what you need to know, and less of what you don't.

Packt is a modern, yet unique publishing company, which focuses on producing quality, cutting-edge books for communities of developers, administrators, and newbies alike. For more information, please visit our website: www.PacktPub.com.

About Packt Enterprise

In 2010, Packt launched two new brands, Packt Enterprise and Packt Open Source, in order to continue its focus on specialization. This book is part of the Packt Enterprise brand, home to books published on enterprise software – software created by major vendors, including (but not limited to) IBM, Microsoft and Oracle, often for use in other corporations. Its titles will offer information relevant to a range of users of this software, including administrators, developers, architects, and end users.

Writing for Packt

We welcome all inquiries from people who are interested in authoring. Book proposals should be sent to author@packtpub.com. If your book idea is still at an early stage and you would like to discuss it first before writing a formal book proposal, contact us; one of our commissioning editors will get in touch with you.

We're not just looking for published authors; if you have strong technical skills but no writing experience, our experienced editors can help you develop a writing career, or simply get some additional reward for your expertise.

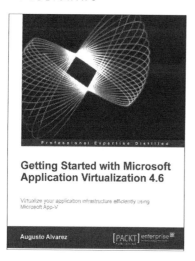

Getting Started with Microsoft Application Virtualization 4.6

ISBN: 978-1-84968-126-1   Paperback: 308 pages

Virtualize your application infrastructure efficiently using Microsoft App-V

1. Publish, deploy, and manage your virtual applications with App-V

2. Understand how Microsoft App-V can fit into your company.

3. Guidelines for planning and designing an App-V environment.

Getting Started with Microsoft Application Virtualization 4.6

Virtualize your application infrastructure efficiently using Microsoft App-V

Augusto Alvarez

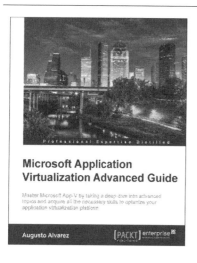

Microsoft Application Virtualization Advanced Guide

ISBN: 978-1-84968-448-4   Paperback: 474 pages

Master Microsoft App-V by taking a deep dive into advanced topics and acquire all the necessary skills to optimize your application virtualization platform.

1. Understand advanced topics in App-V; identify some rarely known components and options available in the platform

2. Acquire advanced guidelines on how to troubleshoot App-V installations, sequencing, and application deployments

3. Learn how to handle particular applications, adapting companys' policies to the implementation, enforcing application licenses, securing the environment, and so on

Microsoft Application Virtualization Advanced Guide

Master Microsoft App-V by taking a deep dive into advanced topics and acquire all the necessary skills to optimize your application virtualization platform

Augusto Alvarez

Please check **www.PacktPub.com** for information on our titles

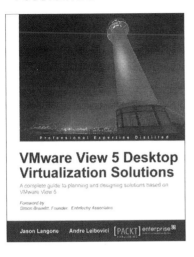

VMware View 5 Desktop Virtualization Solutions

ISBN: 978-1-84968-112-4   Paperback: 288 pages

A complete guide to planning and designing solutions based on VMware View 5

1. Written by VMware experts Jason Langone and Andre Leibovici, this book is a complete guide to planning and designing a solution based on VMware View 5

2. Secure your Visual Desktop Infrastructure (VDI) by having firewalls, antivirus, virtual enclaves, USB redirection and filtering and smart card authentication

3. Analyze the strategies and techniques used to migrate a user population from a physical desktop environment to a virtual desktop solution

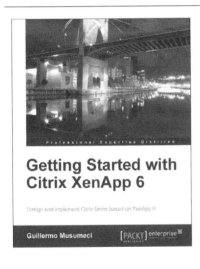

Getting Started with Citrix XenApp 6

ISBN: 978-1-84968-128-5   Paperback: 444 pages

Design and implement Citrix farms based on XenApp 6

1. Use Citrix management tools to publish applications and resources on client devices with this book and eBook

2. Deploy and optimize XenApp 6 on Citrix XenServer, VMware ESX, and Microsoft Hyper-V virtual machines and physical servers

3. Understand new features included in XenApp 6 and review Citrix farms terminology and concepts

Please check **www.PacktPub.com** for information on our titles

Made in the USA
Lexington, KY
20 March 2013